Dear Reader:

The book you are about to read is the latest bestseller from the St. Martin's True Crime Library, the imprint *The New York Times* calls "the leader in true crime!" Each month we offer you a fascinating account of the latest, most sensational crime that has captured the national attention. St. Martin's is the publisher of Tina Dirmann's VANISHED AT SEA, the story of a former child actor who posed as a yacht buyer in order to lure an older couple out to sea, then robbed them and threw them overboard to their deaths. John Glatt's riveting and horrifying SECRETS IN THE CELLAR shines a light on the man who shocked the world when it was revealed that he had kept his daughter locked in his hidden basement for 24 years. In the Edgar-nominated WRITTEN IN BLOOD, Diane Fanning looks at Michael Petersen, a Marine-turned-novelist found guilty of beating his wife to death and pushing her down the stairs of their home—only to reveal another similar death from his past. In the book you now hold, AFRAID OF THE DARK, Tom Henderson details the unraveling of a marriage, and a fatal turn of events.

St. Martin's True Crime Library gives you the stories behind the headlines. Our authors take you right to the scene of the crime and into the minds of the most notorious murderers to show you what really makes them tick. St. Martin's True Crime Library paperbacks are better than the most terrifying thriller, because it's all true! The next time you want a crackling good read, make sure it's got the St. Martin's True Crime Library logo on the spine—you'll be up all night!

Charles E. Spicer, Jr.
Executive Editor, St. Martin's True Crime Library

Titles by

TOM HENDERSON

Darker Than Night

Blood Justice

A Deadly Affair

Afraid of the Dark

Blood in the Snow

From the True Crime Library of St. Martin's Paperbacks

AFRAID OF
THE DARK

Tom Henderson

St. Martin's Paperbacks

AFRAID OF THE DARK

Copyright © 2009 by Tom Henderson.

Cover photo by Blend Images Photography, Veer Images.

For information address St. Martin's Press, 175 Fifth Avenue, New York, NY 10010.

EAN: 978-0-312-94813-9

Printed in the United States of America

St. Martin's Paperbacks edition / December 2009

St. Martin's Paperbacks are published by St. Martin's Press, 175 Fifth Avenue, New York, NY 10010.

10 9 8 7 6 5 4 3

To Kathleen, for putting up with all the gruesome tales she has to keep hearing about as a writer of true crime books does his research and struggles with drafts and rewrites.

ACKNOWLEDGMENTS

Special thanks, on another book together, to prosecutor Donna Pendergast, a true friend and legal bulldog, and to her teammates, Mark Bilkovic and John Skrzynski. All were gracious with their time. Defense attorneys Bob Harrison and Tom McGuire were helpful and gracious, as well, as were medical examiners Carl Schmidt and Stephen Cohle. In particular, I would like to thank Connie and Jerry Wolberg. They welcomed me into their home, trusting me to listen with an open mind about their relative and loved one, despite the verdict. Without them, the crucial interviews with Mark Unger would never have happened. To all of Mark's and Florence's relatives, and their many friends, I offer my condolences. And my apologies, as well, as the guy who comes knocking, hoping they'll talk about the worst tragedy of their lives.

PART ONE

THE LAKE

A CANDLE ON THE DECK

Friday, October 24, 2003

It was, thought Linnaeus Duncan, fixing to be a fine week-end. It was his favorite time of year, the seven-days-a-week of summer hubbub having ended, so a man could relax and enjoy himself and his surroundings.

And, my, what surroundings: a Technicolor forest encir-cling the small lake, and the sun still capable of lifting the temperatures into the 70s if a north wind wasn't blowing in.

Linnaeus (whom everyone called Linn since his days in the service, when they shortened it at mail call) and his wife, Maggie, were part-owners of the Inn of Watervale resort on the south end of Lower Herring Lake, a small lake in north-west Michigan tucked on the other side of some sand dunes, scrub brush and pine trees from Lake Michigan.

Their share of the sprawling complex was eight build-ings on three and a half acres on the lake and another forty acres of undeveloped adjacent property. They rented out seven of the buildings and lived in the other.

Two of the houses were right on the lake, with 160 feet of frontage—a big Victorian with six bedrooms and four bathrooms to the left of a small boathouse and a small cot-tage to the right.

Their other cottages were set back from the water. The remaining twenty-five cottages of the resort were owned by Dori Turner, Maggie's cousin. Though the Watervale looked like one large complex, it was run as two organizations, Dori handling her cottages and the Duncans theirs.

Summer weekends were always busy, with renters checking out Saturday morning and a new batch checking in Saturday afternoon. The resort was about booked up solid from Memorial Day to Labor Day, year after year. Many of its renters had been coming for years. Summer, you could only rent by the week.

Color season offered another burst of activity, which was about done, now. The relatively warm waters of Lake Michigan provided a mini-climate that stretched out the color season into late October, tourists coming to see the bright reds of the sugar maples and the yellows of the beeches and tamaracks, well past the time that forests in the interior of the state had lost their leaves.

This year, though, the Duncans had closed down their cottages early, wanting to get things ready for the winter before they took a short vacation to the West Coast, which they'd just returned from. Before they'd left, Linn had turned off the water to the various cottages, but he hadn't gotten to another end-of-season chore. He decided that today he'd clear the chaise longues and chairs off the roof of the boathouse, which served during the season as a gathering place for guests. That'd leave him all weekend to enjoy himself.

The boathouse roof was about twelve feet above the wide concrete apron that lined the small breakwall along the lake, the water shallow there, about six inches deep.

About 2 p.m., Duncan began lowering the fifteen or twenty pieces of furniture from the roof to the apron, dragging or carrying them across the deck, hoisting them up onto the rail, balancing them while he attached a rope and hook, then lowering them to the apron below as he leaned on the wooded railing.

He left one chaise where it was. It was a big sucker, made

out of two-by-fours, too heavy for him, getting old now, to lift by himself. It had a rustic look, wouldn't harm it much to sit out all winter, so he decided not to mess with it.

Later, his wife told him there was going to be a set of guests up for the weekend—Mark and Florence Unger and their kids. The Ungers had been coming to Watervale every summer for years. Once, when they first started coming, Linn and Mark had shot a round of golf together, a rarity for Linn, who wasn't much to socialize with guests. Not that he was rude or unfriendly, just the opposite. He figured when he was on vacation, he didn't want any motel or resort owners pestering him, so he tried not to pester his guests. His wife handled the bookings and did most of the socializing at check-in.

Even folks who'd been coming for years, Linn only knew by sight, didn't know most of their full names. He certainly knew Flo by sight—who wouldn't, face like that?—but didn't know much about her.

When the Duncans had gotten back from out West, there were several messages from Mark asking about a cottage, and Maggie called him back and explained that they didn't have anything for them, they'd been on vacation themselves, and had shut everything down before they left.

She told him to call her cousin Dori, which he did, and he got a reservation for the Mary Ellen, one of the cottages she owned.

The Ungers arrived in mid-afternoon Friday. Dori didn't check them in, but looked out of her house about 4 p.m.—all the houses or cottages at the complex have names, and the one she lived in was the Johanna—and saw Mark and two boys playing with a dog, the kids and the dog racing around like only kids and dogs can, a happy, joyous scene.

A little later, the Duncans went out to eat. So did the Ungers, a place in town called Dinghy's.

Fred Oeflein had it made. From Memorial Day to Labor Day, he lived at Camp Lookout, a children's camp at the north end of Lower Herring. He owned a software company in nearby Frankfort, a sleepy little town in the off-season, a busy tourist town Memorial Day through Labor Day, and he was part-owner of the camp.

From Labor Day through Memorial Day, for the last twenty years, he'd rented a cottage from the Duncans.

He'd known the Duncans his whole life. A lot of northern Michigan folks move south for the winter, he just moved a lot fewer miles than most of them, from one end of the lake to the other.

It was a good deal for all. He got a place cheap, on the lake, and didn't have to worry about trying to heat his own old, drafty cabin at the camp. They got a trusted friend to serve as care-taker while they were in Florida for the winter.

That afternoon, Oeflein helped a buddy, Tom Turner, fix his bicycle. He got back to Watervale at 8 p.m. and was about to head across the lake to the camp, where he planned to spend the night. In the morning, he had to drain the water pipes that connected the various buildings in the camp so they wouldn't freeze and crack in the winter. No worse work on God's earth than crawling under an old cabin in the woods to hacksaw and solder broken pipes in the spring, lying there on your back in the cold, wet muck.

On the way from his cottage to his small boat for the ride across the lake, Fred saw a candle burning on the roof-top deck of the Duncans' boathouse. He walked over to see what was up, wearing a sort of miner's headlamp to light the way. He knew about a wedding that was scheduled for Saturday, but who was this?

As he got near, a woman hollered out, "Linn?" thinking he was Linn Duncan.

"No, it's Fred," he said.

A candle balanced on the railing, on the far side, overlooking the lake. The boathouse was built into the slope to the lake. From the back, you just went up a couple of steps to the roof. As he walked across the deck toward the couple, they walked toward him, and they met in the middle. They shook hands and introduced themselves. The couple said they were Flo and Mark Unger, from Detroit. Staying at the Mary Ellen. Up with their boys, who were 10 and 7. Just got back from dinner.

Fred apologized for bothering them. It looked to him that he'd interrupted a romantic interlude between the two. "No problem," they replied, in unison.

Florence asked if the Duncans were around. Out for dinner, he said.

There was a strong wind blowing south, coming down out of the hills on the far side of the lake, and it blew out the candle. The lake is oblong-shaped, on just about a perfect north–south axis, and when the wind blew out of the North, it rolled up big waves in a hurry. They chatted a bit. Flo struck Fred as bubbly.

Oeflein said he needed to get going, pointing out his boat. He'd be catching some spray, no doubt, as he bucked into the waves.

"Camp Lookout?" asked Florence.

"Yes."

"Oh, I could never do that. I'm afraid of the dark," she said. She said it sort of casually, but her fear was anything but casual. It had been a dominating motif of her childhood, something her parents grew to accept and deal with rather than try to change.

As an adult, if she was visiting her next-door neighbors at night, one of them had to walk her home, even though their front walks were just twenty yards apart, and they could easily watch her the entire distance from their porch to her front door. Watching wasn't good enough, she had to be escorted.

In the summer, if Mark wasn't home and she wanted to sit out on the deck in the back yard, she'd try to recruit friends from the neighborhood to come over so she wouldn't have to sit out alone. Or she'd come home, realize Mark wasn't there, and call friends on the cell phone, waiting in the car in the driveway till someone would come over and walk her into the house, making sure nothing bad was waiting for her on the other side of the front door.

At Watervale, in summers past, she'd called friends she knew who were on vacation nearby to calm her down when she heard noises at night.

So when she said she was afraid of the dark, it wasn't a throwaway line. She admired Oeflein for his willingness to get into a boat and head into the pure black that filled the air over Lower Herring on a cloudy night. Even on clear nights, there is an up-north darkness over the lake that shocks city dwellers. There are no big cities nearby—Traverse City isn't big enough to diffuse its light this far—and plenty of trees to blot out porch lights, headlights and streetlights. City folks'll look up their first night here in the summer, and say, "So that's why they call it the Milky Way!"

As Oeflein walked down the slope toward his boat, he heard Mark ask her if she wanted a chair or a cushion.

She said no.

Oeflein's small boat was about thirty-five feet to the east of the boathouse. There was water in the bottom, which he started to bail out.

"Do you have a motor on that boat?" Mark hollered out.

"Yes, I do." Oeflein started the small, 9.9-horsepower motor and headed out. He got to the camp about ten, twelve minutes later, built a fire in his cabin, lit the stove, got dinner cooking and turned on the TV. *Dateline* was on, which told him it was after 9.

A little later, he went out for some more firewood. It was raining, now, the night as dark as dark can get.

A MANIKIN IN THE WATER?

Lower Herring Lake is a favorite of local kayakers. The western edge of the 450-acre lake is protected from the prevailing western wind off Lake Michigan by a steep forested slope that crests at rolling dunes.

That cliff-like slope offers flat-paddling and a chance in late fall to get in much easier kayaking than is possible on the many other nearby lakes, where rolling waves and whitecaps in fall usually make for a challenging and uncomfortable paddle.

A late-season kayaker hoping to get in an early morning workout on Saturday, the 25th, would have been happy to see that the brisk winds of Friday night had subsided, though the pewter clouds reflected gray off the water and took the edge off the display of color left on the hardwoods.

Unlike many northern inland lakes that have been lined in recent years by so-called big-foot houses—3,000- and 4,000-square-foot behemoths that fill the small lots almost lot line to lot line—Lower Herring is sparsely populated, here and there small 1930s and 1940s cottages peeking out of the thick forest that surrounds the lake and covers the hillsides that roll away from it.

From a kayak, it's easy to see why the white pine is the state tree. The forest contains a variety of pines and hardwoods and its canopy looks nearly smooth from the water, except for the intermittent white pine daring to tower high above it, having withstood the winter winds and summer storms for decades.

Heading west toward the flattest water from the main boat launch at the northeast end of the lake, the kayaker would have passed a few empty cottages, their aluminum docks dismantled and pulled up on shore, their tow-boats, rafts and Jet Skis trailered home or stored away.

Fred Oeflein might have been spotted at Camp Lookout doing his chores. They might have waved at each other, as kayakers and those on shore will do.

Just past the camp, the kayaker would have turned south and paddled along the glasslike surface of the western edge of the lake. Here there are no cottages, the terrain too steep, pine trees struggling for purchase in the shifting sands.

The water is littered by old trees that long ago lost their foothold and toppled into the lake. Other trees seemed frozen in mid-fall, leaning out over the water at 45-degree angles, roots half exposed. It's a perfect spot for gliding slowly, looking down through the clear water at the fish darting in and around the submerged tree branches.

When the sun is out, this part of the lake is particularly pretty. The hard-packed sand gives the shallow water a yellow-green color that seems in photos to be artificial.

Sixty or seventy yards from shore, the bottom falls away, creating a sharply defined line of blue that tells the power boaters of summer where it is safe to roar along.

At some point, about 9 a.m. Oeflein's small motor would have fired up, and soon after, the kayaker would have seen him go by. The Duncans' white boathouse is a landmark for boaters heading south on the lake. The cottages and houses on the southern shore are tucked back up the slope, hidden by trees and shrubs. But the white rectangle of the boathouse at the edge of the water stands out clearly from wherever you are on the lake.

If the kayaker had been near the southern end of the lake

when Oeflein went by, he or she would have wondered at the commotion Oeflein was heading toward.

This time of year, you'd usually have the lake to yourself. You'd *never* see *this* stuff. Yellow crime-scene tape being strung around. Cops coming and going.

There was something floating in the water, just in front of the boathouse. Was it a body? If so, no one was doing anything about it, or with it. No one was trying to get it out, or give it CPR or whatever you'd do to a body in the water. It just bobbed there in the small waves left from yesterday's blow.

Maybe this was some sort of drill.

And then the kayaker would have seen Oeflein's boat coast up to the beach, its engine idling. The people by the boathouse began waving, but not in the friendly way. They looked frantic. Mad.

They were shouting at Oeflein, but he couldn't hear them until he shut off the motor.

"Move that boat! Get that boat out of here!" said one guy, a plainclothes cop.

"This is where I live," protested Oeflein.

"This is a crime scene, and you have to get that boat out of here!" screamed the cop.

This wasn't a drill. The thing in the water wasn't a manikin. It was Florence Unger. She'd been dead a long time, and there was no need to hurry to get her out.

PART TWO

LOVE, AND DEATH

DROPPING OUT

Mark Unger felt like he was just drifting along, finishing up his third year at the University of Michigan in 1981, completely unprepared, in his mind, for the real world. More lost than drifting, actually. Didn't know what he wanted to do. Only reason he'd majored in communications was that it looked easier than majoring in anything else.

He grew up in the small, tight-knit affluent Jewish suburb of Huntington Woods, just north of Detroit. His household was more affluent than most, his mother, Betty, the owner of a bar and several restaurants on Islamorada in the Florida Keys.

Huntington Woods was too small to have a high school of its own. You either went to nearby Berkley High School or, like Mark, to a private school. He had gone to ultra-exclusive Detroit Country Day School in Beverly Hills, another of the affluent suburbs to the north of Detroit, where he'd been a back-up tight end on the football team, a backstroker on the swim team and a good enough tennis player to make it to the state championships his junior and senior years.

Most of the kids coming out of Country Day were highly motivated. It generally sent 100 percent of its graduates on to college, many to places like MIT, Harvard, Stanford and

Yale. Mark? Unlike his peers, who were plotting out their
Ph.D. track in eighth grade, he didn't try to do much more
than just get along, motivated more by a pick-up basketball
game than the crossword puzzle in the Sunday *New York
Times*.

Suddenly a lack of motivation seemed a problem. Was
depressing. He went to a school counselor and, as he described it later, poured his heart out.

Instead of telling him to buck up, the counselor sympa-
thized with him and told him about an option Michigan
offered to those within a year of graduation. He could drop
out, go anywhere he wanted, re-enroll at another school
eventually and, if he took the requisite number of courses,
they'd count toward his U-M degree.

Unger promptly packed up his 1979 Thunderbird and
headed to Tucson, where his sister, Kim, was enrolled at
the University of Arizona. After four months there, it was
off to Los Angeles. He'd had an internship while in high
school at an old line Detroit ad agency, W. B. Doner, and
friends pulled some strings and got him a job writing copy
at Doner's LA office.

His boss at Doner was an associate professor at nearby
Pepperdine University and convinced Mark to go back to
school, where for kicks he got a job playing music on the
student radio station.

He got the credits he needed, grew tired of LA and in
May of 1983 headed back across country, to Islamadora in
the Florida Keys to work for his mom, Bette Rosenthal,
who had a resort complex. There weren't many better places
for a 23-year-old with no ties and not much ambition.

His first month of waiting tables and tending bar in the
restaurant/bar called the Marina, he made $2,000. He was,
he thought, in paradise. He'd never made so much money,
or had so much fun making it.

Soon, he was managing one of the restaurants, the Harbor Inn, bartending at the Harbor Bar and making even
more money.

Fridays, Ron Harrison, a sportscaster in Miami at WINZ

940 AM, would come out and do a one-hour show at the Harbor Inn, talking deep sea fishing with one of the local captains. Part of the deal was that someone would go on air during the show and promote drink specials and upcoming events. Soon, that someone was Unger.

During football season, Harrison and the captain would pick which teams would win that weekend's football games. The one who picked the most winners got to toss the other into the ocean.

Unger, a sports junkie who, for example, prided himself on knowing the roster and batting and pitching averages of the 1968 Tigers, who'd won the World Series when he was a little kid, knew right off that Harrison and the captain didn't know squat, really, about football. One day Unger asked if he could make picks, too, and suddenly he was getting more air time.

In 1984, Unger talked his way into a regular gig with WFKZ, the voice of the Florida Keys, doing a five-minute sports recap Monday through Friday. It paid $25 a week.

In March of 1986, growing claustrophobic as many transplants do after a year or two in the Keys, of *needing* more than than just one road, Mark returned to Michigan. "You gotta get off the rock," he explained to those who wondered why in the world he'd leave paradise.

There was more to it than that. He'd had a ball bartending, liked the sun, the water, the nightlife and the money, but if he wanted to have a real career, now, at 26, was the time to make a move.

He had some money saved up, but nothing lined up, no plans. He would, he thought, wing it.

Back in Michigan, Unger took a tape he'd put together and gave it to Bob Bass, the general manager at a popular Detroit jazz station, WJZZ, which had a tradition of giving a lot of air time to good, young sportcasters.

"I've got nothing for you. But when my guy goes on vacation, you can fill in," Bass told him.

His guy was Bob Page, a rising star who had, in turn, replaced another rising star, Eli Zaret, who made a name for

himself fresh out of the University of Michigan and then
went on to do sports at a powerhouse FM rock station in
Detroit, WRIF.

That fall, Unger, who had taken a job as executive director of the Michigan Jewish Sports Hall of Fame, was listening to WJZZ in the car and heard Page finish up a show
by saying he was going on vacation for a week.

When Unger got home, he called the station. Page answered.

"Hi, I'm Mark Unger. I talked to Bob Bass and he said
I'm supposed to fill in for you when you're gone."

"My show?" asked Page.

"Yeah."

"Well, it doesn't surprise me, the way things run around
here. You better come in so I can show you what to do."

Unger drove down, Page showed him how to work the
controls, and Unger started the next day, doing one show at
7 a.m. and another an hour later. Never shy, on the first show,
Unger voiced an editorial, ripping the inept Detroit Lions
football team.

Later that morning, Unger got a call at home from Bob
Bass. "I understand you were on the show this morning at
seven," he said.

"And eight, too," said Unger.

"So, when are you coming in to do the afternoon show?"
asked Bass.

The week flew by. Unger was in heaven.

A few months after that, Zaret took a TV job in New
York. Page replaced him at WRIF. Unger thought the WJZZ
job was his. It wasn't. Bass gave it to Fred Hickman, a prominent black TV sportscaster who wanted the radio gig, too,
the station having a predominantly black audience.

The day before Hickman was supposed to start, though,
he entered rehab for substance abuse.

Bass called Unger. "The job is yours."

One of Unger's first games was a Detroit Red Wings
hockey game at Joe Louis Arena. Detroit prides itself as

Hockey Town—the Red Wings trademarked the phrase—
but Unger was one of those rare Detroiters who had grown
up without an affection for or knowledge of the game.

He called his nephew, Lyle Wolberg, a high school student who loved hockey.

"Lyle, you gotta go to the Red Wing game with me. I
don't know anything about hockey. I got you a pass," he said.

"That was a big deal for me," said Wolberg years later.
He coached Mark in the intricacies of the game and his
postgame report came off without a hitch.

Wolberg always idolized Unger. Though Mark was ten
years older, he'd let his nephew play pick-up basketball
with him and his buddies, first when Lyle was a kid, then
as he went through high school and college.

Mark was always the peacemaker if trouble started to
brew, as it can during pick-up games, someone throwing
elbows or coming over the back for a rebound. Mark was
the diplomat, the guy who'd defuse things by saying things
like, "Come on, let's just calm things down." Saying it in a
way that didn't seem like a challenge, that did, indeed,
calm things down.

He was, says Lyle's mother, Connie, Mark's half sister,
"the kid that stood up for the little guy. Who said, 'Come
on, he can play.' He always had a good heart."

Unger loved his work. "I've got the greatest job in the
world," he'd say, a job that granted him entrée to the Detroit
Tigers' press box in the summer, the Lions' football games
on Sundays in the fall and the Red Wings' games in the
winter and spring, not to mention his beloved University of
Michigan football and basketball teams.

The late 1980s were great years in Detroit sports. The
Tigers made the playoffs in 1987, the Detroit Pistons won
the first of back-to-back NBA championships in 1989,
and that year an underdog Michigan basketball team won
the NCAA championship.

Michigan's win was the highlight of Unger's career, for
two reasons. Before the tournament began, word leaked out

that Michigan's coach, Bill Frieder, had accepted a lucrative offer to coach the Arizona State University basketball team the next season.

At a subsequent press conference, Unger asked U-M's athletic director, the legendary former football coach Bo Schembechler, following a bunch of softball questions from his more timid peers, "Coach, are you telling me there's no hard feelings between you and Bill Frieder the way he left the job?"

Meaning, taking the new job before the tournament had even started.

Bo looked at him, and at the throng in front of him, and said, "A Michigan man is going to coach this team."

Frieder was told to leave immediately, just before the NCAA tournament began, and an assistant coach, Steve Fisher, was named interim coach.

Most people thought the turmoil would mean a quick exit for the Michigan team. Instead, it won game after game with the new coach to make it to the finals against Seton Hall in the Seattle Kingdome, a game it won in overtime.

After the game, on the hardwood floor, Unger and one of Michigan's stars, Sean Higgins, embraced.

When they let go of each other, Unger saw Joe Falls, the *Detroit News* columnist, who would later be named to baseball's Hall of Fame, staring at him in disgust. Unger had, in Falls' mind, violated the old sports writers' axiom: No cheering in the press box.

"Fuck you," thought Unger. He was thrilled to hug Higgins. He'd become a star, himself, and he was having the time of his life.

A BORN FLIRT

It had been a lucky, and good, life for Florence Stern. She'd been adopted as a young child by Harold and Claire Stern, he a very successful and politically connected attorney who provided his family with everything they needed and more. Flo was an eye-catching beauty, always laughing, very engaging, a born flirt. "Everyone liked her. There was just a twinkle in her eye," is how Connie Wolberg, a former model, now a travel agent, describes her. Connie met Flo when she started hanging around in high school with Connie's daughter, Amy.

Connie is twenty years older than Mark—Mark was a toddler when Connie got engaged to Jerry Wolberg, and Connie got a kick out of pointing the baby out to her future husband and saying, "There's your brother-in-law."

Flo's younger brother, Peter, had been best friends since grade school with Amy's younger brother, Lyle. Though Flo was three years older than Lyle, over time, they grew close, too. "She was like a sister to me," he said.

Mark first met Flo in 1982 at Connie's house in Huntington Woods, on a visit home from California. Flo was standing by the fireplace and Mark's first impression, something about her body language, maybe, or her obvious self-assurance at 16, was, What a snooty bitch.

The next time Mark saw her was a few years later, at Amy's high school graduation party at Pine Knob Music Theatre, a sprawling outdoor music venue north of Detroit that hosts the biggest touring acts each summer.

Mark felt something just click. He didn't talk to her, but he was intrigued.

The fall of 1987, Mark was recovering from shoulder surgery from an old injury suffered during his stint in the Florida Keys, lying in bed, his girlfriend sitting down next to him chatting when Amy stopped by to see how he was doing. She mentioned Flo, and without his girlfriend noticing, he pantomimed the word to Amy: "Flo."

Two hours later, Amy called him.

"What was that about?"

"I'd like to go out with Flo."

A couple of days later, Amy brought her by, ostensibly just checking in while in the neighborhood to see how Mark was doing. They stayed fifteen minutes. Later, Mark told Amy he'd give Flo a call in a few days.

The next day, to his surprise, Flo, a junior at the University of Michigan, called him and asked him out.

Mark knew how to impress a first date. He took Flo to a Red Wings hockey game against the Pittsburgh Penguins. Parking is hard to come by at Joe Louis Arena, abutting as it does the Detroit River, and most fans stream there from blocks away. Not Mark. His media pass got them a parking spot right next to the arena, and admission through a VIP entrance, where a private elevator took them to their section.

The game was followed by dinner at a nearby jazz club. Mark thought the date went well. He told friends Flo thought she was royalty.

They started dating regularly, though Mark didn't realize he was hooked till he went on vacation in November to the Grand Caymans for five days, with his mother, stepfather and sister Kim.

He was in paradise and all he could think of was how miserable he was.

After he got back, he and Flo were inseparable. She was

either at his place or, more often, he was at hers in Ann Arbor. He'd go to a game, zip over the studio to record his show, then race west on I-94.

In August of 1989, Mark went out of town for the wedding of an old college buddy, and while there, made up his mind he wanted to marry Flo. He came back, bought a ring and hatched a plan to pop the question at an engagement party for another friend.

Flo sulked on the way there.

Unger asked what was wrong.

"We've been going out two years and we're still not engaged," she said.

"When the time's right, the time's right," he said, sandbagging.

There were four couples at the party. He'd given the hostess the engagement ring, wrapped in plastic, beforehand, and she'd hidden it in Flo's dessert, on top of a brownie, under the ice cream and chocolate sauce.

Flo was startled to see something in her food, pulled out the plastic, scraped it off and saw the ring. She burst into tears as Mark got down on his knees.

They were married on February 24, 1990, at Temple Beth El, a big, soaring modern temple in the ultra-affluent suburb of Bloomfield Hills. Though Flo and Mark both belonged to Temple Emanu-El in Oak Park, Flo felt it was too plain to host her big day.

Then it was off to Ixtapa, Mexico, near Acapulco, for a honeymoon of eleven days.

Flo and Mark settled into what everyone they knew thought of as a good, if not idyllic, relationship. He was a local celebrity with his radio job, she got a job at a local jeweler, though her taste for jewelry at an employee discount ate up much of her paycheck. Flo also worked hard at her photography, a hobby she hoped would turn into an art and a profession.

Lyle thought them a perfect couple, something to aspire to when he grew up.

Soon, Flo was pregnant with their first boy, Max. When he was born, Flo asked Connie if they could have the bris at her house. Circumcision on the male baby's eighth day is a rite of passage in the Jewish religion, and the house they were renting was too small and she was more comfortable having it at Connie's house than her own parents'.

She hadn't gotten along with them for years, and while they might be offended not to have it in their house, so be it, said Flo.

Soon, the Ungers bought a house of their own in Huntington Woods—they would be considered poor in that community, and probably should have bought in a cheaper nearby suburb, but they had both grown up there and wanted to be near their many friends and family who lived there.

In retrospect, you could blame the house. "That's when they got in trouble," says Connie, meaning both financial trouble and the beginning of their marital trouble. They could have had the same house in Ferndale a few miles away for half the price, in Detroit for a third. But Huntington Woods was the only place either one of them wanted to be.

You could also blame their need to match the affluent lifestyles of their friends and neighbors, which meant trips to the health club to visit personal trainers, new SUVs, frequent dinners out, and, for Flo, closets full of new clothes, closet floors full of new shoes and boots, and rooms full of newly bought, high-end antiques.

It even meant rooms full of antiques being stored at their friends' houses: Flo was unable to resist a deal, even if she had nowhere to put it and not enough nerve, yet, to show the latest find to Mark.

And Mark wasn't exactly on a budget, himself. Money seemed to be no object for him, either, when he was hanging around with his buddies on the sports beat after games or on the road. If there was a casino close at hand, well, so much the better. Mark loved the adrenaline rush from gambling, and if he ran short of cash during a losing streak, there was always an ATM in sight.

Which made a temptation soon to come his way all the

more tempting, a temptation that would have a big impact on both the Unger family's household income and Mark's state of mind.

One of the sponsors of Unger's radio show was a fast-growing mortgage company named World Wide Financial Services, which was co-owned by his best friend since childhood, Robert Silverstein. Silverstein and his wife, Lori, a speech pathologist, were so close with the Ungers that eventually they became guardians of each other's kids.

One day late in 1991, Unger stopped by World Wide to pick up ad copy. As he waited, the phones rang off the hook. "Can you answer that?" someone hollered at him. "Just take a name and tell them we'll call them back."

Unger did as he was told.

Later, Silverstein told him he ought to think about joining World Wide, become a mortgage banker. Unger told him he didn't know anything about mortgage banking. You don't need to, said Silverstein. You won't believe the kind of money you can make. It's ridiculous.

Though WJZZ was a popular station, it didn't pay its sports personalities much. Unger was making $400 a week, forced to keep his other job with the Jewish Sports Hall of Fame to pay the bills. You were supposed to regard that radio gig as something to do cheap before moving on to bigger things, as Zaret and Page had done, and one whose true worth could only be factored by counting up all the free games and trips and meals.

Flo was adamant about being a stay-at-home mom, now that they had Max. Though Mark had what he thought was the world's greatest job, he took Silverstein up on his offer. In his first six months, he made more than he would have made at WJZZ in several years.

World Wide was a high flyer, filling the radio and TV airwaves with ads touting its quick processing, its execs praised in national publications for their business model and for their exponential job and revenue growth. About 1994, World Wide got into this new product called subprime lending, and a few years later, morphed the business onto a new platform called the Internet, with a business unit called LoanGiant.com.

It was a high-stress, high-paying job and Unger hated every minute of it. He complained that the job boiled down to getting as many people as possible into loan products that rewarded World Wide with high fees, targeting unsophisticated customers who had no idea there might be other, cheaper options available, or that their loan officer had gotten them into a loan they couldn't really afford.

"It's a mill. It's just churn and burn. You do as many loans as as fast as you can every month, and then your life starts over again the next month," Unger'd tell friends.

Flo got tired of hearing Mark complain about the job. And about how much he missed WJZZ. He grew increasingly unhappy. He saw his company as dishonest and racist—it had a largely black clientele with credit problems that precluded traditional bank mortgages, who were pushed into short-term, low-interest loans with high fees for World Wide. When those loans reset in two or three years, the borrowers either had to refinance for more fees, or if unable to do so, lost their houses in foreclosure.

"It was basically taking advantage of poor people," said Connie. "I remember one time he was crying. He said he couldn't stand it, that they had him making out phony W2s so he could get loans through, and it was killing him."

It was years before he was vindicated. In 2004, the state of Michigan ordered World Wide and LoanGiant to stop what were alleged to be fraudulent mortgage loan and documentation practices. In 2005, World Wide filed for federal bankruptcy protection. In 2006, the state's Office of Financial and Insurance Services announced a consent order revoking World Wide's license, ordering it out of business and imposing a fine of $273,255.

The company admitted to numerous violations of state law, including the failure to set up proper escrow accounts, to provide annual statements to borrowers and providing such false information on loan applications as phony net worth, phony income and phony debt obligations.

What was then seen as an outlier—World Wide was the crooked exception to the rule that the funding of sub-prime mortgages was a fine, profitable business niche to inhabit—would by 2008 be viewed in Michigan as the canary in the toxic sub-prime tunnel, a precursor to the financial implosions that took down Lehman Brothers, led to the government takeover of Fannie Mae and Freddie Mac, rocked the world's financial markets for months and led to a federal bank bailout of $750 billion.

If only the world had known what Mark Unger knew as he sadly processed loan after loan through the 1990s.

But not all was lost. Throughout the decade he continued to free-lance for big radio stations around the country, for the Associated Press, for United Press International, for the Mutual Radio Network, covering playoffs and big games for both the local pro teams and Michigan football and basketball teams.

In 1998, Unger went to the doctor about an old injury in his upper back from playing sports. Over the years what had been an occasional nuisance had grown into incessant pain. The doctor prescribed Norco, an opioid, and Soma, a muscle relaxer.

Soon, he was addicted, a condition he kept from Flo as long as possible. He'd wait till he put the kids to bed—that was his job every night, reading to them and tucking them in—before getting high.

The next year, the MGM Grand opened a casino in Detroit, the first of three to open in the city, which became the largest American city to have legalized gambling.

And soon Mark was addicted to gambling, too.

Mark put on weight. He got cash advances on his credit cards at the casinos when his luck was cold. He and Flo, who had been bickering the last few years, stopped sleeping together, and he moved into a spare bedroom. Things were spiraling out of control.

In September of 2002, Unger checked himself into a rehab facility across the state in Grand Rapids. He didn't want to. He didn't think he had a problem. He wasn't an alcoholic. He *liked* the drugs and the gambling. But Flo and a doctor they knew did an intervention with him. He knew if he wanted to save his marriage, he needed to get clean. He did it for Flo, not for himself.

In February, sober for five months and much trimmer, Unger returned home. It wasn't a happy homecoming, though. Flo had gone to work in the meantime as a mortgage banker, too, for Flagstar Bank, a national operation headed in the Detroit suburb of Troy. She hated it. And hated Mark for having made it so she needed to take a job.

Mark was still madly in love. After his stint in rehab, Flo looked more beautiful than ever. As unhappy as Flo seemed—and she wasn't shy about expressing it—he still had hopes they could turn things around, that there was still a happy ending possible.

FILING FOR DIVORCE

Soon after Mark went into rehabilitation, Florence began confiding in close friends, first that she was contemplating a divorce, then that she had made up her mind.

She and Kate Ostrove had hit it off in 1992, when they were working at a shopping center in Troy, a few miles from Huntington Woods. Flo worked at Barneys, Kate at Neiman Marcus. They had a lot in common, including a love of antiques.

In November, two months into Mark's stint in rehab, Flo told Kate she was getting a divorce. It was a loveless marriage, she said. She was very unhappy, he was no longer attractive to her—on the contrary, he repulsed her—and she was fed up with Mark's addictions to drugs and gambling, and with their financial troubles.

Flo had gone back to work and wasn't happy about it. She loved being a stay-at-home mom, but if she went ahead with the divorce, she'd need a steady source of money.

She was a fine photographer, too. It was more than just a hobby, but free-lancing at it was no way to keep the kids fed and clothed. A friend of hers named Joanne Pintar owned a decorating store called Home, and Flo hung some of her photographs there for sale, but the income was sporadic, at best.

Kate asked one day, "Are you going to file for divorce while Mark's in rehab?"

"No. I'm not going to do that. I'm not going to kick a dog while it's down," she responded.

After Mark got out of rehabilitation, the Ungers started marriage counseling, though it had no effect on Flo's resolve, much of it resulting from her resentment over having to work while Mark sat at home or, all too common, was over at the club working out, or, once the weather broke, out playing golf at the municipal course in the neighborhood.

Mark was good about some things—he'd make the kids breakfast and pack their lunches, sometimes pick the kids up from school. But the other household chores were hers. Making dinner, doing the dishes, the laundry, the dusting. He was too busy golfing to do those things, too, she'd complain to her friends.

One day Max called her at work at the bank, terrified. He had come home from school and there was some strange man in the house. His dad wasn't there. What should he do? Florence raced home from the bank. Turned out the stranger was a cable TV technician Mark had let in the house before going golfing.

That he took off to golf, leaving the stranger in the house, knowing the kids would be getting home soon, infuriated her.

Flo told Kate that she wanted to spring the news about the divorce to Mark during one of their counseling sessions. She was nervous how he would react if she told him when they were alone.

On August 26, 2003, Florence's attorney, Ada Kerwin, filed for their divorce in the Oakland County Circuit Court.

Kerwin specialized in family law for the Detroit law firm of Clark Hill. One of Flo's close friends, Amy Folbe, who was also an attorney, had recommended her. Flo had asked Folbe to handle the divorce, but Folbe declined. For one thing, they were part of the same close-knit community and she knew the divorce would cause rifts. For another, the very prominent, old-line Detroit firm that she was with, Honigman Miller Schwartz and Cohn L.L.P., was expensive, and Folbe doubted if Flo could afford it.

There was no hope of saving the marriage, Florence told her. This was no ploy to get him to change his ways so he'd go back to work and get them back to their old lifestyle. She was through.

She told Kerwin about Unger's addictions and that in her mind, he was still addicted. He had traded his addictions to gambling and Vicodin for an addiction to therapy. It had come to define his life. He was, she said, spending an inordinate amount of time with his rabbi, in group therapy, in individual therapy, in this meeting and that meeting. He was so self-involved that he had no time for work and not enough time for the family.

Florence asked for joint legal custody between her and Mark, and that she be granted physical custody of 6-year-old Max and 9-year-old Tyler.

Since Michigan is a no-fault divorce state, as long as Florence didn't change her mind, there was nothing Unger could do to stop it. The real legal fight would be over custody and child support.

About the time the papers were filed, the Ungers had a therapy session scheduled. Florence told her friends that she would break the news to Mark there, in front of what she hoped would be a calming influence.

In the middle of the session, she broke the news. Mark was dumbfounded. He had no idea of the depth of her unhappiness. The counselor wasn't a calming influence at all. Mark blew up and stormed out.

Susan Witus was one of Florence's many close friends from high school. They were both fitness buffs and four or five mornings a week they drove to the Beverly Hills Racquet Club together to work out.

Witus was one of those Flo confided in about the divorce and how she'd planned to spring the news on Mark. Witus was close to Mark, too, and apprehensive about what would happen that night, half expecting the call she got at 10 after 7.

It was Mark. He was sobbing, almost hyperventilating.

"Flo wants to get divorced. I shouldn't have gone into rehab. I knew this might happen."

"What are you doing right now?"

He told her he was in the car, driving home.

"You should pull over."

"I don't know what to do. I don't know what to do."

"I think you should go back to the session, because otherwise you're going to be talking about this later at home, or fighting about it in front of the kids. Go back to the session and talk about it in the privacy of the therapy room."

"Okay," he said. Then, "Did you know?"

"I had an idea," she said.

Mark returned to the counseling session.

A week or so later, he called her again, and told her she needed to back him up. She needed to talk Flo out of it.

"I'm sorry this is happening. I know it's hard on the kids. I know this is very hard, and it would be nice if she gave it more time," she said. "But, Mark, you know Flo. Her mind is made up."

"But you need to go to bat for me."

"Well, I can try, but it's not going to make a difference. Her mind is made up."

After that, Witus called Flo on her cell phone. She didn't want to call her at home and risk Mark answering and getting into another embarrassing conversation.

On September 15, Unger was served with a copy of the divorce complaint and Friend of the Court paperwork.

Unger hired Andrew Rifkin, an Oakland County divorce attorney, who filed a response on October 7 saying that Mark wanted the two to try to work out their differences.

Kerwin had been on both sides of hundreds of divorces. Boilerplate was always answered by boilerplate, with the special pleadings left for the judge to hear. The response by Mark's attorney should have been a simple statement denying the breakdown in the relationship. She assumed language about reconciling their differences for their best interests and their kids' was at Mark's insistence. It was more than a hint to her that things might get sticky.

The response also said that in the event things couldn't be resolved, Mark wanted physical custody and that "reasonable parenting time" be awarded to Florence.

On Tuesday, October 21, both sides met for a hearing before the Friend of the Court, which occupies a separate building in the sprawling Oakland County government campus near the once-prosperous city of Pontiac. The city is now a struggling, decaying, hardscrabble place suffering more than most communities in southeastern Michigan by the collapse of the auto industry and the city's namesake brand.

They met in a very small room, Florence, Mark, the attorneys and a Friend of Court referee. The hearing was to make sure that such things as financial information were being exchanged, to smooth out support or visitation issues, and to encourage parents to attend what was called a SMILE Program, which encourages them to lessen their animosity and make things easier on the children.

Kerwin was struck by Mark's demeanor. He was exceptionally quiet, giving grunting, short answers, avoiding eye contact, staring down at nothing in particular.

His flat demeanor changed in a hurry after the meeting. Divorce proceedings include what are called interrogatories, questions asked in written form.

Unger's addictions and his fight against them were well known to family and friends, but he'd asked Florence not to bring them up during the divorce. He had, he thought, an agreement with her that she wouldn't.

Florence had been reluctant to have them be part of the interrogatories, but Kerwin had explained to her why they were crucial.

Rather than mail the interrogatories to Rifkin, Kerwin handed them over at the hearing. Unger's drug and gambling addictions were at the heart of the questions, in agonizing detail.

Anyone who has ever gone through a divorce can imagine the sense of betrayal Mark felt later when Rifkin gave him the interrogatories to read, and he saw that his emotional and physical troubles, and his battles against them, had been turned into, for example, the lawyerly verbiage of Question No. 21:

For each and every addiction or substance abuse problem you now have, or ever had, including but not limited to alcoholism or addiction to other drugs, prescription or otherwise, please state:

A. The nature of said addiction or substance abuse problem, and the dates during which you were/are affected with it.

B. Whether you have ever been diagnosed as having any addiction or substance abuse problem, including but not limited to: Alcoholism or addiction to other drugs, prescription or otherwise. If so, state the diagnosis, date it was made, the person making the diagnosis and their professional affiliation.

C. Whether you have ever been in any kind of treatment program, whether inpatient or outpatient, for treatment of any addiction or substance abuse problem, including but not limited to: Alcoholism or addiction to other drugs, prescription or otherwise. If so, sate the name, address, and the telephone number of the facility or program and the dates of your treatment.

D. Whether you have ever received any prescription for any type of medication as a result of any kind of addiction or substance abuse problem, including but not limited to . . .

One hundred and one questions later, Question 122 asked:

Please describe the type, extent and nature of your addictions.

Question 123 asked:

Please provide the following information regarding
any and all individuals with whom you counsel regarding your addiction and your efforts at recovery
for your addiction:

    A. Name, address and phone number.
    B. Date counseling began.
    C. Frequency of contact.
    D. Nature of contact.
    E. Cost per visit.
    F. Total cost from inception to current date.

Question 129, in parts A through H, asked Unger to
name all the gambling institutions he'd visited since January 1, 2001, including the dates of each visit, the amounts
he'd bet, the amounts he'd won or lost, the source of funds for
his gambling, the dates and amounts of money charged to
credit cards, the dates and amounts of any money withdrawn
from savings, checking or investment accounts, amounts
borrowed against retirement, amounts borrowed from other
sources and any and all credit card, bank or credit union
statements that listed any funds used for gambling.

One can imagine the anger that might boil over into fury
if Unger gave any thought to the amount of billable hours
that went into drawing up those interrogatories and the likelihood that he'd be footing the bill for both Kerwin's time
drawing them up and Rifkin's bill fashioning a response.

The irony that the interrogatories were passed out at an
introduction to the legal system that included an offer to
join the SMILE Program was lost on Kerwin.

The hearing was the last time Kerwin would talk to her
client.

"I DON'T WANT TO GROW
OLD WITH MARK"

Laurie Glass was Florence Unger's best friend, and had
been since Laurie'd moved to Huntington Woods when she
was 10. They lived half a block apart, saw each other most
days, talked to each other every day. Mark was her friend,
too, though she was far closer to Flo.

In spring of 2003, just before the kids got out for summer vacation, Florence confided in her that she wanted a
divorce. Mark hadn't been doing anything except hanging
out, working out, going to therapy and golfing since he'd
returned from rehab.

Flo was upset about his work ethic. She didn't like her
job and hated that he didn't have one and didn't seem interested in getting one.

Forget the money, though. She told Laurie that the ba-
sic, undeniable, unchangeable thing was: "I don't want to
grow old with Mark."

Simple as that.

On September 26, about 4 p.m., the beginning of Rosh
Hashanah, Mark Unger surprised Laurie with a call. She
was in the kitchen, baking a holiday cake with her son.

She answered the phone and, no preliminaries, Mark
asked, yelled, really, "Do you believe in this divorce?"

"That's not a yes or no question."

"Bullshit."

"Mark, let's talk." Trying to calm him down, she repeated, "It's not a yes or no question. I know you're upset . . ."

"You need to step up to the plate. You need to speak to Florence. You need to tell her this is going to kill the kids."

"I believe she has thought of the children, she has belabored this decision quite deeply," said Glass, sounding perhaps more formal than she intended.

"You need to talk to her, you need to tell her this is going to hurt the kids."

Finally, to get him quieted, to be relieved of the call and get back to her son and the cake, she said, "I will commit to you that I will speak to her, but I want to reiterate to you that I feel she has thought about the children."

Glass was shaken. She called her sister, needing to talk about it, not believing Mark had called her yelling and screaming.

A few minutes later, while she was still on the line with her sister, call-waiting told her she had another call from Mark. He was crying. She tried to calm him down. "I know you're very upset. I know you're against a divorce."

"Just promise me you'll speak to her."

"I will."

"Okay. I'm going to hang up the phone. I don't want to have to yell at you anymore."

Unger would have yelled further had he known Glass' participation in a plan to help Florence set aside some money. Glass was a bookkeeper and money manager, and she helped Florence balance her checkbook. She gave her advice on ways to hide money from Mark, such as buying gift cards for places she knew she'd need to shop for herself or the kids in the months ahead. The cards were small and easy to hide and got money out of bank accounts that Mark could go after.

One night, Unger showed up on Laurie's front porch at 10 p.m. and rang the bell. Laurie was putting her kids to bed and was upstairs in her son's bedroom, immediately over the porch.

It wasn't a neighborhood where people came knocking at 10 unless they had bad news. She got up and ran downstairs as her husband, David, opened the door. It was Mark, crying. She turned around and went back upstairs, let her husband deal with it.

Laurie told Flo she was worried about Mark's deteriorating behavior.

Flo had continued to do things socially with Mark, going out to dinner or a movie, though she claimed they were no longer having sex. "I'm just trying to keep the peace," Florence would say to her friends. "I'm just trying to get out of this as friends, for my children's sake."

Laurie counseled Flo that going out together was not the wisest choice. She was sending mixed signals. By being friendly, it was keeping Mark's hopes kindled for a reconciliation.

Flo would cut her off: "I'm just trying to keep the peace."

They stopped talking every day. Laurie felt uncomfortable calling her at home, now, afraid she'd get Mark and he'd cry or start in getting her to talk Flo out of going through with it.

On Monday, October 20, they talked briefly. Laurie had been out of town for a long weekend, and Flo called her to talk for a minute on the way to the bank. The next call she got about Flo was five days later. It wasn't from Mark.

"YOU DON'T EVEN
WANT TO KNOW"

Glenn Stark had been good friends with the Ungers for about five years. His wife, Kathy, was part of Flo's large circle of women friends. Until August that year, he and Kathy had lived four blocks away from the Ungers. In many suburban communities, that might as well have been twenty miles. But not in Huntington Woods, where it seemed everyone knew each other, if not through their own histories or jobs, then through their kids.

They were one of the couples Flo would call if she got home at night and Mark was out, sitting in the driveway till she recruited someone to indulge her and come over and walk her into the house. The Starks were happy to do it, found it endearing.

The Ungers and Starks attended the same parties, went out to dinner together, attended synagogue together, had gone on vacations together. Flo and Kathy talked nearly every day by phone.

Florence felt comfortable enough with them to be honest about her fear of the dark. They were happy to oblige her; they thought her truly one of the finest people on earth. Asked to describe Flo, without hesitation Kathy would say, "Lovely. Funny and kind and generous. And as warm-hearted as a person can be."

The move to Bozeman, Montana, by the Starks and their kids, Ken and Ben, the previous summer, a drastic change of life and scenery, to be sure, had been sparked by a vacation there in 2000.

Like many first-time visitors to Montana, the Starks had been enchanted by the big sky of the high plains east of the Rockies and by the forests and craggy peaks of the Rockies themselves. After they returned they couldn't get the idea of moving there out of their minds.

Their friends probably thought their talk was just that: talk. Glenn was a financial services professional who had grown increasingly unhappy with his job. Instead of the rat race and the stress of the financial world, he dreamed of owning his own restaurant. So did his wife, who had an extensive culinary background, doing catering, teaching cooking classes and writing cookbooks.

Finally, in the spring of 2003, talk turned to reality. They put their house on the market at a time when Huntington Woods houses often sold before they were even officially listed, for more than the asking price.

Their house sold quickly, too. In August, they moved, knowing they wanted to open a restaurant, but not having a specific place in mind. Kathy and Flo called each other frequently.

Flo told her of wanting a divorce, of how bad things were getting in the marriage, of her fights with Mark. Both Kathy and Glenn advised her to work harder at getting along with Mark, not to patch up the marriage, but to be more accommodating, to not make so many waves, to make it easier on each other and the kids.

In October, from the 14th through the 22nd, Stark was back in Michigan, tying up some loose ends of his financial services business and meeting with would-be suppliers for the delicatessen he and his wife were opening.

Stark spent most of the trip in the affluent nearby suburb of West Bloomfield, at the house of a friend named Harold Rosen, a co-worker from his recent days as a financial planner. But Glenn had made plans to spend Tuesday night at the Ungers' home, with Mark and Flo and their kids.

Stark had known for some time the Ungers' marriage was troubled. Earlier during his visit back to Michigan, Mark had brought it up, and Stark gave him some candid advice: He told him he thought Mark needed to start thinking of a life without Flo, to envision life without her.

"I can't do that," Unger replied. He loved her too much.

That night, Mark struck him as withdrawn, Florence as unhappy. The Ungers had almost no interaction the entire night. The kids, Stark and Flo spent most of the night watching TV. Mark spent most of the evening in other rooms or out of the house.

He and Mark usually found conversation easy. Tonight, the lack of it and the tension in the room made him uncomfortable.

At one point, he asked Mark out of earshot of the others if he was uncomfortable having him visit, would he rather he stayed elsewhere?

"No, I'm not mad at you, you're not the one divorcing me," said Unger.

At one point, Stark, Flo and the boys were sitting on a sectional. Mark was on a chair. He got up, the remote control falling onto his bare foot.

He yelled in pain, cursed and stormed out of the room. It struck Stark as an exaggerated reaction. It wasn't his foot that was hurting.

Florence looked at him and rolled her eyes. Stark interpreted the gesture to mean: "This is what I deal with all the time."

Joan Frank and Florence met for breakfast on October 16 at a Coney Island restaurant in Royal Oak, just across Woodward Avenue from Huntington Woods.

The Detroit area prides itself on being the world's epicenter for Coney Island hot dogs, despite the New York–sounding name, and has numerous chains and independent restaurants claiming to be the best, all serving the same hot dogs in natural casings slathered with chili, chopped onions and mustard.

Generations ago, Greek immigrants opened two hot dog joints next to each other in downtown Detroit that still serve hot dogs and provide work for newly arriving relatives. As the suburbs spread out from the center city in the '50s, so, too, did the Coney Islands, becoming a staple of every strip mall and shopping center.

Frank was caught in the middle of the Ungers' marital woes. She owned her own communications business, doing marketing and public relations. She had known Flo since their kids were in preschool together in 1995, and she and her husband, Steven, had become close to the Ungers.

They went to synagogue together and twice had taken vacations together in northern Michigan, once to a newer, ritzy place called The Homestead, once, for a week, to Watervale.

Mark had been one of Frank's clients, too. After making the transition from a job he loved to one that had him rolling in dough, early in 2002 he hired Frank to help promote him. Get his name out there so that someone thinking of a mortgage might think of him. The professional relationship had ended when Mark went off to rehab that fall.

Soon after Mark left for the rehab center in Grand Rapids, Joan's son had an activity not far from the Ungers', and she decided to spend the time visiting Flo.

Until Mark's departure, he had tended to the Ungers' bills. A bunch of them had arrived, seeming to come at once, as bills do, and as she chatted with Joan, Flo started opening them up. One after another, most with big balances due. Huge balances, to Flo's mind. The total the Ungers owed was beyond anything she could have imagined. Neither she nor Joan added the bills up, but the total had to be in the tens of thousands. Many tens.

Joan was shocked, too, though she tried to calm Flo by projecting an extra sense of calm, herself. Don't panic, was the message. It's manageable.

She offered to help. Mark would need to start making money when he got home, and she could help there. When Mark got back, she could once again help market him as an expert in the still-booming mortgage business. Do some publicity, maybe set up a Web site, put some press materials together, and so forth.

There were several community newspapers in close proximity and she could pitch them on features about Mark. After all, he was a local celebrity, the radio sport guy turned mortgage broker, radio star turned entrepreneur. That was a pitch you could easily sell a small weekly, or even a daily like the Royal Oak *Daily Tribune*.

One night, Flo, the Franks and another of their friends were out to dinner. Flo's cell rang. It was Mark, calling from Grand Rapids. Soon they were privy to an embarrassing conversation. It was clear Mark was accusing her of being out with another man. Flo kept saying it wasn't true, she was with the Franks.

Flo got frustrated and hung up. Her phone rang immediately. Mark. Grilling her about who she was with. She hung up, again.

He called back. "No, Mark, I'm here with Joan and Steven. Do you want to talk to them? Do you?"

He didn't take her up on the offer, which was a relief for the Franks. The calls ruined what had been a fine night out.

After Mark got out of rehab, Joan, eager to retain a client and eager to help Flo, called him on the phone. She told him she had some ideas to get his career kick-started, some marketing things they could do. She wanted to come over at some point soon and discuss them.

Mark seemed interested, but never followed up. He had a good reason for not wanting to hurry back into a work world of mortgage banking that he'd hated: He'd bought two disability insurance policies in the 1990s. One paid almost $8,000 a month, tax-free, up to age 65, if something caused him to lose his job in the mortgage business. He could get a job in any other field and still collect. The other paid more than $2,000 a month, but stopped as soon as he got any job.

About the time he left for rehab, Unger filed two claims, and both were honored. His ship had come in—$10,000 a month tax-free—so why not sail on it?

But to Flo and her friends, he was starting to look like a lazy bum. Though she was a beneficiary of the easy income, too, it bothered her. She told her friends she thought it was a scam.

"Is he looking for anything?" Joan asked Flo at one point, meaning work.

"I'm done," said Flo. "I can't do this anymore. I'm fed up."

Florence had always worked out, often at the toney Beverly Hills Racquet Club. The Franks were members there, too, and they'd run into each other regularly.

After he got out of rehab, the Franks started running into Mark there all the time, too. Very soft when he'd left, he'd become something of a workout nut. He'd hired a professional trainer—another bill to add to the pile—and worked out regularly.

The decision to file for divorce made for some awkward situations socially. Flo not only talked about the divorce and how she felt about Mark with Joan, but with Steven, too, in phone calls or, much more frequently, in e-mails. Once at the racquet club she told Steven that Mark had been acting like Jekyll and Hyde—nothing violent, but crazy mood swings. There came to be a conspiratorial feel in the air when they got together.

The two couples would be out to dinner and Mark would excuse himself to go to the bathroom, and Flo would start talking about getting the divorce filed, or how she couldn't wait or how miserable she was, and when Mark would return, an awkward silence would engulf the table.

After she filed, Mark freaked out when he found out all their acquaintances knew her plans, feeling betrayed that Flo had spread the word on the one thing he could least face. Flo told Joan that it'd be best to act as if she didn't know, to avoid adding the Franks to the list of people he was freaking out about.

The topic of conversation at their breakfast on the 16th was Watervale, and an upcoming trip the Ungers were taking there, from October 24–26. Flo didn't want to go, but she didn't want Mark taking the kids alone. A week earlier, she had asked Joan if she and Steve would go up with them, and Joan had said they had plans, but maybe they could change them.

"You know, I wish we could get out of this commitment, but there's no way," she said, now. "I tried. I just can't do it."

"Bummer. I don't want to go with Mark alone," said Flo.

Joan asked her about the divorce. Things are heating up, Flo said, and Mark's been getting nasty. Life was not good.

"You never want to be where I am," became a constant refrain to Flo's friends. She was bad company, these days.

Earlier, Joan had suggested the two families celebrate Thanksgiving together, at the Franks'. Flo said she didn't want her parents, Harold and Claire, to be alone for the holiday. Bring them, too, Joan had offered. Great, said Joan. They would get together after the Ungers got back from up north to plan the menu.

Lori Silverstein was another one of those Flo had confided in about the marriage. She liked Mark, and Mark would call her to talk about the marriage, too, of his continuing amazement that Florence wanted to end it and of his determination not to have the kids go through it.

At one point, after Flo had filed the papers, she gave Mark some advice: It might be better for him and the kids once the family was broken up into two households. Two positive households instead of one unhappy household filled with stress.

He would have none of it. That was sheer fantasy, he said, two happy households. That wouldn't be the way it would work out.

On Tuesday, October 21, Lori stopped by to visit Flo. At one point, Mark came in the room, and he and Flo struck her as exceptionally cordial, much nicer to each other than they had been lately.

She mentioned something to Flo about it, and Flo said that having firmly decided a divorce was the only choice she had, she figured she might as well be as nice as possible.

Wednesday morning, Mark called Lori and was ebullient about how things were working out. "We've never gotten along better. Look how great we're getting along," he said. "Can you believe this is what she wants to do when we're getting along so well?"

Cheryl and Ron Loeb had lived in Huntington Woods for thirty years, and had lived next door to the Ungers for eight. The couples didn't socialize much, but were good neighbors. Ron had golfed with Mark a few times. Flo and Cheryl visited each other for coffee once in a while. Their kids played at one another's houses and in the summer the Unger boys played in the Loebs' pool.

Over the years they had helped Florence with her fear of the dark, no matter that their city was one where crime was nearly nonexistent, where to run afoul of the law meant a speeding ticket for five over the limit on one of the shady sidestreets, or getting a citation from the ordinance officer for putting the garbage out front the day before your scheduled pick-up.

When Florence was over at their house at night, though her front porch was just forty feet from the Loebs', she wouldn't make the walk home on her own. Unabashedly, she'd ask Ron to escort her from front door to front door. If he wasn't there, she'd ask the Loebs' son.

The first time Florence asked, Ron said he'd stand on the porch and watch her, make sure she got home okay. It wasn't good enough. Florence asked for the escort.

In the months following Mark's rehabilitation, Flo's conversations with Cheryl tended more and more toward her unhappiness with her husband and the marriage. She was clearly resentful, angry that their lives seemed to have flip-flopped. She wanted to be at home for the kids when they returned from school. But that was Mark's role, now.

On Wednesday, October 22, in the midst of doing some yard work and walking from the back yard to the front, Ron saw Flo in her garden and said, "Hi, Flo, how are you doing?"

And instead of giving him the usual "Fine, how are you?" she looked over at him. She was crying, and she said, "Not very well."

"Is there anything I can do?" he asked.

"No. Things here are very bad."

"Maybe things will work out," he said, embarrassed, not sure what to say or do. "It'll be okay."

Flo told him that she and Mark and the kids were going up north that weekend. She didn't want to go. "I'm scared," she said.

At 1:30 p.m., on Thursday the 23rd, Florence met Gary Scholnick for lunch at the Red Coat Tavern, a popular restaurant known for its burgers, just up Woodward Avenue from Huntington Woods in Royal Oak. It was less than a mile from her office at the local Flagstar branch.

He'd been a close friend of Mark's since childhood, and was a good friend of hers, too. He was also the insurance broker who'd sold Mark his disability policies.

He got there first. She arrived, found his table, sat down. She'd been crying.

It was a client, she said, who'd gotten her so upset. He'd called her and was trying to take advantage of her, dickering with her about rates. She hated that stuff.

Then there was Mark. They'd been discussing how to divide their belongings the day before and it turned into a big fight. And now they were all going up north on Friday, not something she was looking forward to.

"If you don't want to go, don't go," he said.

"I need to go," she said. She said her lawyer had told her

to show family unity, and she wanted to show the kids they would have a family, divorce or no.

And then she went back to work.

About 4 p.m., Flo called her older brother, Peter Stern, who lived in Northern Michigan. He was an emergency medical technician in the artistic resort community of Glen Arbor.

Peter had known Mark was going through tough times with gambling and drug addictions, but didn't know until a few months earlier that his sister's marriage was in deep trouble.

He'd had to go to the Detroit area for a few days in March and stayed with Mark and Flo. It was obvious things were way out of kilter with the marriage, the silences, the lack of interaction. "They're just not a team," Stern thought.

Flo told him they were deep in debt.

How much?

A lot.

"If you sold your house and got a divorce, would you still be in debt?" he'd asked her.

"Yes, we would still be in debt."

Which was saying something, considering housing values in Huntington Woods. Their house had to be worth $200,000, probably more. How could they be so far in debt?

Over the next two months following his visit, Peter had left Flo a series of unanswered messages on her home phone. Finally he asked his dad what was going on, that he was concerned Flo hadn't been returning his calls. Their father relayed the message and Flo finally called Peter, and said to call her only on her cell, that Mark was erasing all her messages at home.

In September, Peter needed to remortgage his house and Flo told him she could get him a good rate. "And, oh, by the way, I'm getting a divorce," she said, and then abruptly said she had to go, and hung up.

For the next three weeks, because of the refinancing, Peter and Flo stayed in close contact. She told him Mark was threatening to sue for full custody of the kids and was going to leave her with $1,000 a month. She told her brother she'd live in a box before she let her kids go.

So when Flo called and said she and Mark were getting ready to drive up to Watervale on Friday, Peter was surprised. Flo said she didn't want to go, but she was.

Peter asked her if she wanted to stay at his place, instead.

No, she responded.

After work Thursday, Flo ran into Cheryl Loeb in Imelda's Closet, a women's clothing store in Birmingham. She was looking at boots when Cheryl spotted her.

"How are you doing?" asked Cheryl.

"You don't even want to know," Florence responded. She was glum. She told Cheryl she and the boys were going up north with Mark, clearly not excited at the prospect.

They changed the subject to boots. Flo settled on a pair of brown ones, but had to order the size she needed.

Saturday morning, Cheryl Loeb was at Detroit's Metropolitan Airport, awaiting a flight to Chicago. Her husband called her on her cell. It was about Flo.

Flo also ran into Kim Lifton on Thursday morning. A freelance writer, Kim had been introduced to Flo while Mark was in rehab by Mark's cousin, Marci Zussman. Zussman knew that Lifton and her husband were looking to do a refi on their house to fund a bathroom remodeling and wanted to funnel the work to Flo.

The Liftons thought Flo a bust as a mortgage banker—she didn't seem to know much about what she was doing—but they hit it off as friends.

That morning Kim invited Flo over for Shabat Friday night.

"You don't want us there. We're not good company these days," she replied. Besides, she said, they were going out of town.

There was an e-mail awaiting Flo when she got home that day. It was from Steven Frank. He knew she was upset about the trip and he wanted to buck up her spirits. He told her how proud he was that she hadn't rolled over and taken the easy way out by just staying with Mark, that she was fighting hard for her happiness.

Flo e-mailed back, talking about giving in:

> Yeah, sometimes that sounds so much easier. But I just can't settle, anymore . . . You know, there are a lot of nasty things that I can do—I don't want to have to do it, but if he tries to take the kids away from me, and the house, I'm going to have to get nasty about the divorce.

Flo also spoke about "settling" for a life with Mark in earlier e-mails and conversations she'd had with the Franks. On October 1 she'd e-mailed the Franks while in a funk, depressed about her job, which wasn't going well. She hadn't been in the mortgage business long and didn't have a so-called "book of business," repeat customers who could be relied on to provide a base for both her and the bank.

Her boss had been pressing her to generate more loans. He wanted her to staff a booth at an upcoming home-builders' show, which was about as pleasant a thought for Flo as grabbing a spot in line for tooth extractions.

> I am icky today. Mood swing central. I need to find business or I'm going to go nuts. Maybe I should just settle, like I have been for years. Today it seems like it would be easier," she e-mailed.
> XO, Flo.

Flo and Kate Ostrove talked on the phone. When Flo told her about the upcoming trip, Kate told her she thought it was a bad idea.

She didn't want to go, Flo said, but she wanted to reassure the kids, show them that their parents could still be friends.

* * *

About 11 o'clock Friday morning, Susan Witus and Florence had their first phone call of the week. Susan had recently had a baby, and the week before, Mark, Flo and Glenn Stark had stopped by after dinner for a visit. They all had some ice cream and spent a pleasant couple of hours; here it was just a week later and it seemed they hadn't talked in forever. It was rare for them to go more than a day or two without talking.

Susan asked her how she was.

"It was the worst week of my life," said Flo.

Susan asked about the Friend of the Court hearing. "That must have been stressful," she said.

"That was nothing compared to the rest of my week."

"Why. What happened?"

"I've been crying on the bathroom floor for the last two nights. We've been warring all week," said Flo.

They ended up talking at length. It wasn't just things with Mark that had made it a bad week. Things weren't going well at the bank. She hadn't been writing many loans, was under pressure from her boss to start producing, a big deal she was counting on had just fallen through.

Things were so slow, she said, she was contemplating getting rid of her personal trainer at the club. But Mark had a personal trainer twice a week, so why should she have to give up hers?

"Maybe I should just live off his disability," said Flo.

There are disabilities, and then there are disabilities. The irony that by some definition of "disabled," Mark was now able to finance his efforts at the club to get into the best shape of his life went unnoticed.

To Susan's surprise, Flo said she and Mark and the kids were leaving later that day to go up north, to Watervale.

"Why?" asked Susan, who had vacationed there with the Ungers twice. She knew how nice it was, and how important it had been to the Ungers over the years, but going under these circumstances?

"I made a promise to the kids and I'm going to keep it."

"You know, the weather is supposed to be really bad. It's supposed to be raining."

"I don't even care. I just want to go up there and chill."

Also to Susan's surprise, Flo talked about trying to decide on a Christmas vacation with Mark and the kids. She'd just bought some skis, so maybe they'd go to Blue Mountain, a ski resort on Georgian Bay in Ontario. Or maybe they should go to Florida. The snow or the beach? She said she was struggling to make up her mind. And then there was their first court appearance over the divorce. That was coming up in December, too, and might get in the way of a vacation.

Earlier in the week, Mort Meisner, a close friend of both Florence and Mark, who coached Max's Little League baseball team, called Mark.

"Hey, Mark, how you doing?" he asked. His friends had been worried about him.

"You'll never guess what happened. I was in my underwear today and Flo said, 'Mark, you've really lost some weight.' I told her, 'Because I want to be your man, again.' "

"Did you hug her?" asked Meisner.

"Are you kidding? I want to take it one step at a time."

On Friday, Meisner called Flo and asked her if they were still going up north.

"It'll be good to get away with Maxie and Tyler. It'll be fun," she said.

She sounded in good spirits. Meisner thought her tone might bode well for Mark.

During the drive north on Friday, Flo called Kate Ostrove. She said they'd just stopped at her kids' favorite place to eat and were about an hour from Watervale. She surprised Kate, then, telling her the kids were very excited about the trip and she was very happy. It had been a while since Kate had heard her use those words.

* * *

Marci Zussman and Flo had been fast friends since Mark introduced Flo at a holiday dinner ten or eleven years earlier as his future wife. They saw each other almost daily and only in the rarest of circumstances went a day without talking on the phone. Though Mark was her first cousin, she was far closer to Flo.

They went antiquing together and garage sale-ing and to the local flea market most Sundays.

One of Zussman's girlfriends had a house in Charlevoix, a city of summer home and cottages for the wealthy on Lake Michigan, in the far northwest corner of the state's Lower Peninsula.

The friend was going there this weekend to close the place up for the winter, and Marci was going with her, but they had to wait until Friday evening to leave because the friend's son had a soccer game.

Mid-afternoon Friday, Zussman got a call from Flo, teasing her for still being back in Huntington Woods. The Ungers were almost to Watervale.

"I'm here and you're not," she said, meaning, as Zussman took it, "I'm up north and you're still stuck in the city." Kind of a nah-nah, nah-nah-nah. Not mean-spirited. Just glad to be there.

Zussman was happy to hear the tone in her voice. Flo sounded happy and content, she thought, not words associated with her lately. Good for her. Zussman had been to Watervale, herself, in July the previous year, her and her kids spending a week with the Ungers. It was, she knew, a great place to come alive.

About 3:30, the Ungers pulled into the driveway in front of the office in Watervale, the road in from the highway a riot of fall color, the trees that surrounded all the cottages and cabins of the resort in full color, too.

Maggie Duncan checked them in.

About 4, Dori Turner looked out from her house and saw a sight that warmed her heart—Mark and the two boys were playing with a dog, the faces of the kids and the dog reflecting equal measures of unbridled joy as they raced around, the kids trying to tag the dog, the dog easily eluding them, circling around and chasing back at them.

Was there a nicer, prettier sight than that? Kids, dogs and full color season as a backdrop?

The Duncans went out to eat Friday night and got back about 9:15. There'd been a waitress there who used to work at Watervale, but Maggie couldn't remember her name. It'd bugged her all through dinner.

When they got back home, the lights in the Johanna were out—Dori, her cousin, and some of her friends who were up for the weekend had all gone out for the Friday fish dinner at the Villa Marine Bar in Frankfort. When Dori returned a few minutes later, Maggie called her to ask her what the girl's name was.

Dori looked toward the water. It was misting out and pitch black. She noticed that the low-wattage light that was always left on at the Duncans' boathouse roof in front of the Johanna had burned out and there was nothing you could see.

About 9:30, Maggie went to bed to read. Linn stayed up awhile, as was his habit. It was quiet on the lake, a relief from the frequent late-night chatter of the summer guests on the roof of the boathouse, extending their day as long as they could, extending the Duncans', too, with their talk.

At 10, Dori took her dog out for a walk. It was still raining. There was a light on in the Mary Ellen.

After watching the 11 o'clock news, Linn turned out the light and joined his wife. Dark night, cool fall weather, no tourist tomfoolery, great night for sleeping.

A BODY IN THE WATER

At 7:38 a.m., the phone rang. Linn would remember the time the rest of his life. He wondered why the phone was ringing, wondered, too, why he'd slept in so late, usually up and at 'em by then.

Better not be a buddy calling him to ask about golf, not this early. Getting ready to be irked if it was, he picked up the receiver.

"Hello."

"This is Mark Unger." And then sobs.

"Hello, Mark."

"She hasn't come home all night." Meaning Flo.

"What would you like us to do?" asked Linn.

"Well, we'd like you to go look for her."

Linn looked at his wife and told her what it was about. "What do you think we should do?" he asked.

"Well, let's get dressed and go help him."

Linn hung up the phone. Maggie threw on some jeans and a sweatshirt and went out to the living room. She looked out over the lake, the first thing she did every day, but there was no peace to be gained from the view today.

She looked over at the boathouse and saw that the chaise longue had been moved from where Linn left it when he was moving furniture the day before. Maggie could only see the back of it. It had been over in a corner, but was considerably over to the left, now. And it wasn't flat like he'd left it, either, the back was up.

Florence is probably down there, she thought, mystery likely solved.

Same thought Linn had had. He'd come into the room, was standing next to her and looking at the boathouse, too. Gee, maybe Flo's on the chaise. Maybe she fell asleep there, and that's all this is, just a wife falling asleep in a chair.

"Let's go take a look," said Maggie, who headed out the door and toward the boathouse. Linn, who had to put his shoes on first, followed fifteen or twenty seconds behind.

Maggie got to the chaise, saw that it was empty and kept on walking to the railing overlooking the lake—and looked down.

A body floated in the water, face down, bobbing to the gentle wavelets of the still morning. Flo? There was a halo of deep pink on the surface of the water around her head. There was a quilt on the apron below. By then, Linn was at her side. They both stared down, knowing what they were looking at, but it taking a while to sink in, unreal.

She turned to him. "What should I do? Should I call 911?"

"By all means," said her husband, still staring. "Yes, you go up and call 911."

Maggie stood there, seemingly lost in thought, frozen by the moment, for twelve or fifteen seconds, then turned around and walked back to the house and a phone. She seemed calmer to Linn than he was, his voice a lie to his own ears, if not to hers. He stood there, then realized he was crying. He stared down, "doing some cursing to myself," as he would describe it later. After about thirty seconds, he thought, "I better go down and take a look."

Maggie called the 911 operator, sounding anything but calm. She told her where she was, what she'd just seen, they needed to get someone out here.

"I believe it's a— It is a suicide or a drowning or something," she said.

The operator asked her, "Was she depressed, lately?"

"Yeah, she has been, I believe. It looks like she had a quilt. My husband said it looked like she came down here to sleep and got a quilt, and whether she just went over the side, I don't know."

By now, Linn was at the edge of the water, about two feet from the body. The body was angled off to the northeast, the head aiming out, the hair floating on the surface.

The pink jumped out at him. It just looked so incongruous, pink water. And the body seemed to be floating extra high. He looked at the body's calves, out of the water, and the shoulders, out of the water, and the head floating high on the water, too.

Linn stared at the body for maybe two minutes. Half the concrete apron was taken up by a boat hoist that sits in the lake during the season, to hold a boat out of the water so you don't need to anchor it. It was stored on the apron for the winter.

Linn saw that next to it were two yellow candle stubs, maybe two inches long. Next to the candles were the quilt and some small bits of broken glass. He picked up the quilt and underneath it was a puddle of pink water. He hung it up on the hoist, something he did reflexively, thinking later he shouldn't have touched it, but wanting, then, to be neat.

Linn headed back to the Mary Ellen, walking west up the slope in the remnant of an old narrow-gauge railroad bed that used to run along the lake to haul lumber to Lake Michigan. The railroad had long since been dismantled, but a well-trod path remained, and Linn headed along it.

Mark was walking toward him. Their eyes met and Mark picked up his pace. Linn was thinking: What do you say? How do you tell someone there's a body floating face down in the water and it's probably your wife?

So Linn's thinking as Mark's walking and they meet in front of a cottage called the Cecilia, two down from the Mary Ellen, and Linn touches him on the chest and says, "Mark, you're not going to like it. She's in the water."

Mark went, as Linn would describe it later, "ballistic."

Dori Turner was up and dressed, in her bedroom when she heard godawful screaming. She looked out the window and saw Linn and Mark Unger.

Mark was screaming and hollering—people around the corner of the lake later said they could hear him and thought something horrible had happened to Linn, that he must have had a heart attack—and Dori saw him take off on a beeline, diagonally across the sloping yard toward the boathouse.

Unger ran out of Dori's view, behind shrubs and trees in full color and down beneath the slope of the hill, running directly to the body. He got to the water and jumped in.

Dori ran out on the porch. "What's wrong? What's happened?" But Linn didn't answer. He followed after Unger. When he got to the apron, Mark was in the water, leaning against the concrete, his head in his arms, crying.

It didn't look like he'd touched the body, or had rolled it over to make sure it was Flo. Her body looked undisturbed from when he'd been staring at it a few minutes ago.

Mark got up, came over to Linn and they hugged, both crying, now. They separated. Mark's jacket was on the apron and Linn picked it up and hung it on the boat hoist, too.

The two walked back up the slope. Maggie came out of the house with a chair for Mark to sit on. Later, Linn wouldn't remember how the chair had gotten there. At the time, it seemed as though one minute Mark was standing, next he was sitting in a chair, sobbing, in a blanket Maggie had wrapped around him.

"THIS IS NOT RIGHT"

At 8:20, fifteen minutes after the 911 call had come in, the North Flight EMS crew from Paul Oliver Hospital in the nearby port town of Frankfort arrived, two women and three men. Linn led them down to the body, still bobbing on the wavelets.

The right arm was bent under the body, the hand visible on the other side, by her left shoulder. The left arm was bent, elbow jutting out away from the body, hand under the abdomen.

One of the men, Mike Trailer, got on his knees, reached out and touched one of Flo's legs. It struck Linn as peculiar. "Why'd he do that?" he asked.

"To see if she's still alive," said one of the women.

If there was a chance she was still alive, they should have been racing in the water, pulling her out and acting with some sense of purpose, Linn thought. But there wasn't a chance. She couldn't have been there face down all that time and be alive, seemed obvious to him.

Trailer poked her instead of pulling her out of the water because he wanted to disturb what might be a crime scene as little as possible. He wanted the body to stay exactly where it was till they were done working the scene.

Trailer later would describe her leg as "rigid, stiff and

cold." He got up, saw pink fluid on the concrete apron, in a pool about a foot in diameter. Blood, he thought, diluted by the rain earlier.

He looked at his co-workers and said, "I think we better back off. This is not right." Normally he would check for a pulse to confirm she was dead, but he knew there was no point.

Duncan left the EMS crew to their business and walked back up the hill.

Neighbors started accumulating. One was Jim Ryan, who lived down Watervale Road from the resort. He and his wife, Eliza, had been coming to the area on vacation since 1996 and a year earlier had bought a place and moved there from Minneapolis.

A little after 8 that morning, he'd been in the kitchen with his wife when they'd heard loud shouting. The phone rang. It was Dori Turner. She was crying. "Please come over to Maggie's right away," she'd said. By then, Dori knew Florence was dead. She'd been told before that Mark had been in rehab, and she knew Ryan was a long-time member of Alcoholics Anonymous, so she thought he might be a good shoulder for Mark to cry on.

The Ryans lived just down the road from the resort and normally would have walked, but this time drove over. There were emergency vehicles parked, lights going. A man he didn't know was sitting in a chair on the lawn, wrapped in a blanket. Jim walked toward Maggie.

"There's been a suicide," she said. A woman. Her husband and two boys were there. Maggie told Jim, knowing he'd had his own history with alcohol abuse and was an AA counselor now, that the husband supposedly was recovering from some problems with alcohol or drugs.

Another neighbor, Sharon Trens, Dori's cousin, came over and said the man was wet and needed to get into some dry clothes, and Jim walked over to him, figuring he had to be the husband they'd told him about, and said, "How you doing?"

"I think I'm going to be sick."

The man got up and went over to the side of the cottage and leaned over, like he was going to throw up. Then he did something that struck Jim as very peculiar—he kneeled down and started rolling around on the fallen leaves. Had he gone back to drinking? Or on some kind of drugs?

Ryan walked over.

"Were you sick?" Meaning, had he thrown up?

"No."

So what was all the rolling around about? Ryan helped him back to the chair. He asked Unger if he'd had a chance to talk to his boys, yet.

"No."

He hadn't talked to Flo's parents, either, and he needed to.

CALLING THE STERNS

About 8:45 a.m., the phone rang in the Huntington Woods home of Flo's parents, Harold and Claire Stern.

The Sterns were still in bed. Claire picked up the telephone. Mark was on the other end. His voice was odd, panicky. He asked to speak to "Papa," the name the grandkids had given Harold.

"Where's my daughter?" asked Claire Stern, knowing instinctively to ask the question.

"Let me talk to Papa."

"I want to know where my daughter is." Knowing, the way you *know* these things, from his tone, from her gut, that something was very wrong.

"My God, you've killed my daughter," she said, angry.

"Let me talk to Papa."

Harold grabbed the phone and started to talk. Unger interrupted. "She's in the water. She's in the water."

Later, Stern would remember nothing of the conversation past that point. Mark saying, "She's in the water," and then . . . what? A blur. Everything a blur.

The Sterns got up and got dressed. About 9:30 or 10, Ada Kerwin, Florence's divorce attorney, stopped by the Sterns' house. She had gotten a call about Flo from Amy Folbe, the attorney who had recommended Kerwin to Flo.

A little later, Laurie Glass stopped by, too. Mark's cousin, Marci Zussman, had called her to tell her Flo was dead, and she'd raced over to the Sterns'.

Huntington Woods is a tight-knit community. Word of Flo's death raced through the city, by e-mail, cell phone, land line and "Did-you-hears" on sidewalks and over fences.

The city is just two miles north of the Detroit city limits, but to drive through the one city and then through the other, you'd think they were on different continents.

Huntington Woods is just 1.5 square miles, with a population in 2000 of 6,151—96.96 percent white then, and .68 percent black. Detroit's population of 951,270 was 82.7 percent black and 12.26 percent white.

Huntington Woods is bounded by Ten Mile Road to the south and ends a mile north, at Eleven Mile Road. East to west it is just a mile and a half wide. Its chosen nickname is the rather mundane "City of Homes," which doesn't exactly differentiate itself from the suburban cities that surround it. Other nicknames are "City of Trees," and, because of its large Jewish population, "Chanukah Woods." One resident is quoted on the Wikipedia Web site listing for the city as saying, "You don't understand, they don't let bad things happen here."

Residents are generally upper-middle or upper class, with a median family income of $97,055 and a per capita income of $45,264. In nearby Detroit, median family income was $33,853 and per capita income was $14,717.

There is no trace of the swamp the city was built on. The homes are brick and large, but not ostentatious. Most Detroit suburbs are laid out in strict east-west/north-south grids. Here, the streets meander in curves beneath tall, broad-trunked trees that provide thick shade in summer, the cicadas at dusk humming with what strikes visitors as an ear-piercing electric whine, one that residents rarely notice, or if they do, appreciate as a sign of the season.

It is common for generations of children from the same family to go to Burton Elementary School and live in houses around the block or down the street from where their parents and grandparents grew up, just as the Ungers had.

But on this day the Sterns were distraught. They talked about their grandchildren and what should be done about them. Letting them stay with Mark was out of the question; conclusions had already been made that this was somehow his fault.

Kerwin drove over to the police station to get on the record with the local authorities what had happened up north.

Meanwhile, Benzie County Sheriff's Deputy Troy Packard, who'd been sent out by dispatcher Nicole Lamerson, arrived at Watervale a little after 9. Rosy-cheeked, he looked more like a high school linebacker than a cop.

Lamerson had said to him, "Are you ready for the first one of the day?"

"Alrighty," he'd answered.

And she'd responded, "You're going to love it." Meaning, some excitement for his Saturday morning, not a typical resort area call about a missing Jet Ski or a cabin break-in. Explaining that a woman had called about a possible suicide.

Packard, a uniformed patrolman, had been with the department for all of ten days, having been hired from Manistee County just to the south.

He found Trailer down on the boathouse apron. Trailer told him they needed to secure the area. "We've got an unusual death," he said. Packard saw the quilt hanging on a railing by the boat hoist. It looked to be stained with blood. A red liquid had dripped off the bottom and onto the concrete and formed a pool around bits of broken glass.

Packard told the EMS crew to clear the scene. He looked up and saw that the railing around the roof of the boathouse was broken. He walked back to the Duncans and told those there not to go back to the boathouse or the lake.

He then walked farther up the slope to Unger, who was crying.

Unger told him he wanted to go back to the Mary Ellen

to check on his boys, make sure they were all right. Packard said that was fine, and he, Unger and Ryan walked over to the cottage.

Max was on the couch downstairs, Tyler upstairs in the bedroom.

Linn Duncan walked in the side door. Max, wrapped in a blanket, was watching a movie on a small player. Linn wasn't sure what you called it—a CD player?—it looked like one of those little laptop computers with a screen that flipped up.

Duncan stood there five minutes, then thought, Shoot, I'm not doing anything but standing around, might as well go home.

Unger went up and got Tyler and when they came back down, Packard told him he needed to go back down to the lake and secure the scene. He told Ryan to stay with Unger and make sure he was going to be okay.

"Have the boys eaten anything, yet?" Ryan asked Unger.

"No."

"Maybe we should go to breakfast first and get the boys something to eat," said Ryan, and they all walked over to the dining room at the Watervale Inn. No one else was there.

Unger sat down at a table with his boys. Ryan kept his distance. He could see Mark tell them that their mother was dead, the kids' hysteric reaction. Not something you'd ever want to witness.

There wasn't any point, then, to ordering breakfast. Who was going to eat? So they walked back to the cottage.

"There's some alcohol in the cabinet, a bottle. You might as well dump that," said Unger to Ryan. "I'd feel more comfortable if you dumped it out."

It was amaretto. It was more than half full. "Did you have anything to do with that last night?" asked Ryan, meaning the bottle. Or, rather, what was gone from it.

"No. It's not mine. It's my wife's."

"Did it have anything to do with what happened last night?"

"No. She didn't drink last night. She hardly drinks at all."

Ryan poured it down the sink, thinking, Hmm, he's supposed to be in recovery, she didn't drink, so why is the bottle nearly half empty? Light drinkers don't usually travel with their own bottles of opened booze. Just struck him as odd.

Whether it was watching the alcohol get poured out, or just a need to talk, Unger told Ryan he was an alcoholic, but he'd been sober for fourteen months. Still went to meetings every day. Got his medallion for achieving a year of sobriety. He'd given it to Flo and she was thrilled to get it.

"I got sober for Flo," he said.

"You need to do it for yourself," said Ryan. "You can't do these things for somebody else."

Ryan had been in a recovery program for more than twenty years, and had worked for ten years as an inpatient counselor at a hospital in Minnesota.

Unger said he wanted to pack up and leave, seemed, to Ryan, eager to get going. Unger told the boys to get their stuff together, they needed to leave.

"This isn't a happy place for us. We should go," he said.

He started working the phone, too, making and getting calls. He asked Ryan to make one of his calls for him, to his brother-in-law, Peter Stern. Could Ryan call him and tell him the news?

Why he wouldn't call his own brother-in-law himself, Ryan had no idea. But he did as Unger asked.

Stern, who was with the township fire department, got a page about 9:30. Thinking it might be about some fire or accident, the page surprised him. It was a message to call Ryan, who sounded strange, sort of evasive. It was about Flo, he said, there'd been an accident, but he couldn't bring himself to blurt out the real news.

"Well, did everyone die in a car accident?" asked Peter. Worried, but being flip, not really thinking the worst.

"No. Just your sister," he said, getting right to it. Ryan told him there'd been an accident, his sister had been found in the lake and had apparently drowned. He didn't say what he'd been told, that it was a suicide.

"Is there any foul play suspected?" asked Stern. The question shocked Ryan. Foul play? Murder?

"Not as far as I know. As far as I know, it's suicide," he said.

Stern said he'd be right there.

"What did he say?" asked Unger.

"Well, he was shocked and upset," said Ryan.

A few minutes went by. Unger made another call or two, then seemed to realize the boys hadn't made much progress. "Come on, boys, you got to get packing."

PACKING THE CAR

Packard got out his yellow crime-scene tape and made a wide perimeter around the boathouse area, anchoring it on one end around a tree west of the scene. He called dispatch and said to call the nearby Michigan State Police post to send out whoever was on duty that day. He said it was a very suspicious scene—"We got blood everywhere," he said. Blood and a broken rail on a deck and a body floating in the lake.

He needed a detective out here, maybe the sheriff himself, to assess the scene and decide whether to call in the state police crime lab team. Calling in the state police is common at suspicious death scenes in small northern Michigan communities whose local resources are limited and whose police tend to be young and inexperienced.

State Trooper Rick Doering arrived a little later. About 9:30, Sheriff's Deputy Detective Ken Fallowfield arrived. He wasn't supposed to work Saturday, but he hadn't finished some paperwork in the detective's bureau the day before. He wanted to get it out of the way and had come in this morning.

Lamerson heard he was in the building, called him on the phone.

"What do you guys have, radar?" asked Fallowfield, meaning, How did you know I was in the building?

"Guess what we've got?" she said.

"A murder?" said Fallowfield facetiously. More like a leaf blower gone missing.

Lamerson told him Packard said there was blood everywhere, and that the original 911 call said some guy's wife, who had been suicidal, hadn't come home all night.

"You're kidding. Where at?"

"Watervale."

"Jesus." Watervale? Famous local resort?

So he had raced on over. Packard took him to the boathouse deck. Fallowfield examined the broken support pillar. It was fractured and splintering outward toward the lake, but not broken clear through.

Fallowfield looked down, over the edge. He saw a woman, face down in the water, wearing what looked like some sort of running suit and a pink halo. He saw what looked like diluted blood on the concrete, broken candles, bits of broken glass. What struck him was a void between the blood on the concrete and the lake. If the woman had bled on the apron—and that seemed a certainty—how did her body get in the water without leaving a trail of blood?

Clearly it was a scene that warranted state police crimelab technicians, and they were summoned from the lab in Grayling, seventy-five miles away.

Meanwhile, another member of the Benzie County Sheriff's Department, Detective Sergeant Tom Kelley, who ran the detective bureau, arrived on the scene. Like Fallowfield, he was supposed to be off duty, but Lamerson had called him to tell him what was up.

Soon, the county's volunteer dive team arrived. The sheriff, Robert Blank, had called Chris Wooten, the dive team leader, and said their services might be needed, there was a report of a body in Lower Herring.

Wooten called the members of his team, which met them with their scuba gear at the sheriff's department, then drove over together. Once there, they were told the site was being treated as a crime scene, to please hang around, but they wouldn't be going in the water for a while.

Fallowfield borrowed Packard's camera and started shooting the scene. He went down to the concrete apron. The circle of blood was about twenty-four inches in diameter. The blood in the pockmarks of the old concrete was redder, less diluted by rain or lake water.

Having turned the scene over to Fallowfield, Packard went back to the Mary Ellen.

The boys and Unger were sitting on the downstairs couch. Unger had changed out of his black sweat suit into jeans and a red top. He told Unger he needed to ask him some questions. He asked what they had done last night, when was the last time he'd seen his wife.

To both, Unger answered, "I don't know."

What time had he called the Duncans?

"I don't know."

What time had he woken up?

"I don't know."

Then, "It's just too hard to talk about."

Packard stopped the questioning. The boys were eating cereal. Unger paced the room, constantly making and receiving calls on his cell. Packard wandered around the cabin, seeing what there was to see.

It was routine cabin stuff. Mostly, Packard watched Unger. When he went out to the screened-in porch, Packard followed. Unger would be in the middle of a conversation, then erupt in emotion, starting to cry, saying, "I don't know, I don't know," and in the middle of that, call-waiting would let him know there was another call.

And switching to that call, saying "Hello" like everything was normal. He took another call, began crying and hollering, said goodbye, turned to Packard and started talking in a calm voice.

Sheriff's Deputy Sergeant Beth Baesch arrived. She was a supervisor for night patrol, and had been off duty at a kids' soccer game that morning when she got the call to get over to Watervale and help work the scene. It was her job to interview Max and Tyler, everyone figuring it'd be easier for them to talk to a woman.

They were distraught. But Max, probably happy to talk about the recent past to keep his mind off the present, was an easy interview.

Max told her his mom was supposed to stay in the downstairs bedroom, his dad upstairs. His mom liked to go to the boat house patio and she went out there with her blue blanket. His dad went, too. His mom had on her fleece and his dad had on his favorite black coat.

He and Tyler watched one movie and in the middle of the second one, his dad came back in. He watched it with them for a few minutes and told them it was time to go to bed. He tucked them in and said their mom would be back in a little bit. The boys watched movies on their own little DVD players.

As they'd been lying there a while, their dad came back in and kissed them, again. Their mom or dad always came back in a second time, and Max had been sort of asleep and wasn't sure if it was his mom or dad until he felt whiskers. His dad told them he'd been listening to the Detroit Red Wings hockey game on the radio and the score was 3–0 Detroit.

And the next thing he knew, it was light and he looked over and Tyler was already up and downstairs with his dad.

And his dad took them over to the Inn, where he told them what had happened. "He said, 'She never came up, and they found her in the water,' " Max told Baesch.

She asked him if his mom and dad had been getting along.

"Sort of not getting along." Then adding, "If they fought about dinner, does that count?"

Had his parents talked about a separation, or a divorce, last night?

"No. Everything was fine," said Max. He told her his mom was a loan officer at Flagstar Bank, his dad didn't work except for sometimes doing sports updates on the radio, and added that he was in the fifth grade at Burton Elementary.

And that was it.

Meanwhile, Packard stuck close to Unger, listening to his string of phone conversations. He talked to his sister, then to a funeral director. The call to the funeral home puzzled Packard. So soon?

In between calls, Unger kept saying he wanted to leave. He needed to go home. He needed to get his sons out of there.

Packard went back outside and saw a Ford Expedition, Unger's car, parked by the cabin with its tailgate open. He went over and looked inside. It was packed with belongings, including duffel bags. Packard pointed the car out to Kelley. The car looked like it was ready to roll.

After Peter Stern got off the phone with Ryan, he called a friend named Ellen and asked her to drive him to Watervale. They got there a little after 10.

He could see the crime-scene tape strung out across the path to the lake, well up from the water. He walked toward the tape. But then, afraid of seeing his sister's body, of having *that* be his last memory of her, he stopped and stood there, waiting. For what, he had no idea.

He spoke to a series of police officers and answered some routine questions. He kept saying, "This is fishy." Later, when he tried to recall details, a lot of it was just a haze.

At some point, his father called. It had been decided that Mark couldn't keep the kids. For now, they should stay with Peter. When he left Watervale, he should take them the twenty or twenty-five miles to his house in Glen Arbor.

Mark was off with other police and Stern was relieved not to have to see or talk to him. At one point, someone told him Mark wanted to speak with him. He ignored the request as long as he could and kept his distance.

THE WORD GOES OUT

Connie and Jerry Wolberg were at the Birmingham Temple. Every other year she organized a three-day conference on one topic or another, and this year it was "Jews and Non-Jews: The Love–Hate Relationship."

During a morning break, they turned their cell phones on to check for messages. Each had a bunch. Her cousin Marci had called, her sister Kim, her son. They knew something bad must have happened and went into an empty room to find out what.

She called Marci, who told her the news.

"What! What!" Connie kept screaming. "Nothing registered," she'd say later.

She called Mark, but couldn't reach him. Jerry called Lyle. Finally, Mark called.

"I kept saying, 'How are the kids? How are the kids? Are the kids okay?'" she'd say later. "He'd be crying and crying and at some point, he'd stop."

"Can I come up?" asked Connie.

"No. I'll come down when I can."

Susan Witus was out and about early Saturday morning. When she got back, there was a message to call Laurie

Glass. Laurie's husband, David, answered and told her the news: Florence was dead.

She hung up and began sobbing intensely. Her husband, Brian, heard her and came running. She told him what had happened and told him he had to go to Watervale. He needed to go look after Flo's kids.

Lyle, Mark's nephew, and his wife, Cheryl, lived around the block from the Ungers. Lyle and Cheryl had 3-year-old twins, and Cheryl had given birth to a daughter, Maya, three weeks earlier. They'd last seen Flo on Wednesday night, when she'd walked over to visit the new baby. Cheryl had put the twins down about 8 and Flo had stayed another three hours before walking home.

Flo and Cheryl were close friends. Frequent antiquing buddies, they loved to share girl-talk over a glass or two of wine. Flo had gone through an amaretto stage, and it hadn't been hard for her to get Cheryl to share that with her, too.

The drinking, Wolberg didn't mind. The antiquing could drive him to distraction. He made a very good living, but, nonetheless, he hated seeing the bills come in. They'd have fights on occasion over the spending. Or when Lyle would see some obviously pricy antique taking up a new spot in the house. Often, though, the situation would be diffused with the explanation, "Don't worry. It's Flo's. She just can't take it home right now because she doesn't want Mark to see it."

It was close to 10, and Lyle and one of twins, Katie, were walking out the door to drive to a tennis class Katie was taking at the Beverly Hills Racquet Club. Cheryl was staying home with Maya. Cheryl's cell phone rang. It was Marci Zussman.

Lyle heard his wife start shrieking, and then: "Oh my God, I can't believe it!"

She told him the news. He calmed her down a bit, then called Mark's cell phone. No answer. Panicked himself, not sure what to do, not wanting to break his promise to

Katie that come the weekend, Daddy would do something special with her—the twins were jealous at all the attention Maya had gotten the last three weeks—Lyle loaded his daughter into the car.

On the way, Lyle's cell phone rang. He looked at the screen. It was Florence's number. A jolt there, of hope, of fear. Could it all be some horrible mistake and Flo was calling to put everything right? He answered. It was Mark. He was crying.

"What happened?" asked Lyle.

"She's dead! She's dead!"

"What happened?"

"She's dead!"

"Where are the boys?"

Mark was incoherent. Somehow he got the gist of it across.

"Mark, you gotta get the boys out of there," said Wolberg. Picturing Flo in the water, the horror of the scene.

Wolberg told him he was coming up, he'd be there as soon as he could. He hung up the phone and called a friend, Glenn Cantor, and told him what had happened and that they needed to go.

The class lasted forty-five minutes. Wolberg sat in the club. He couldn't get cell phone coverage. There was so much he needed to do and nothing to be done but wait for the end of Katie's class.

Wolberg raced home after the class, threw some stuff in his Volvo station wagon, then drove over to Cantor's. Brian Witus was there, too. Wolberg knew him by reputation but had never met him. He was an attorney and had told Cantor, "You may need me."

They hit the road, a little after 11. Witus called Glenn Stark out in Montana, thought he should know. Stark's reaction shocked Witus.

"*He* did it!" said Stark, nearly hysteric. "*He* did it!"

Later, Stark would say he just *knew*. Or thought he knew. When he heard the horrible news, he instantly thought there was no accident at the heart of it, no set of fluke

circumstances, no blameless cause. The word shouted out
to him: MARK!

Seymour Schwartz's cell phone rang at 11:30. He was a
defense attorney, and that morning, Schwartz was across
the state from Beulah, in the small town of Standish,
near Lake Huron, in the middle of the biggest trial of his
career.

Two brothers, Coco and J. R. Duvall, had been accused
of killing a pair of Detroit-area deer hunters in 1985. Back
then, the case had made headlines for months, the hunters
having left for a weekend and never been seen again. The
only more famous missing person in recent Michigan history had been Jimmy Hoffa.

Finally, a state cop named Bronco Lesneski, working
on his own time, broke the cold-case open and Schwartz
was representing the accused killers, who were alleged to
have had words with the hunters in a bar, later followed
them down the road, pulled their car over and beaten them
to death with baseball bats. The brothers didn't have much
money, so Schwartz agreed to take a house as payment.
(*Darker Than Night*, St. Martin's Press)

Schwartz had known Mark since they were boys. For
years, they'd shared coaching duties on Max's Huntington
Woods baseball team.

After Mark got out of rehab, Schwartz had offered to
drive with him to Alcoholics Anonymous. "He was new to
it, and I was ten, eleven years in. He was doing terrific,"
said Schwartz.

The call was a mutual friend, telling him Florence had
died and asking him if he wanted to drive over and help out.
Deep into the trial—and, coincidentally, going up against a
state prosecutor named Donna Pendergast, who would soon
take an interest in Unger—Schwartz declined.

He couldn't get his mind off Mark and his loss. "He just
doted on this woman," he said to himself, and would say to
others later, in the ensuing months.

* * *

Flo's cell phone, which Mark was carrying, rang. Packard watched him answer it. It was Stark, calling from Bozeman. Unger had called him earlier, left a message: "Call me as soon as you get this message, on Flo's cell phone."

Meanwhile, Witus had already reached Stark.

"What happened to her?" Stark asked Mark, getting right to it, no how-you-doing, his voice emotional.

"I don't know."

"What happened to her?" asked Stark, again. "Did you let her go for a walk by herself?"

It must have seemed a puzzling question to Unger.

"No," said Unger.

"Did she do this to herself?"

"No. No way."

"Is this a homicide investigation?" asked Stark, getting right to it, again.

"Stop it! Stop it!" Unger said. "You're scaring me. Stop it!"

"Mark, I'll look into your eyes, and I'll know."

"Okay. Okay. I gotta go." Unger hung up.

"What was that?" asked Packard.

"A friend from Montana," said Unger, matter-of-fact. From the one end of the conversation he could hear, it hadn't sounded like a friend.

Fallowfield returned from the lake, took a photo of the packed car and had Unger recount his version of events.

Unger told him he and Flo had gone out to the boathouse about 8 and he'd gone back to the cottage to check on the kids and put them to bed. He came back out, Flo wasn't there. He went back to the cottage and fell asleep watching TV.

The next morning, he woke up, Flo hadn't come back and he called the Duncans, who had found her in the water.

Fallowfield left, called the county prosecutor and said he needed to meet him, there'd been a suspicious death and he needed a search warrant. Weird thing is, he said, there's nothing resolved here and the husband already has the car packed and is ready to drive to Detroit, his wife's body still in the water.

Sergeant Kelley kept busy. He interviewed both Linn and Maggie Duncan, he interviewed Peter Stern, and then he drove Mark Unger to the Benzie County Sheriff's Department to interview him in his office, away from all the turmoil.

Before he left with Kelley, Unger agreed to let Stern take Max and Tyler to his house, get them away from Watervale, where their mother was still floating.

(Unbeknownst to Mark, Kelley had told Stern not to let Unger see the boys later, and he'd called the Leelanau County Family Independence Agency to tell them what had happened. Shortly after Stern got home, a worker from the agency showed up at his house to make sure it was suitable for the boys and to order him not to let Unger take the kids.)

Kelley didn't read Unger his rights. He was free to go with Kelley or not, free to cut the interview short, free to walk out, so there was no legal need to warn him about anything.

Kelley handed Unger some paper and a pen and told him to write down his version of the weekend's events. Unger filled in two pages, handed them back to Kelley, who read on page one:

> We came up Friday night for the weekend. Went to dinner at Dinghy's, came back to Watervale, watched DVD with kids. Walked to the deck. I came back to cabin to get kids to bed. Went back to the deck. She wasn't there. Went back to the cabin. Fell asleep, watching DVD. Got up in the middle of the night when Tyler called. Woke up this morning, no Flo. Called Linn and Maggie. Linn told me he found her.

And on page two:

*I ran down there. I tried to get her out, but blood
started coming out. Started crying.*

Kelley signed his name to it as a witness and wrote
down the time: 12:35 p.m. Just 12:35? Hard to imagine how
so much could get crammed into one bad morning.

Kelley looked the brief report over, noticing more what
was missing than what was there. It wasn't much of a narrative, lots of blank spots, looked like, a long night and a
long morning compressed into a few sparse sentences. He
started asking Unger questions, getting him to go into
some detail.

Unger's delivery alternated between bouts of sobbing,
Kelley offering him Kleenexes from the box on his desk,
and a quiet, matter-of-fact tone.

He said he'd carried the candle out to the deck, Flo taking a blue blanket. After a little while he'd gone back to tend
to the kids, tucked them into bed, sang them some songs,
read to them. Sang them an extra song. Read them an extra
story. When he went back out, it was drizzling.

"What time was this?" asked Kelley.

"I don't know."

"Well, in relation to midnight."

"Way before midnight."

He looked for Flo, didn't see her, did see the lights on in
the Duncans', figured Flo had gone to visit them, so he returned to the cottage.

Then what?

Then he watched some DVDs and fell asleep on the
couch. During the night, Tyler had some problems, made
some noise, he went up to comfort him and ended up falling asleep next to his son.

Had he at any point gone back out to check on Flo?

No.

Next thing he knew, it was 7:30 a.m. No Flo. He called

the Duncans and a little later, he was walking outside and Linn was walking toward him from the boathouse and touched him on the chest. Unger said Duncan told him, " 'It's really bad. I think Flo jumped off the deck.' "

While they were talking, Mark kept fiddling with his cell phone, looking down at it, punching in numbers, trying to make calls but having trouble getting any bars or enough reception to get a call through, and getting agitated by it.

At one point, Kelley led Unger outside so he could get better reception and make his call. It struck Kelley as odd that in the middle of being questioned about the suspicious death of your wife you weren't exactly paying full attention.

"Were you the last one, then, to see Flo alive?" asked Kelley when they were back inside.

"I guess so."

Now's the time, thought Kelley. He'd been told by others that the Ungers were going through a divorce; he'd been told, now, that Mark was the last one to see Flo alive. He pulled out his Miranda card and read Unger his rights.

If Unger had asked for an attorney, the interview would have had to end, by law. But he didn't. Kelley told him he'd heard they were getting divorced. And that he'd heard Mark had been having problems with drugs and had been in rehabilitation.

Unger cut him off, told him he didn't want to talk about this anymore. Wanted to go back and be with his boys. Wanted to get them and take them home.

Kelley, remembering the packed car, thought without saying. You want to get your boys and go home, eh, while your wife is still down in the water?

But said, politely, "You know, sometimes things happen in our lives that we don't mean to happen. Sometimes, basically in desperation, things happen." Kelley had been a cop for thirty-three years, had by now what others would describe as a grandfatherly approach to his interrogations, quiet and pleasant.

"If you've got something to say to me, if you've got something to ask me, then ask me," said Unger.

"Okay. Did you push her off the deck?"

"What kind of question is that?" said Unger, flaring up, like it had come out of the blue, never mind his having just been read his Miranda rights.

He said he was through. He wanted to go back to the cottage. So Kelley drove him back to the lake, where it was early afternoon and Florence Unger's body was still bobbing.

BOXER SHORTS

After Unger returned, Dori Turner took a tray of food over to the Mary Ellen, with coffee, milk and cereal. She went in the kitchen door. Mark was in the front room, sitting on the sofa with the boys, one on either side of him, their backs to her.

Tyler turned to his dad as she walked in and said, "Daddy, my heart is broken."

Unger looked at her and said, "Broken hearts mend, don't they, Dori?"

At 2:25 p.m., the technicians from the Grayling crime lab arrived, two forensic scientists named Frances D'Angela and Jennifer Patchin, and a lab specialist named John Bowen. The women were civilian employees, Bowen was a state police sergeant and a fingerprint specialist.

They talked to the police who were already there, then walked slowly around the scene, D'Angela shooting photos with her 35-millimeter camera, Bowen backing those up with shots from his digital camera. She noticed the broken rails bowing outward at the front of the boathouse deck and shot them. The rails were low, only two feet high or so, not much of a barrier. Bowen dusted very fine black powder on the rails and the deck, brushing it on with a clean ball of cotton.

Patchin took notes as they proceeded.

She saw paint chips from the broken rails on the boathouse roof, near the chaise longue, and, when they went down to the concrete apron, saw what looked to be matching paint chips, a wood splinter, and an earring.

As they made their way around the scene, periodically, Bowen would set down his camera, get out a note pad and sketch the surroundings.

D'Angela took samples from the blood on the concrete, sticking cotton swabs into the little pockmarks in the concrete where the blood was less diluted, then letting them air dry. Patchin picked up the wood splinter, which Bowen measured to be forty-seven inches from the boathouse wall, and the earring, which was seventy inches from the wall. It had a post, for pierced ears, and seemed to be silver with a clear gemstone.

Later they would confirm it was Flo's, matching the one in her left ear.

With the help of one member of the dive team Bowen made some measurements. The center of Florence's head was forty-one inches from the edge of the breakwall. The center of her right knee was sixteen inches from the wall. From the front boathouse wall to the breakwall, it was one hundred and thirteen inches. It was twelve feet, six inches from the top of the railing on the roof to the concrete apron. It was a drop of thirty inches from the edge of the concrete down to the water.

The team then moved on to a search of the Mary Ellen, which revealed nothing more suspicious than a pile of kids' DVDs.

Patchin tested various things with luminol, a chemical that luminesces when it comes in contact with blood. She did the covered porch, the thresholds of all the rooms, the bathroom walls and floors, the towels in the bathrooms, the blankets on the couch, the stairs to the second floor. Nothing.

At some point, the crime lab people brought out what looked to be a one-piece paper suit they had brought with them from Grayling—it was actually much stronger than paper, a suit that lab technicians might wear to keep from contaminating samples—and asked Unger if he would sign a consent form to let them have his clothes. And put this on, instead.

He said sure and, with all the tumult in the Mary Ellen, went over to the Duncans' to change there. Unger asked Linn if he could use their bathroom, and to his and Maggie's surprise, he came out of the bathroom before he'd put the suit on, and asked, "How do you like my SpongeBob SquarePants Halloween boxer shorts? Max and Tyler gave me these."

Maggie had no idea who or what a SpongeBob was, but she knew that the last thing she wanted to be doing right now was looking at Mark in his underwear.

"Well . . ." was all she could muster. She offered him a seat on the couch and got him a glass of cider.

Wolberg, Cantor and Witus would have made record time getting to Watervale but for a bit of miscommunication. At one point along the way, they were told on the cell that Mark was at the sheriff's office in Beulah. After waiting in the lobby there for twenty minutes, though, they were told that Mark was no longer there, that, instead, he'd been driven back to the resort. They got directions and made the short drive to Watervale.

They found Mark at the Duncans', looking incongruous, at the least, in his jumpsuit. Mark started crying. He hugged Wolberg and wouldn't let go and Wolberg started crying, too, and they hugged and cried for a few minutes. Seemed longer, later, when Wolberg thought about it. Mark hugged Glenn, then Brian, and they all cried.

The Notre Dame football game was playing on TV, Wolberg noticed, one of those things you remember later. So it had to have been before 4. That's about when the game would have ended.

Mark wasn't free to go, yet. Witus and Wolberg stepped outside to check things out. Yellow crime-scene tape stopped them from getting too close to the boathouse. Sergeant Kelley was there and they introduced themselves. Witus' phone rang. It was Glenn Stark, again—he'd kept calling them on the drive north, his reaction a source of amazement and another bit of incongruity to a monstrously incongruous day—and now he demanded to talk to the police at the scene. Witus gave the phone to Kelley, who talked to Stark briefly—they couldn't hear Kelley's end of the conversation—before giving the phone back.

Stark told Kelley, as he'd told everyone he'd talked to since he first found out, that Mark had done it.

About 4:30, Patchin asked Unger to consent to a fingernail swab and a buccal swab of the lining of his mouth.

Just before Patchin could begin, Unger asked:

"Is Flo still in the water?"

"Yes," said D'Angela.

Unger began sobbing loudly. D'Angela noticed: no tears.

About then, the search warrant was issued for the car and its belongings.

Kelley and Baesch unloaded the dog crate, some lawn chairs, a bag with Florence's personal effects, the duffel bags and assorted stuff for the kids. In the back, behind the second-row passengers' seat, on the floor under all the other stuff, was a pile of wet men's clothes—black sweatpants, a pair of white socks, brown slip-on moccasin slippers and a red, long-sleeve sweatshirt.

Packard wondered why you'd load wet clothes into the car first, then pile everything else on top.

Finally Mark was told he could go. Wolberg called Peter Stern, told him he was at Watervale, and asked him if he could fetch the boys and drive them back home.

"They're in my custody," said Peter, his tone a surprise to Wolberg.

"I have to go see my boys," said Unger to Wolberg. "I've got to go see my boys." Wolberg told Stern they would be there soon.

On the way to Glen Arbor, Mark said, "Pull over." He

wanted to talk to them, but not in a moving car. He took them step by step through the events, starting with the night before and right on through everything that had happened that morning. It was a mystery, he said. She'd been out on the deck and he'd checked in on the kids and then she was gone.

Stern's phone rang off the hook. His family. Mark's family. Mark trying to get through to him, again and again. Wolberg. At first, after Mark and his friends arrived, Peter refused to let Mark see the boys.

"Come on, Pete, he needs to be with the boys. You're going to be there," said Wolberg. None of this made sense. Why was Pete mad at Mark? How can you keep a dad from his kids, especially on a day like this?

Peter relented.

Harold and Claire Stern arrived soon after. Unger told the elder Sterns how sorry he was. He seemed in shock, disoriented. He didn't offer up anything about what had happened, but asked them if they had any questions for him.

They did, no doubt, but they said they didn't. They were livid, sure he was the cause of Flo's death, but tight-lipped. They didn't want him there. They didn't want to talk to him. Peter didn't want him there. He didn't want to talk to him. They wanted him and his friends gone.

They sat inside the house, staring at walls, enveloped by the awkward silence and the thick, sluggish movement of time.

At one point, the Sterns got up and went outside. Mark followed them out. He had a question for them. They knew, he said, how much Flo loved the north country. How much she loved Watervale. That she loved it so much, it would make her happy to have her ashes spread there. Would it be all right if he had Florence cremated? Would they agree to that?

The question was almost as shocking as the morning's phone call. Cremation? First, it was a violation of Jewish law. Second, they knew how upset Mark had been when his own father's fifth wife, a Lutheran, had had him cremated. Mark had been outraged.

"No, I don't want her cremated," said Mrs. Stern.

"Okay, that's fine, whatever you want," said Mark.

Wolberg wanted Stern to let him drive Max and Tyler back to Detroit. He knew Mark's mother, Betty, and the boys' aunt, Kim, were flying in. He wanted the boys to be able to see them as soon as possible, get back to their home and surrounded by as many family and friends as possible.

Stern told him no.

He was able to convince Stern, finally, to at least let Mark spend the night there. The boys needed to be with their father that night, surely he could see that. Cantor, Witus and Wolberg checked into a motel.

Late in the afternoon, the Duncans went around the lake to have dinner with some friends. They sat out in the back yard with binoculars, watching the last of the police procedural being conducted in their yard. What they saw was:

At 6:00, Chris Wooten, the head of the county's dive team, in a wet suit but minus his tanks, entering the water, next to Florence's body. Two others in wet suits, Doug Warnke and Craig Mayo, joining him. Wooten using a tape measure to take measurements of how the body was angled in relationship to the small breakwall.

At 6:36, the three men in the water picking up the body, making sure to keep it positioned the way it had been, right arm folded under her, and handing it up to some men on the concrete apron.

Patchin standing on the apron, watching the body as it came out.

What the Duncans couldn't see, but the police could, was that despite all the time in the water, there was a lot of blood around Florence's right ear, and blood drained from her nose and ears as she was lifted. And there's nothing like blood in the water to rile up sharks, and cops. And, perhaps one day, a prosecutor.

They carried the body up the hill, loaded her into a ve-hicle and drove her off to McElduff-Jewett Funeral Home.

Two days later, after the police were done taking their photos, making notes and measuring various distances, they took down the crime-scene tape, and the Duncans were free to go out on the boathouse deck again.

That's the first time Linn, who went down to take some photos of his own, noticed the damage to the railing: two support posts were splintered. He'd missed it in all the hubbub Saturday. The damage was new. On Friday, when he'd lowered all the patio furniture over the railing with a rope, the posts were fine. Something had happened to them in the meantime.

A CALL FROM MARK

Sunday morning, Peter Stern borrowed a car from a friend—his truck wasn't suitable—and drove the boys and Mark back to Huntington Woods. The Ungers traveled together, but wouldn't be staying together when they got back home. The boys would stay, at least temporarily, with the Sterns.

Wolberg drove Witus and Cantor back to Watervale. One of them needed to drive Mark's car back and pick up the family's stuff, at least the things the police would let them take.

They walked up the steps of the boathouse and across the deck to the railing. Wolberg noticed some black powder. Fingerprint powder, he thought. They wiggled the railing and noticed its give. They stood against it, surprised at how low it came on their legs. They looked over the rail at the cement below, picturing what had happened, imagining the body in the water. It was creepy.

They walked down and stood on the concrete, the bloody stain a reminder of everything bad. Wolberg needed to get out of there.

They went to the Mary Ellen and were surprised they could just walk in. They saw Mark's keys and picked them up. They picked up the Ungers' things that weren't already in the car and then headed out for the long, quiet, depressing ride back to Detroit.

Laurie Glass' phone rang at 6 p.m. It was Mark. He started crying and couldn't speak.

"I wouldn't believe it was true until you called me and told me, yourself. I was worried about you yesterday," said Glass.

"That's okay, they were just doing their job," he said, referring to the police. "It's because of the divorce. I'm okay."

Mark told her that he and Flo had been out on the deck, and she had asked him to go check on the kids.

"You know how she was, how she always worried about the kids," he said.

He started crying, again. "That's the last time I saw her," he said, sobbing.

Unger told her about falling asleep with the kids and waking up in the morning when Tyler stirred. He realized right away, he told her, that something was wrong. He could tell Flo hadn't been there. Nothing had been touched. He ran downstairs, sort of hoping the car wouldn't be there. That'd be an explanation for her absence. Maybe she'd gone off somewhere, mad at him, maybe to her brother's place.

But the car was there. He ran over to the Inn to see if she was there, but it was dark and he couldn't see much. So he called Linn Duncan, "and the next thing I know, he said, 'Mark, something terrible has happened.'

"I said, 'What, what?' and he said, 'It's bad. It's really bad. Flo has jumped and killed herself.' And I ran down there and she was face down in the water."

Unger told her he tried to pull her out, but she was too heavy. "Blood was rushing up at me. She was so heavy, and blood was rushing up at me." He went back to the cottage to get out of his bloody sweatpants, got a blanket and took it back to the lake.

"I don't know, I thought I could keep her warm," he said. "The next thing I knew, the police were there. It's all a blur from there."

SITTING SHIVA

Shiva, the seven-day Jewish period of mourning, began on Monday, at the Ungers' house. Normally, it would start after burial, but because of the investigation, the need for an autopsy and the resulting delay in burial, shiva was held first.

Early in the morning, Amy Folbe was carrying the garbage out as Mark walked by, on his way from the Wolbergs' house to his own. There was tension between them.

"What happened, Mark?" she asked.

"I think it had something to do with the chair," he said. Without elaboration, he continued on his way.

At one point during shiva, when he had a chance to talk to her alone, Mark came up to her, crying very hard. He stopped crying, gave her a hug and said, "You know, I really hated you."

"Why?"

"Because you're the one who convinced Flo to get a divorce."

"Mark, she always wanted a divorce."

Mark went back to his chair.

Joan Frank had gotten the call Saturday from her oldest friend, Liz Groskind, another Huntington Woods resident, that Flo was dead. She waited, shocked, unbelieving, until Monday to call Mark at home.

He answered the phone crying. Joan said she wanted to talk to him, and Mark told her to come over. She went over that afternoon, her husband meeting her in front of the house.

They went to the office upstairs to talk, but the kids were there, so they went down the hall to what had become Mark's bedroom during the Ungers' estrangement.

"Let me tell you about the weekend," Mark began, taking them back to Friday afternoon, describing the drive up, that they got to Watervale, that Flo loved the cottage, this charming cottage, not the one they had stayed at when the two couples had vacationed there together, but a different one, new to them.

Breaking the flow at one point, though, by blurting out, "Why would someone do this to her? Who could have done this to her?"

Which surprised Steven Frank. The death had struck everyone they knew as either an accident, or something horrible Mark had done. Now, he was suggesting someone else had killed her?

But then he returned to his narrative, in detail. They had checked into the cottage, then headed into nearby Frankfort. They'd had a nice time at dinner, come back and gone for a walk.

"Things were good. We had a nice conversation," said Mark. "And, you know, she said to me, 'I'm worried about the kids.' And I said, 'What are you worried about? They're doing great.' You know, she even let me put my arm around her."

She let him put his arm around her? Joan didn't believe it for a second. No way she would have let Mark do that. She had told Joan repeatedly over the preceding months how repulsed she was by Mark. She wouldn't have sex with him. Wouldn't share a bedroom with him. Had grown to detest him, really. She had begged Joan to join them because Flo couldn't stand the thought of a weekend alone with him, and the first night there, she welcomes his arm around her?

Joan cut him short. "I need to know what happened. I can't be at peace . . . I need to know what happened."

Mark thought he'd been doing just that and took her question as an affront. He started yelling.

"No, that's not what I'm saying," said Joan, trying to calm him down. And then, "Maybe she had an aneurism."

"No, she didn't have an aneurism."

Lyle Wolberg, who would serve as Unger's caretaker and confidant the next few weeks, walked into the bedroom, and that was the end of the conversation.

AUTOPSY

On Monday, October 27, while shiva was being held at Florence Unger's house in Huntington Woods, Dr. Stephen Cohle conducted the autopsy on her body, which had been driven south from Benzie County to the Blodgett Campus of Spectrum Health centers, tucked into an affluent area east of Grand Rapids, near the shaded campus of private Aquinas College.

Grand Rapids is the second largest city in Michigan, a big city with big-city expertise at dealing with the dead and unraveling the mysteries of how they got that way. Florence Unger was morgue No. 446, the number referring to the count of the dead who had been brought there in 2003.

Cohle is the county's forensic pathologist and chief medical examiner, but his office also handles about 150 forensic examinations a year for counties throughout western Michigan and northern Michigan, even the faraway Upper Peninsula. Most counties can't afford their own forensic pathologists and many use his office for their suspicious deaths. He'd been doing autopsies for Benzie County for about twenty years.

Frances D'Angela was there, to collect Florence's clothing and take it back to the lab. Lending a hand were a staff assistant and a medical student.

Cohle examined the body, but only after studying preliminary police reports, to give the body and its presence in
front of him crucial context. He knew the woman had been
in the process of getting a divorce, that she and her husband
had rented a cabin at a resort, and that the woman had been
found floating face down in six inches of water.

That knowledge was necessary because his job was to
decide the manner of death, too—accident or homicide—
and that meant far more than just cold tissue and signs of
trauma. It wasn't enough to determine that she'd drowned,
but how. And how in just six inches of water? Not likely,
except for incapacity. So, incapacitated how?

Cohle began by inventorying the personal effects that
had arrived with her, down to the one white metal earring
in her left ear.

She had been weighed with her clothes on, while they
were wet. He guessed that her real weight was 135–140
pounds, not the 150 the scale read.

Her clothes were stripped away and a series of photographs taken, a series that would continue throughout his
long and often loud task.

Her body was stiff with rigor mortis, which told him
she'd been kept well refrigerated since her death. That was
good. There would be little tissue deterioration to interfere
with his work.

He palpated her face and wiggled her nose to see if
there were obvious fractures. There weren't. He pulled
up her upper lip and pulled down her lower lip to examine her teeth and gums and look for trauma there. There
was none.

She had black eyes, clearly not a result of lividity, most
likely, he thought, the result of fractures in the floor of the
skull, which helps form the roof of the orbital eye socket.
Each eyelid was swollen, the right eye more so.

The right side of her face, in front of her ear, was bruised,
too, and there was a small abrasion on her ear.

Cohle picked up a razor, one of many tools he was adept
with, and shaved her head. He saw more bruising, above

the right ear. The abrasion on the ear and the bruising were both consistent, he thought, with a fall.

He found another abrasion on her right hip, bruising on her right forearm, very small, superficial scrapes on the back of her left hand and a more severe scrape on the little finger of the right hand.

Cohle then picked up his bone saw and began cutting through her breast bone. To pull out and examine the organs, he needed to sever the esophagus, the food tube that connects the throat and the stomach.

He pulled out her stomach and found evidence of bruising on it, too, where it had hit her spinal column in the fall to the concrete apron. He emptied her stomach, which was fairly full, holding about 600 milliliters of food, more than a pint. Since the food hadn't had time to pass into her small organs, she had likely died within a couple of hours of her last meal.

There was no water in her stomach, indicative that she wasn't conscious when she'd entered the lake. A drowning person who is conscious will hold off gasping as long as possible, hoping to get to air, but eventually will make a desperate gasp that usually forces some water into the stomach.

The small blood vessels in her lungs were congested with water. She'd been inhaling blood as it leaked into her nasal cavities, which meant that she'd been unconscious, and that she'd been on the deck awhile before she'd entered the water.

Had she rolled right into the water, she would have drowned before that much blood could have gotten in her lungs. And it would have taken at least twenty minutes, maybe thirty, for that much blood, oozing slowly, to be breathed into her lungs.

You could imagine a scenario, unlikely, perhaps, where she'd landed on the apron and later rolled into the water. Perhaps she'd regained consciousness and tried to rise, but, with her injuries, fallen back down and rolled off the apron. But that seemed unlikely.

He weighed her organs and—no surprise here—her lungs were much heavier than normal, having been saturated with water and blood. Her right lung weighed 880 grams; the average is about 300. Her left lung weighed 670; the average for the generally smaller left lung is 250.

Cohle also took samples of blood, urine and eye fluid. The eye fluid would be examined for alcohol, the blood and urine for a comprehensive blood screen. (The tests came back negative for alcohol, positive for ibuprofen, caffeine and niacin, a vitamin found in a lot of foods.)

He sliced off bits of each organ, heart, lung, liver, and so forth to be placed in a one-quart jar filled with preservative. That was standard procedure, in case any subsequent investigation required more detailed organ examination. Those pieces, as well as slices of the brain, would be stored for three years, then destroyed.

The remainder of the organs would be put in a bag and placed back in her body when he was done.

Inside the pelvis, Cohle saw what he guessed to be about 150 milliliters of blood, about six ounces, near the bladder. She had fractured the right side of her pelvis when she fell, too.

Cohle then moved back to her head, where he made an incision from ear to ear across the back. He pulled the skin up and over her head. Before he removed her brain, he examined the inside of her scalp for more evidence of trauma. He found two more noticeable patches of bruising.

He used the bone saw to cut off the top of her skull. Before he removed it, he looked for evidence of injury, or tumors. The brain is covered with a tough, opaque, white fibrous membrane called the dura mater. He used a tool that looked like a combination of pliers and forceps to pull the dura mater loose.

Normally, in 90–95 percent of his autopsies, he'd pull out the brain, now, and examine it in what is referred to as a fresh state by laying it on its back on a board and slicing into it with a big knife.

But in this case, with its suspicious nature, he wanted to

do a more careful examination of the brain tissue in what was called a fixed condition, which meant immersing it in formaldehyde for two weeks. The chemical would toughen up the brain tissue, making it easier to cut into thinner slices and inspect more minutely.

With the dura mater and the brain removed, numerous skull fractures were evident, including some at the base of the skull, which would have leaked the blood into her eyelids.

When the sawing and the weighing were done, and her organs placed back in her body and the scalp pulled back down over her head, when Florence Unger's body was finally free of the things of this world, Cohle wrote down her cause of death: craniocerebral trauma.

Then came the manner of death, of which, under Michigan law, there are five possibilities—accident, suicide, natural, homicide and indeterminate.

Cohle wrote . . . nothing. He wanted to wait on that one, see what turned up when he looked more closely at her brain.

Two weeks later, he took Florence Unger's now-toughened brain out of the formaldehyde. Looking at the top of it, before he began cutting, he could clearly see evidence of cerebral edema. The convoluted folds at the surface of the brain had flattened out under pressure from leaking blood vessels below. Her brain injury would have been fatal. He doubted she could have lived for more than an hour and a half after her fall.

He cut off the brain stem and laid the brain topside down on top of a cutting board, then cut slices off every quarter inch, from front to back, and laid them out in sequence, the first slice from the left lying to the far left.

The slices from the right side showed bruises, but they were subtle, indicating that she hadn't lived long after the fall.

As for the manner of death . . . he still wrote nothing. Somehow Florence Unger had gotten into that water. Given her injuries and the time she'd lain there unconscious, it seemed impossible that anything she had done on her own would have gotten her off the apron. She'd lain on the concrete for maybe half an hour, unconscious. And then she'd gotten into the water.

He'd mull it over awhile. There was no need to hurry. There was an ongoing investigation that could still turn up something definitive, or at least more evidence to help sway him from indeterminate to homicide. They might all get lucky and get a confession. Florence Unger was certainly in no hurry.

Cohle mulled it over and he mulled it over, and on November 19, twenty-three days after he'd first seen her body, he wrote "pending investigation" on his autopsy report and decided to mull it over some more. He was nothing if not methodical.

OFF THE HOOK?

Florence Unger's funeral was held the day after the autopsy, Tuesday, October 28.

The Starks flew in from Bozeman. At the gravesite, Mark received the mourners as they put dirt on her casket. Kathy and Glenn were the last in line. After they threw in their handfuls, they had no choice but to acknowledge Mark, think of something to say despite their discomfort and suspicions.

Mark walked up to Kathy and Glenn and threw his arms around them and hugged them both at once.

Both Kathy and Glenn stiffened, didn't return the hug. Couldn't even look at him.

"Look at me, damn it," said Unger.

Glenn wouldn't. He and Kathy walked away and that was the last time the old friends would have direct contact with each other. But not the last time they would share a room.

Lori and Robert Silverstein had gone to see Mark on the Sunday night he'd returned from Watervale. They'd been there to console him, and hadn't asked any questions about what had happened. There were too many people in his house, in any event.

It wasn't until after the funeral that Lori and Mark finally discussed the events of the weekend.

He said they'd been out on the deck when this boatman came up to them, struck them both as odd, and as the boatman headed off across the lake, he and Flo shared a laugh, wondering what in the world someone would be going out in a boat in the rain for?

And after the boatman motored off, Flo got restless and worried about the kids and asked him to go check on them, and when he came back, she was gone.

Mark told her that the landlady's light, which had been out earlier, was on, and he thought maybe Flo had gone to say hi to her, so he went back and lay down with Tyler to watch a movie. He fell asleep and didn't wake up until morning.

Soon after, all hell broke loose.

It struck Lori as reasonable. Why not? What was the alternative?

After Florence's death, Mark stayed with Lyle and his wife, who lived around the block from the Wolbergs, their back yards abutting.

The Unger boys were staying with the grandparents and no one thought it wise to let Mark stay by himself, so he slept on a couch at the Wolbergs'.

Cheryl had given birth to a daughter, Maya, on October 1. She was a colicky baby and cried much of the night. Mark, who was having a hard time sleeping, told the Wolbergs to sleep if they could, he'd take care of Maya, who'd wake up crying every hour and a half or so during the night.

"He did the night feeding. He'd walk her around the house, bouncing her up and down. He had the magic touch," said Lyle later.

Gary Scholnick was the Ungers' insurance broker. In addition to Mark's disability policies, Florence had two life insurance polices, one for $500,000 and the other for $250,000.

While sitting shiva at the Ungers', Scholnick brought up
the topic of the policies and said that he could start processing the claims if Mark wished. Unger looked at him
like he was coming out of left field. Later Scholnick would
think Mark had been stunned that the subject had been
brought up at such a time. Scholnick just thought he was
being a good friend and a good agent, and let it drop.

In November, Mark had Scholnick begin processing the
paperwork. Scholnick filled out the claims and Unger came
in and signed them. But since the manner of death had still
not been determined, payment was being delayed.

The delay was substantial. One check was eventually
mailed out in March of 2005, the other the following
October.

Weeks went by, Florence Unger's death still *the* topic of
conversation. It had cleaved the local Jewish community
down the middle, on one side those who *knew* Unger had
killed his wife, on the other those who *knew* he was incapable of such a thing.

It was common knowledge that the state's attorney general's office was involved on an unofficial basis, which was
common with potential homicide cases in small jurisdictions that don't often handle much more than cabin B&Es
and drunk driving cases, especially those involving complicated forensic evidence.

There were rumors, too, that Oakland County somehow
was involved, that prosecutors there were figuring out how
to intercede, despite the hundreds of miles that separated
the jurisdictions.

Speculation was rampant. Was Unger going to be
charged? If so, when?

Meawhile, Mark had been told to get a good attorney,
and he got one of the best. His mother Betty, who lived in
Florida, was wealthy and she let him know that money, if
needed, would not be an object.

Attorney Robert Harrison was one of the best, and one

of the most expensive, a former Wayne County prosecutor with three decades of top-notch defense work on his résumé.

He promptly arranged for Unger to take a lie detector test with a former state cop, Christopher Lanfear, now heading up his own private detective agency. The test took place at 5 p.m. on November 3.

Lanfear began with a control question, then asked five questions.

One: "Do you know for a fact who did kill your wife?"

"No."

Two: "Did you personally kill your wife, Flo?"

"No."

Three: "Did you do anything intentionally that caused her injuries?"

"No."

Four: "Did you do anything accidentally that caused her injuries?"

"No."

Five: "Are you deliberately withholding information you have about Flo's death?"

"No."

Lanfear immediately typed up a two-page report for Harrison that summed up the meeting, including the questions and answers, and finished with:

> It is the opinion of the undersigned examiner, based on the analysis of the polygraph examination of Mark Steven Unger, that he is being truthful to the pertinent test questions.

Harrison forwarded a copy on the the attorney general's office in Lansing.

Right before Christmas, Mark stopped in at Lori Glass' house for a visit. By now, she had her suspicions, too. She and her husband and their friends had hashed it out over and over, they'd read the newspaper reports, seen the TV coverage, heard it on the radio. There seemed to be holes in his story, at least things that needed better explanation.

What really bugged her was this: If what he said was true, why wasn't he angry? Angry at those whispering behind his back? Angry at whoever might have done it? If it was true that someone had dragged her body into the water, and it wasn't him, then why wasn't he raging at whoever had done it?

She asked him point blank, her husband with her in the room: How did Flo's body get in the water?

It was just a narrow strip of concrete, he said, from the boathouse wall to the water. She must have landed on it and rolled into the lake. He held his hands up to show them how big the strip was, holding them six to eight inches apart.

"Can't you just see it?" he asked. "I can picture her wrapped in a blanket, pulling this lounge chair backward on the deck, and she must have gone too far and fell over the rail."

Joan Frank continued to see Mark at the Bloomfield Hills racquet club, with his personal trainer or on his own, but they were just that: sightings, with perhaps a nod, both of them busy with their workouts and no time to chat.

On New Year's Eve, Joan was shopping in a store called Party Time. She and her family were spending the night with the Unger boys and Flo's mom and dad, and Joan wanted to get the boys some funny hats and those curly things that straighten up when you blow into them, for when the crystal ball on TV came sliding down. Try to keep their minds off another holiday without Flo.

Joan's cell rang. It was Mark.

They exchanged how-are-yous and Mark said, "I went to the cemetery today for the first time."

"For the first time?" she said, not sure how to respond. He hadn't been there since the funeral?

"Yes, for the first time."

"For the first time?" she repeated, incredulously. Flabbergasted is how she would describe it later.

"Yes."

"I thought I'd have a connection, but I didn't."

She certainly wasn't in the mood to ask him to elaborate, and he offered nothing further. They said their goodbyes.

Late in February, early now in 2004, Mark called Joan, again.

"I have great news," he said. "But you can't tell anyone."

Someone he knew with an in at the attorney general's office had passed on the word. "They have decided not to charge me," said Unger.

Joan was shocked. Felt like she'd been punched in the gut. She didn't respond. No polite "That's nice" or "Glad to hear it." It wasn't nice. She wasn't glad to hear it. She was one of those who thought he'd done it.

Silence on her end. Mark said goodbye.

PART THREE

TAKING AIM

ON THE HOOK, NOT OFF

The "someone" with an in at the attorney general's office might not have had as much of an in as he or she thought, because things had been proceeding apace since Flo's death.

There were other ways to come at Unger besides directly. While friends and family of Florence chafed at the lack of seeming progress and the passage of weeks, and then months, without word of whether charges would be filed by the Benzie County Prosecutor's Office, custody proceedings in Oakland County gave officials there a chance to investigate the death.

And the state AG's office in Lansing had been on top of the case from the beginning. The department's star prosecutor, Donna Pendergast, who lived in suburban Detroit and kept abreast of breaking news stories there, had called Benzie County Prosecutor Anthony Cicchelli a few days after Florence's death.

"It had the making of a difficult case," she would say later, explaining why she called. She knew Benzie's prosecutor ran a small operation without much of a budget, "a one-man shop" as she described it.

But it was a fine line between offering help that might be crucial to solving a case and coming across as a pushy big-city star coming to the rescue of the rubes.

Besides, a big, high-profile case can win elections for local prosecutors, and some of them will do anything to hold on to them. Others, knowing they don't have the tools, the time or the expertise to investigate and prosecute tricky forensic cases, are happy to pass them up the food chain.

"Do you need any help?" she asked after chatting about the case.

"Oh, no," said Cicchelli.

A week or so later, Pendergast's supervisor, Tom Furtaw, called her and told her to give Chiccelli another call.

He'd decided maybe he did need help, after all. Most of the testimony and evidence that would go to motive wouldn't be found in Watervale, it would be found in and around Huntington Woods, likely involving talking to dozens of friends, family and other potential witnesses, and Chicchelli didn't have the budget or time for all the trips to the Detroit area that that would require.

Meanwhile, Flo's father, Harold Stern, a well-known long-time attorney in the Detroit area, had met with an Oakland County prosecutor, Deborah Carley, who headed up the division that handled family-court cases. Stern was convinced his son-in-law was a murderer, and wanted Unger stripped of the custody of his boys.

Carley was eager to start the legal process against Unger, rare though it may have been to initiate custody proceedings against a father who hadn't been charged with anything. Not to mention that the respected medical examiner who'd conducted the autopsy couldn't decide on the manner of death.

By all accounts, Mark had been a great father. No one disputed his parenting skills or his devotion to his boys. What they disputed were the circumstances of his wife's death, and his role in it.

Carley assigned Assistant Prosecutor Mark Bilkovic to the case, against his wishes. He thought it was foolish to begin proceedings in family court before any conclusions had been reached on the criminal front.

To take Unger's kids away, they would have to link Unger to his wife's death, and Bilkovic felt the wisest path to that was for the state attorney general's office to wrap up its investigation and, better yet, wait till there was a trial and conviction.

The AG's office was livid when it found out about Carley's plans. Pendergast had once worked for Carley and they didn't get along, so there was that. But it was going to be a dilution of resources. To build a case in family court, they'd need the testimony of the AG's investigators and the state police, and they needed to focus their time and efforts on a criminal case, not a civil one.

Bilkovic voiced his concerns, strongly, was overruled and went about his work in good-soldier fashion. Carley told him to use whatever resources he needed. Things seemed stalled on the criminal front; if she got her staff going in Oakland County, it might jump-start things in Lansing and in Benzie County.

"We were going to have to prove he'd murdered his wife to terminate his rights, and she was bound and determined to do it," said John Skrzynski, who was chief of the felony division of the Oakland County Prosecutor's Office. "She got the whole ball rolling."

A storm was brewing for Mark Unger. Not only did Oakland County want to take his kids away, the county's former star prosecutor, Donna Pendergast, had taken the case over from an undermanned office in Benzie County.

The state's AG's office was anything but undermanned, and Pendergast was a master at marshalling its resources.

One day in November, Dr. Ljubisa Dragovic, chief medical examiner and chief medical pathologist for Oakland County—the second largest in the state behind Wayne County, which includes the city of Detroit—was paid a surprising and, to him, mysterious visit by Detective Sergeant David Wurtz of the Oakland County Sheriff's Department, a member of the county's crime task force and a regular visitor to Dragovic's office.

Wurtz had two photos with him he wanted Dragovic to

look at. One was of what looked to be a stain on concrete. The other was a deck and some broken railing. Neither contained any people.

Dragovic told him the two photos made no sense without context. "What do you want here? What are you interested in?" asked Dragovic.

"Well, what do you think of this picture here?" said the sergeant, showing him the one with the stain. "If I told you it's a bloodstain, what can you tell me?"

"Well, if it's a bloodstain, obviously someone was bleeding on that spot. That would be the conclusion. But give me some details."

"Well, I'll see," said Wurtz. And he left.

Two days later, he was back, this time with several others from the sheriff's department, and with more photos.

Over a series of meetings, Dragovic looked at all their photos of the crime scene and photos of Florence Unger's autopsy and read a copy of the autopsy report.

Dragovic said he'd need to look at microscopic slides of her brain and lung tissue, too, when they became available.

Lieutenant Steven Rains of the Michigan State Police was based in Lansing and oversaw the department's eight traffic-crash reconstruction experts around the state, specialists in biomechanics and applied physics who helped determine what had happened at the scene of traffic fatalities.

Trooper Rick Doering had contacted Rains earlier, asking him if he could bring his tools to the scene of suspected homicide at Lower Herring Lake, the chief tool being something called a Sokkia Total Station, a device that sat on a tripod and measured angles and distances. Road crews use them, surveyors use them, and so do police.

Early on November 21, Rains drove up from Lansing, picked up Trooper Jerry Hillborn of the Traverse City post and went to the Benzie County Sheriff's Department in the reconstruction unit's work van, arriving at 10 a.m. to meet with members of the sheriff's department, including Sergeant Tom Kelley, and with State Police Detective Sergeant Walter Armstrong of the Manistee post, Trooper Blair DuVall of the nearby Honor post and technicians from the Grayling crime lab. And Pendergast.

It was Armstrong's first involvement with the case, having been asked by Kelley to come by and help out. He would eventually be put in charge of the state police investigation.

Those gathered reviewed the events of October 24 and 25, looked at photos of the scene and then drove to Watervale, arriving there at 11.

Rains took a walk-through of the scene to determine the best spot to set up the Sokkia in order to get clear views of the breakwall, the water's edge where the body had been, the boat hoist, the concrete apron, the boathouse roof and its broken railing, places where there had been blood and the Watervale Inn and cottages.

All the angles and distances were recorded electronically and later downloaded into a computer program that would create a detailed, scaled diagram.

At some point two insurance company representatives showed up and came down to the boathouse, too.

After taking all the measurements he thought he'd need, Rains went out on the boathouse deck with Hillborn to conduct load tests on intact portions of the railing, using something called a load cell, an instrument normally used at crash scenes to measure such things as the coefficient of friction for particular road surfaces. The load cell helped determine the speed that vehicles had been traveling when they crashed.

On the deck, Rains and Hillborn attempted to simulate a body leaning against the rail. They placed a bicycle seat against the rail, then placed the load cell against it and a T-shaped handle against the load cell they could then push against.

As they pushed, a digital readout told them the pounds of force per square inch that were being applied. Eventually, they built the force up to 198 pounds, at which point the railing and the connecting support posts began to bend outward, toward the lake. Florence Unger, they had been told, weighed 130 pounds.

What if someone had been propelled into the rail? It wasn't a scientific test—Rains would later describe it as a layman's test—but the 185-pound cop got in front of the rail, got comfortable and balanced, then aggressively kicked the top rail with the bottom of his left foot. The rail didn't break, but there was a sharp noise and some nails started to pop out.

So, the railing would have supported a leaning body without a problem, but was not up to withstanding a real display of force.

AN UNUSUAL VISIT

On January 8, 2004, a team from Oakland County visited Watervale, again. Lieutenant Clay Jensen of the Oakland County Sheriff's Department drove a county car, with Dragovic and Rob Zivian, an assistant county prosecutor in the juvenile division, along for the ride.

Pendergast drove up from Lansing and met them.

It was one of the coldest days of the winter, down around zero, windchill 15 or 20 below, maybe lower at the south end of Lower Herring Lake after the wind had ripped across the ice and snow that covered it.

Dragovic paced the scene. He walked atop the boat-house and examined the railing. He went down and peered into the scaffolding of the boat hoist. He bent over the concrete. He stared out at the ice on the lake. He went back up and walked around the deck, again.

He had dealt with hundreds of drownings in his career. Early on, he'd worked at the shores of Chesapeake Bay. For much of his career he had been surrounded by water, by Lake Saint Clair, by the Detroit River, by the hundreds of lakes that dotted Oakland County.

Water provided a means of accidental death. And it provided a means to make death *look* accidental. A body in the water wasn't just a body for him, it was a body waiting to be linked to a mystery.

They were all bundled up, but the wind cut through their clothing, and by the time he was done forty-five minutes later, they were frozen about solid. Wanting him to hurry up, but no one having the temerity to say a word to the irascible medical examiner.

Finally, he was done.

They got back into their cars and headed south for the ninety-minute drive to Grand Rapids to meet with Dr. Cohle, and for Dragovic to see what he could see in the slides of Florence's brain tissue.

Word had been left with Cohle's secretary a few days earlier to expect them. He wasn't looking forward to it.

Cohle is barrel-chested and thick-armed, a competitive power lifter who wears a Beckwith's Gym T-shirt to work and blends the physical with the cerebral as an expert chess player. He has an affinity for Porsche Boxsters and a vanity license plate that reads "4ENSIC."

Cohle is also a co-author with Tobin Buhk of two books detailing the forensics of his most interesting cases, and with Roger W. Byard and Vincent J. M. DiMaio, of a medical text on sudden death in childhood and adolescence.

Cohle's path had crossed Dragovic's before, and not pleasantly. According to Cohle, in a previous case, involving a woman accused of killing a police officer, one of Cohle's colleagues had testified for the prosecution, and Dragovic for the defense. Later, Dragovic had belittled his colleague, saying he wasn't skilled enough to get a job in Oakland County.

Worse, he'd said something similar about Cohle's former wife, while they were still married. She, too, had disagreed with Dragovic, and she, too, had been belittled. Cohle considered Dragovic a talented jerk with a false sense—no, not *sense*, *certainty*—of his infallibility.

The whole thing had a taint to Cohle. He'd conducted more than 6,000 autopsies in his career, maybe 2,000 of them for other jurisdictions. He'd never heard of a circumstance where officials from a county hundreds of miles from a suspected crime scene had interjected themselves into a case.

It wasn't just odd, it was unheard of. He wasn't surprised that the state attorney general's office was involved. That was common. But another county? What kind of politics had been brought to bear here? he wondered. "Clearly politics played a role in driving this case forward. This was unique in my career," he'd say later.

Cohle had the slides ready when they got there at 3:30. They all crammed into his tiny, cluttered office, filled with files and books and trays of specimens and scientific equipment. "What's going on, here?" he said to himself. "Why do they have all these people here?"

Dragovic looked at the slides and then stated, politely but bluntly—doubt was not something that much preoccupied him—that Cohle was mistaken. Florence Unger hadn't died because of brain trauma. She had died of drowning. The trauma likely *would* have killed her, but drowning *did* kill her.

The injury was a proximate cause of death, he told Cohle. Drowning was the immediate cause of death.

"Look, you've got to take that into consideration," said Dragovic.

"Okay," Cohle said, noncommittally. It was clear Dragovic hadn't convinced him. Dragovic asked Cohle to have more slides made for him and to mail them to him in Pontiac when they were ready.

Later, Cohle would say: "It became clear to me that they wanted me to say she'd drowned. That someone had dragged her into the water. That was a reasonable hypothesis, but not provable. I couldn't say that. Was it possible she was alive and dragged into the water? Yes, but I couldn't prove that. Dragovic was trying to convince me that it was a drowning, but he had no scientific basis for it."

What was going on, he thought, was something Cohle characterizes as the cultural difference in the way medical examiners conduct their business in Michigan. Those in the southeastern part of the state, in the big counties, "pretty much testify the way prosecutors want them to."

Dragovic, he thought, was just trying to deliver the goods for his prosecution team. Cohle, on the other hand, prided himself on his independence.

Dragovic brandished a copy of the autopsy report of November 19, the one where Cohle had written in for manner of death: "pending investigation."

If Dragovic couldn't convince him to say that the cause of death was a result of drowning, he could still try to get Cohle to change his temporary opinion about manner of death, from indeterminate.

As he began to argue that point, Cohle cut him short. He had, he told his visitors, signed an amended autopsy report on December 23. They must not have seen it. On that one, he'd written in one new word: "homicide."

In finally making that determination, Cohle didn't need to have the same certainty as a jury. He just needed to feel that the evidence pointed at murder. It didn't need to point strongly. On a scale of 1 to 100, 51 was enough.

The crime-scene photos had swayed him. The pool of blood on the concrete apron was twenty to twenty-four inches from the water. Though he couldn't rule out that she'd somehow gotten into the water on her own, it was highly unlikely.

"I ruled it homicide, but I wouldn't have objected if I was working with another pathologist and he said the cause was indeterminate," he explained later. "I reluctantly ruled it a homicide. If I was on a jury, based on my findings alone, it would have been hard to say, 'This is murder. This guy has to go to prison.'"

Half an hour after they'd arrived, the visitors from Oakland County left for their three-hour drive home, the journey shortened by their excitement. They'd come to persuade Cohle that it had been a drowning and had failed. But their real mission had been to get him to say it was a homicide, and, lo and behold, he'd done it six weeks ago.

BUILDING A CASE

Cohle may have ruled the manner of death a homicide, but he did it after lengthy deliberations, and reluctantly. He would tell those who asked that he couldn't imagine a jury convicting Unger and sending him to jail based on his findings.

Pendergast and the state would need more than Cohle's reluctant ruling to convict Unger, especially given the rumors that his wealthy mother, Bette, who owned a resort complex on Islamorada in the Florida Keys, was ready to pay for the best defense her money would buy.

On February 26, State Police Detective Sergeant Walter Armstrong, State Police Trooper Rick Doering, Sergeant Kelley of the Benzie County Sheriff's Department and assistant Oakland County Prosecutors Mark Bilkovic and Rob Zivian met at Watervale with Jason Hertzberg and Brian Weaver, two engineers of Exponent Engineering, a firm in Chicago hired by the Oakland County Prosecutor's Office to run tests on the railing and support posts on the boathouse roof and take wood samples back to their lab.

Meeting them were two private investigators hired by defense attorney Harrison, Chris and Mike Neihardt, as well as two engineers working for Harrison, John Zarzecki and David Ruby, who would later conduct their own tests on wooden pieces of the deck railing.

Zarzecki was a chemical engineer for Soil and Materials Engineers, Inc. of Ann Arbor, and over the years he'd tested old wooden structures to help with restorations, including many for the National Park Service. He also was a frequent expert witness in lawsuits involving issues of material integrity.

He'd developed an expertise in a field known as nondestructive testing, which involves a wide range of high-tech ways such as X-rays, ultrasound, fluorescent penetrants and pulse radars to assess a material's strengths without having to damage its integrity.

Ruby owned a structural engineering firm, Ruby+Associates of Beverly Hills, Michigan. This was a bit far afield from Ruby's usual job-site visit. His firm had designed the structures and foundations for major projects across the U.S., including the John Hancock Center and Sears Tower in Chicago, the Renaissance Center that dominated the skyline in downtown Detroit and the Peachtree Center in Atlanta.

One of the specialties of Ruby's firm, which brought him into this case, was designing what were called tie-off systems for large companies, such as General Motors. Federal law required any employees who had to work more than six feet off the ground to be harnessed and tethered to prevent falls.

The harnesses had to be tied off to rails or other load-bearing devices that could hold up to 5,000 pounds, which was what was needed to stop a 200-pound man with a fifty-pound load at the end of a 10- or 12-foot fall.

Ruby and Zarzecki were there to work out the loads that the railing and support posts on the boathouse roof could support. They were told to stay off the deck until the police and Exponent people were done with their work. The Exponent folks struck Ruby as weird, acting maybe like the CIA or Secret Service, haughty to the point of rudeness.

Right off, matter of courtesy, Ruby asked them if he could have their business cards for future reference.

"We're not giving any cards," one of them snapped.

The boathouse was cordoned off with yellow police tape, and Ruby and Zarzecki were told to stay outside it. They wandered down to the lake and strolled around, slowly—and painfully, given the windchill and the temperature—killing time for several hours.

They watched as the prosecution team examined the deck and railing, at one point cutting out a piece of railing on the right side of the deck. It wasn't easy work. The deck was under eight inches of ice and snow, and ice coated the railings all around. It was just a brutal day.

Finally, after 3 p.m., they were allowed onto the deck. That far north, it gets dark early in February, and soon it was dusk. They started with a vertical post at one end of the rail and pushed it to see if it had any give. It didn't. Neither did the second or the third. The fourth post, in the middle of the front of the deck, overlooking the lake, had a lot of give, though. Zarzecki was able to move it back and forth by five or six inches, without applying much pressure.

One of the cops saw them touching the rail and told them to stop. Take pictures or notes, but keep your hands off.

They got down and looked at where the post went into the surface of the deck. The post was nearly completely rotted away. A hard push and it would have broken in two.

Long icicles hung from the deck roof. Ruby later measured them at between twenty-four and thirty-six inches.

Ice-damming, thought Zarzecki, a sign that water wasn't flowing off the deck the way it should, but was getting trapped along an edge, or seeping in between layers and building up, a common and wood-destroying problem in Michigan winters, particularly near lakes, where high humidity added to the trouble.

On April 2, the Exponent team came back to Watervale to gather more pieces from the deck. Zarzecki came back, too. It was 8 a.m. and Zarzecki noticed the deck was slippery. "Greasy" was how he'd describe it later. Though it was early in the spring, algae was already well entrenched.

He'd lived on a lake for fifteen years and his deck would get the same way, had to douse it with bleach every few weeks to keep the algae at bay.

It was their show to run, the Exponent engineers told Ruby and Zarzecki. Once they were done with what they wanted to do on the deck, then the two of them could have at it, too.

Zarzecki asked them if he could have a couple of posts if they didn't want them, namely the third, fourth and fifth posts from the left. The Exponent engineers told them they could take one, two or three, they were taking the others.

The Exponent guys pulled out a small chain saw and cut out sections of the railing and deck. Zarzecki pulled out a video camera and filmed them. He also took photographs.

The Exponent team cut off all the railing and posts around the perimeter of the deck, not just the lakeside portion. Zarzecki found it interesting that as they cut off the railing by the lake, some of the posts just fell over, so rotted at the bottom that without the horizon railing attached, there was nothing keeping them vertical.

It was plain to Zarzecki, who was also a licensed builder, that whoever had last rebuilt the deck had been a woeful craftsman. The support posts for the deck railing had been feebly attached to the deck, and what should have been four-by-fours were pairs of two-by-fours nailed together.

Moreover, the surface deck had been laid over another deck at some point. It should have been edged with a strip of metal flashing that should extend out about three-quarters of an inch from the wood, to ensure that water running off in warmer weather or snow melting in colder poured directly off the building and onto the ground below. There was no flashing. Without it, water would run down the front of the top deck and seep in between it and the old deck and never make it to the ground.

When Exponent was done, Zarzecki went up on the deck where post number four had been, in the middle of the ice dam he'd seen on his first trip, and with his bare hands was able to rip away pieces of the decking, it was so rotted, the nails just pulling out, no problem.

Green mold was rampant in the exposed one-by-sixes of the lower deck, and thick moss was growing.

Dragovic thought it would be a matter of weeks till he got the slides. But they weren't mailed out until May 3. Soon after, he got a call from Kevin Simowski in the state attorney general's office, asking him if he had formed a conclusive opinion about the cause and manner of Florence Unger's death.

He had.

Could he put something in writing?

"Sure. When do you need it?"

"As soon as possible." He told him to drop it the mail, addressed to Pendergast.

"Okay, in a day or two, I'll send you an opinion."

On May 17, Dragovic wrote his report and mailed it off. The second to last sentence read:

This decedent landed on the cement dock underneath, sustaining massive head trauma.

The last one read:

It is further my opinion that the decedent's unconscious body was subsequently placed into the water, where she drowned as a result of submersion.

Two days later, Mark Unger was arrested and taken for arraignment in the 85th District Court in Beulah. He was charged with an open count of murder and released on bond pending a preliminary examination, which was scheduled for July 6 in the same court.

A CAREER MOVE ON HOLD

The prosecution team was assembled in an unusual fashion. It was headed up by Pendergast, of course. Eventually joining her were Mark Bilkovic and John Skrzynski, much to the surprise of both.

Bilkovic had feuded with his immediate boss, Deborah Carley, over her pushing a custody hearing in family court before Unger had even been charged with the crime. It reeked of political pull, but, worse, was tactically stupid. She had insisted, and for a while he had soldiered on.

He'd begun interviewing family and friends in preparation. Meanwhile, Pendergast and Attorney General Mike Cox were ticked off at Carley and Oakland County Prosecutor David Gorcyca, too. Early on, the AG's office had held a strategy session with state cops and its own investigators to map out strategy in the Unger case. Carley got wind of it, but the AG's office made it clear Oakland County folks weren't invited.

Gorcyca insisted on proceeding, with or without state investigators. The prosecutor's office assigned its own investigators to the case. It put out a press release criticizing the state. Cox and Gorcyca stopped speaking to each other, or so went the scuttlebutt that reached Bilkovic.

"I was not happy with the decision," Bilkovic would say

later of the insistence on trying to prove Unger an unfit parent before he'd been proven a deadly husband. The county's case was three-pronged—that he had gambling problems, he abused prescription drugs and he'd killed his wife, though by all accounts he was clean since leaving rehab, claimed to no longer be gambling and had not been charged with her death.

"I thought it jeopardized the criminal case if we did the family case first," said Bilkovic.

In March, Oakland County Family Court Judge Linda Hallmark refused to dismiss the custody case against Unger, but ruled that evidence relating to Florence's death was inadmissible because he had not been charged with it.

The decision angered Gorcyca, who appealed the ruling, telling the press that it was "a death blow" to proceedings.

Quickly, though, reason prevailed. In May, Carley and Gorcyca agreed to put the custody proceedings on hold pending Unger's trial, provided he voluntarily give up custody of the two boys to the Sterns. He reluctantly agreed.

Oakland County was now on board with the state AG's office as the criminal case moved forward. Bilkovic was assigned to Pendergast's team and given the task of continuing his interviews with friends and family in and around Huntington Woods. Pendergast would oversee interviews up in Beulah, with the police, EMS folks and civilians who had been in and around Watervale the weekend Florence Unger died.

Bilkovic, though, was still unhappy. Nearing the top of the office's pay scale, not enamored with his boss and office politics, he worried that the long trial preparation, followed by what looked to be a long and complicated trial, would interfere with the evolution of his career.

He was chafing to quit the office and go into private practice, yet this looked to be one of those career cases. He went back and forth, back and forth, and in April decided to quit the office. He was going to go into private practice as a defense attorney, chosing the functional name of The Law Offices of Mark Bilkovic.

Skrzynski was one of his bosses, too, and while he admired Bilkovic's skill in the courtroom, and thought him the best prosecutor in front of a jury he'd ever seen, and a pretty good guy, they weren't close.

Skrzynski could be irritating. A former English teacher, he would critique Bilkovic's briefs with a variety of colored highlighters, on the lookout for mismatched verb tenses, misplaced modifiers and, Lord forbid, misspellings. The pink highlighter was his favorite, and when Bilkovic got his drafts back, it was a color he feared.

But he wasn't afraid of telling Skrzynski he was quitting—it was Pendergast he was worried about.

"I thought she'd come through the phone and strangle me," he said later. To mollify her, he made a half-hearted offer he was sure she'd turn down. If she wanted, he'd work with her as a special prosecutor.

A week later, she called him back. She wanted to keep him on, and Cox had agreed. His new career as a defense attorney was on hold, and was back trying to put people in jail.

The team was set. Or so they thought. There would be a surprise down the road.

"JUSTICE NOW FOR MAX
AND TYLER"

Just as Florence Unger's murder had divided the close-knit community of Huntington Woods into those who were sure Mark had done it and those who knew he hadn't, so did news that the county had taken Mark's kids away.

Mort Meisner, for one, was livid. A long-time friend of Mark's, they'd coached their kids' baseball teams together for years, since the kids were 4 and in T-ball. Meisner was head coach, Mark a base coach.

Meisner, who owned his own public relations and marketing firm, immediately started an e-mail newsletter railing against the proceedings called "Justice Now for Max and Tyler."

"I told Mark, 'This isn't for you, it's for the kids. You haven't been convicted of anything,'" he said.

That made him a pariah to those who sided with the Sterns. "I was excommunicated," he said. Old friends stopped talking to him. Some of his kids' friends were no longer allowed to play with them. The Sterns wouldn't let Max play on the team that season, and he was no longer allowed to come over to the Meisners'. When Meisner's son had his bar mitzvah, Max wasn't allowed to attend.

Meisner was well-known in Detroit media. A local kid, Oak Park High School class of 1971, University of Detroit, class of 1975, he started his career as a production assistant at WXYZ-TV, the ABC affiliate, then moved to management positions in Chicago and St. Louis before returning to Detroit in 1988 to become station manager at the CBS affiliate for a decade.

Under his direction, WJBK was known for its news values and racked up numerous Emmys for investigative journalism, generally something of an oxymoron in the if-it-bleeds-it-leads nature of local TV news. Meisner is regarded well enough in the industry that he serves as agent for some 100 on-air personalities around the country.

He was one of those Mark had called the day Florence's body was found. As usual for a Saturday morning, Meisner had been working out at the Beverly Hills Racquet Club and checked his cell phone when he finished dressing, about 10 a.m.

There was a missed call from Mark and a message: "Mort, it's Mark. Call me. It's Floey! It's Floey!"

What struck Meisner as odd was no one from the state police, the state AG's office or the county prosecutor's office ever called him to ask him what Mark had had to say.

"I'm sure they looked at his phone logs and saw who he called. I was shocked no one called me about it. It just goes to show how shoddy it all was," he said.

He'd been in the news business a long time. He knew about death and murder and the vagaries of human emotion. Unlike many of his neighbors and friends, he didn't think he *knew* what had or hadn't happened at the boathouse.

"Ninety percent of me believes Mark doesn't know how she died. The other ten percent thinks he does. I don't know. Maybe she told him she was having an affair. Maybe they struggled and she fell and he got scared. Is that possible? Sure. Do I believe it? No. The main reason I don't believe he did it was, he worshipped her. Worshipped her. Mark felt he hit the lottery getting a woman who was so pretty."

But what Meisner was sure of was, the system wasn't playing fair, though he regarded Florence as a good friend.

"As much as I liked Mark, I was better friends with his wife. I talked to her more than I talked to him," he said. When Unger had been in rehab, Meisner would take Florence out for lunch occasionally.

She confided in him about her unhappiness with Mark and her thoughts about a possible divorce. "I'd say, 'Look, you put up with Mark when he was on drugs. And you've put up with him while he's in rehab. Why not give him a chance when he gets out?'

"She'd say, 'I don't know.'"

She'd also, as she did with other friends, tell him about what she described as an unhappy household, her adopted parents cold and aloof. Her father, Harold, was a hard-driving, ambitious attorney known for stewing silently; her mother, Claire, had survived the holocaust as a child by spending much of her time hidden in closets. Who knew at what cost emotionally?

Meisner assumed Flo's flirtatiousness grew out of a need for affection and reassurance. "She could be a tormented soul. She could be very unhappy," he said.

Mark's mother, Betty, would fly up from Florida and babysit Max and Tyler when needed. Flo preferred that to asking her own parents to watch them, and the Ungers eventually built a room on to their house to accommodate her.

Flo's body language was clear, said Meisner, when her parents came to Max's Alley Cats baseball games, which were played at a diamond in the adjacent suburb of Berkley. She'd act as if she didn't know them. They'd walk in and sit in the bleachers along the first-base or third-base line and "Flo'd sit out in the right-field corner on a folding chair," he said.

Mark would be the one, unlit cigar always clenched in his mouth, his trademark at the games, to go over and say hi.

Seymour Schwartz, the defense attorney whose son, Sydney, also played on the team, also noted the coolness between the Sterns and Flo. It was common knowledge, he said, that Flo hadn't gotten along with her parents for years.

"Mark would always come up to his in-laws and say,

referring to the nearby concessions stand, 'Can I get you anything?'"

Schwartz says Mark's consideration to his in-laws was typical of how he treated the kids and their parents. "Mark was great with all the kids. He was generous with his time and praise. And he never missed a game," he said.

The baseball league at the time had asked a local association for a donation to help pay for a new scoreboard. The association said it would help out, provided Unger was removed as coach.

"We refused to take his name off anything," said Schwartz.

Meisner's friendship with Mark centered around baseball. "I've never been so much as out to lunch with him," he'd say later. After an exciting win or a tough loss, Meisner would usually call Mark later to talk about the game. "I can't tell you how many times I'd call him and he'd be putting his kids to bed or reading them a book. He was Mr. Mom and Mr. Dad. Florence loved her kids, but she was wrapped up in her photography and other things. She wasn't the one to drive them places."

She also had what Meisner perceived as a bit of meanness at times. Soon after Mark had gotten home from rehab, Flo invited the Meisners over for dinner. Mort was surprised to see Flo drinking wine in front of him. "It was almost in a flaunting way. Most people in that situation would be more supportive of their husband, you know, not wanting the temptation there. I told my wife on the way home, 'God damn it, why did she have to drink?' It was another way of pushing his buttons."

WEARING THE WHITE HAT

Donna Pendergast was used to getting the big cases. She both lived for them and hated them. She got insomnia working on them, lying there in bed going over details, working loose threads, mad at the accused and righteously indignant on behalf of the victim. Her stomach got worked into knots, her fists would clench, she'd lie there trying to sleep, then give up to work the case. She'd spend weeks irritable, angry, in the mood for revenge, taking the horror of what had happened to someone as personally as you can.

Michigan Attorney General Mike Cox had hired Pendergast in August 2003. He'd been her boss when he was head of the homicide unit in the Wayne County Prosecutor's Office. When he recruited her to Lansing, he told people she was the best prosecutor in the state, and he wasted no time giving her a chance to prove it.

One of the most notorious cases in recent memory in Michigan was nearing trial that summer—the arraignment and preliminary hearing in district court had already taken place when she joined the office—but Cox pulled the state prosecutor who was working what very well might be the case of a lifetime off it and handed it to her.

It was the case of the missing deer hunters, one that had attained something approaching mythical status in

Michigan. The disappearance of two deer hunters from the Detroit area in the woods of northeastern Michigan in 1985, near the small town of Mio, had a particular resonance in the state.

"Up north" is where folks generally flee from the metropolitan Detroit area—on weekends in the summer to rent a motel room on a lake, or, if they're lucky, for the family cottage; in winter for the downhill and cross-country skiing and snowmobiling; and, by the hundreds of thousands the last two weeks of November, for the annual deer hunt.

Detroit is the place you flee from, with its congested highways or fear of crime. "Up north," as everyone calls it, is the sanctuary.

So when David Tyll and Brian Ognjan, two friends since childhood, left their families to go hunting a week into deer season and were never heard of or seen again, it wasn't just another possible murder or crime. It was *special*. It was *scary*.

Over the next eighteen years, state police investigated tips that came in from thirty Michigan counties, ten states and several provinces in Canada. Dive teams searched ponds, lakes, streams and rivers. Aerial searches were done over six counties. There had been at least five searches by cadaver dog teams over the years in four counties. Interpol had looked for David Tyll's missing Ford Bronco around the world. Thousands of hours of relentless investigation yielded nothing.

Still working the case in April of 2003—mostly on his own time, after work, or early in the morning on the way to his office in the resort town of East Tawas on Lake Huron—State Police Sergeant Bronco Lesneski finally broke the case open, getting an eyewitness to tell him the tale of how the two men had had words with the wrong guys, brothers named Coco and J. R. Duvall, in the wrong bar and had been beaten to death with baseball bats in a snowy field.

The case was a prosecutor's nightmare—no bodies had ever been found, there was no blood evidence, no DNA, no forensics. Nothing but two guys who fell off the face of the earth and one eyewitness, an admitted drunk who had been kicked out of the bar the night she claimed to have seen the murders.

Pendergast had developed a reputation for cold-case slayings—"Justice is a concept that never gets cold," she says—and the deer hunters' case was the coldest of her career.

Pendergast was—in the words of the headline of a *Detroit Free Press* profile that ran at the time in big type across most of the front page of the Metro section—"Born to prosecute." As Joe Swickard wrote in the story, "Defendants can hear a cell door's cold clank when she enters a courtroom."

It could have been taken for overwriting, but she got her guilty verdicts for the Duvalls, and Swickard got to say, "I told you so."

As the Unger trial approached, Pendergast was 48, though she could pass for ten years younger. She was tall and blonde, with striking, aquamarine eyes. But looks didn't rack up an 89–2 record in murder cases.

Pendergast grew up in a northeast neighborhood of Detroit known as Copper Canyon. The city once required its cops and firemen to live in the city, and many of them lived in that neighborhood, as close as they could legally get to Eight Mile Road, the street made famous by Eminem and the dividing line between city and suburbs.

Donna's father, Bill, was a cop who survived both twenty years on the streets and another twenty years at headquarters downtown, where Byzantine politics could make street life seem like punks' play. He retired with the rank of detective sergeant.

He was a tough guy, and, recognized early on, his daughter was, too. "She'd stand up and back me down, so I figured she'd either be a prizefighter or a lawyer," he said in the *Free Press* profile.

In high school, Donna worked as a life guard on Belle Isle, the big island that sits in the middle of the Detroit

River. During law school at Detroit's Wayne State University, she tended bar in Greektown, just around the corner from police headquarters and, down the block, the Frank Murphy Hall of Justice, where she would later work.

Pendergast studied labor relations as an undergrad at the University of Michigan, planning on a career in labor law. But a course in advocacy in law school changed her mind. She wanted to be a prosecutor. One who did it as a lifer, not just as a stepping stone to a lucrative career as a defense attorney.

She landed her first job with the prosecutor's office in Oakland County in 1987, signing arrest warrants and prosecuting drunk drivers and speeders in the county's numerous district courts, where misdemeanors and traffic offenses were handled. Felonies got kicked up to district court, where, in those days, just two women were on a staff of fifty-seven.

She soon made it three. At first, the cops and sheriffs who frequented circuit court regarded her with skepticism or disdain, reacting perhaps to her looks. If they thought they could intimidate her, it wasn't a thought they entertained long. The daughter of a cop, she spoke like a cop. She was soon accepted.

She got her first murder conviction in 1989. By the time she was recruited to be his star prosecutor by Wayne County Prosecutor Michael Duggan in 2000, she had won some fifty more.

Among them were several that made the national news and were played up big on the various cable court shows.

One was a conviction of Jonathan Schmitz. While on *The Jenny Jones Show* for an episode on secret crushes, a man named Scott Amedure proclaimed a crush for Schmitz. After they'd flown back to Michigan from the taping, Schmitz went to Amedure's house and shotgunned him.

Another was the murder case that became a true-crime book for St. Martin's in 1997, *The Coed Call Girl Murder* by Fannie Weinstein and Melinda Wilson, about an Oakland (Michigan) University student named Tina Biggar, whose secret life as a call girl named Crystal ended in her murder.

Another—one that continues to haunt her—was of a couple of young psychopaths named Aaron Stinchcombe and Russell Oescher. They lured a pair of 12-year-old girls from a slumber party and then killed them. While chanting, "Wind-up toy, wind-up toy," they twisted the head of one of the dead girls.

Pendergast was met with hostility and resentment by many of her colleagues and by many of the judges, too, when she joined the Wayne County staff. The defendants in Wayne County circuit court are mostly black. So are a preponderance of the employees. The color of Pendergast's skin and hair didn't help. Neither did the fact that she was coming in from Oakland County. She was regarded as some white interloper spoiled by the pace of the suburbs, who would be chewed up and spit out by the caseload. Too refined, too pretty, too privileged.

She was making too much money to suit her colleagues, too. It had been a practice in the office for years that all new hires—no matter how much experience—started out at level one on the pay scale. Duggan, new to the office and vowing to shake things up, wanted her on his homicide team. He knew he couldn't get a star to come in from Oakland County at a cut in pay, so she started at level four. Her colleagues filed a grievance with the National Labor Relations Board.

They would, slowly and grudgingly, learn what her predecessors had learned in Oakland County. She came prepared, her direct and cross-examinations were organized and relentless, without coming across as mean-spirited, and she could connect with juries, even black ones.

As Cheryl Matthews, who went on to become an Oakland County circuit judge, told Swickard, "She was absolutely prepared for every witness. Her opening and closing statements and questioning of expert witnesses were the best. Of course I snuck up to watch her work. It's important to steal from people who know what they are doing."

In Wayne County, she proved she could handle a docket that seemed nearly infinite. While some judges there have reputations for short days and four-day weeks, prosecutors work at hyperpace. Often, they have to get subordinates to pick their juries because they're arguing other cases right up until the next case starts.

Pendergast made good money as a prosecutor. She could have tripled or quadrupled her pay as a defense attorney.

Not Pendergast. "The thought doesn't appeal to me. I like wearing the white hat," she said. "I know everyone needs a defense, but . . ."

BORN TO BE A DEFENSE ATTORNEY

Robert Harrison was, says John Skrzynski, born to be a defense attorney. He has the look of a wise uncle and is possessed of a booming, deep voice that resonates throughout a courtroom, never a need for anyone in the back row to strain to hear.

In his sixties, he still has a passion for the law, and for his clients.

Mort Meisner paid him a visit before the trial to take his measure, get a feel for what kind of attorney Mark had hired.

At one point, while talking about the case, Harrison pounded the table in his office and said vehemently, "If he gets convicted, it'll be the biggest goddamn injustice I've ever seen!"

Meisner went around the table and hugged him. "My friend is in good hands," he said. Later, Meisner would say, "It was kind of corny, but I was so moved."

Harrison was born in a hardscrabble Detroit community known as Delray, a neighborhood of immigrants who arrived eager for work at Ford Motor's sprawling Rouge complex nearby. The air was often thick with smoke from a multitude of factory chimneys, each spewing its own colors and foul smells.

He got his undergraduate and law degrees from Wayne State University, a large commuter school near downtown Detroit, and began his career at the Wayne County Prosecutor's Office in the fall of 1967. He quickly climbed the ranks, being named chief trial lawyer four years later.

In 1972, he went into private practice as a criminal defense attorney in the new firm of Harrison, Friedman & Roberson, which quickly became the hottest law firm in town.

And one of the most unusual, a model of diversity well before that became a buzzword, in a community known for its racial polarizations. "We had an Armenian Protestant, a Russian Jew and a black Catholic," says Harrison. He was the Armenian, Bernard Friedman was the Russian Jew and Dalton Roberson was the black Catholic.

They were all stars.

In 1974, Roberson became a district judge, and Friedman later was appointed to the federal bench and became chief judge of the eastern Michigan region. Harrison, though, wasn't tempted by the bench. He loved being a defense attorney and loved big cases.

After Roberson left, Harrison merged his firm with another very high-profile firm, one hardly so beloved by the community. It was run by Norman Lippitt, who represented the Detroit Police Officers Association during one of the most turbulent times in the history of the city.

The nearly all-white department was seen as an occupying force by many in the black community throughout the 1960s and 1970s, a community that was on its way to becoming the majority ethnic community in the city as white flight to the suburbs continued apace.

A famous incident involving Detroit police was detailed in the 1968 best-seller by John Hersey, *The Algiers Motel Incident*, about a horrific event during the 1967 riots. Three black youths were killed and two white girlfriends and seven others beaten, allegedly by Detroit police and members of the U.S. National Guard.

Another involved a shootout at the New Bethel Baptist

Church in Detroit, where a radical black attorney named Ken Cockrel successfully defended Alfred Hibbitt, who was accused of shooting two Detroit cops in a 1969 shootout.

Cockrel won an acquittal for Hibbitt, arguing that the Detroit Police Department was racist, and he successfully defended himself against contempt charges, despite calling the judge a "lawless, racist, rogue bandit, thief, pirate, honky dog fool," by proving that the Wayne County Jury Commission systematically excluded black jurors.

In 1970, Cockrel successfully defended Hayward Brown, who killed an on-duty Detroit cop who was a member of an undercover unit. Cockrel claimed, and the jury believed, that Brown had fired in self-defense because of fear in the black community of the unit's vigilante ways.

(A self-described Marxist-Leninist, Cockrel was part of revolutionary change in the city. He was elected to Detroit's city council in 1977 and a generation later, his son, Ken Cockrel Jr., became mayor after Mayor Kwame Kilpatrick pleaded guilty to two felonies involving perjury in a civil lawsuit to cover up an affair with his chief of staff.)

The merger of the two law firms was both controversial—it seemed an insult to some that a high-profile partner in what had been the city's most diverse law firm would join forces with one almost reviled in the black community—and lucrative. The steady work for the police association would ensure a good living and enable Harrison to take on other big cases that might not otherwise pay enough to justify the time.

The irony was that if those were criminal cases in Wayne County, a reliable tactic by the defense was to put the arresting officer or investigators on trial. Juries in Detroit were generally considered to be very sympathetic toward black defendants and much more willing than their counterparts in the suburbs to be open to allegations of police malfeasance.

So Harrison got good at defending cops and at attacking them. And based on the potential witness list for the Unger trial, there would be plenty of police to take aim at.

* * *

Tom McGuire had been a friend of Harrison's since their first year of law school. McGuire had spent a stint with the Wayne County Prosecutor's Office before going into private practice, specializing in product liability and medical malpractice. He had retired the year before the Unger case, but came out of retirement to help his old friend, who was in need of an expert on medical issues.

"He was driving his wife crazy and she begged me to get him on the case so he'd have something to do," joked Harrison. McGuire's wife, Mary Ellen, had been Harrison's office manager for many years and was retired, now, herself.

McGuire had a reputation for quickly grasping complicated science, of being a tenacious cross-examiner who couldn't be bamboozled by gobbledegook, of being witty and charming when needed, and relentless, even ferocious, when needed, too. And if there was a need for sarcasm on occasion, he was very good at that, as well.

They made a good team—Harrison cool, authoritative, almost grandfatherly; McGuire hot and decisive.

DROPPING THE FIRST BOMB
AT THE PRELIM

The preliminary examination in the case of *State of Michigan* v. *Mark Steven Unger* began on Tuesday, July 6, 2004, in the 85th District Court in Beulah, Judge Brent Danielson presiding.

The preliminary exam in Michigan is nearly always a formality. The prosecution has a very low bar to clear to get a case moved to circuit court, which handles felony cases.

Was there reason to think a crime was committed? Was there a modicum of evidence linking the defendant to the crime?

A long series of witnesses was heard over two days, including local and state police who had worked the Watervale scene, the Duncans and Dori Turner, Fred Oeflein, Jim Ryan and a slew of the Ungers' friends and family.

Most of it was perfunctory. But not all.

After a long recess, Glenn Stark took the stand at 3:16 p.m. Tuesday, and if any of the reporters were wondering what their leads were going to be, they wouldn't for long.

Stark told the court that he and his wife, Kathy, had lived in Huntington Woods until moving to Bozeman, Montana, the previous August, that they'd been friends with the Ungers for five years and had been aware of the impending divorce.

"Did you ever speak to Mark about Flo's wishes for a divorce?" asked Mark Bilkovic.

"Yes."

"Did he make any requests of you with respect to the divorce?"

"Yes. Initially he asked me to talk to Flo and try to help them reconcile. I told him I didn't think it was my place to be in that situation."

Bilkovic asked him about his trip to Michigan just before Florence's death. Stark said he'd gotten in on Wednesday, October 15, and had left the following Wednesday, the 22nd.

"During that time, did you speak with Florence Unger?" asked Bilkovic.

"Yes, many times."

"And did you ever see Florence Unger during that period of time?"

"Yes, I did."

"When you spoke with her, did she express any concerns to you that she had over Mr. Unger's behavior?"

"Yes. She told me that Mark's behavior had been increasingly erratic. She told me that he would turn very quickly, from, I believe what she referred to as perfect-husband behavior to angry, despondent, withdrawn."

"Did she ever use the phrase with you, 'Dr. Jekyll and Mr. Hyde'?"

"Yes, she did."

Bilkovic asked him about the night Stark had spent with the Ungers, the Tuesday before he went back to Montana. Stark said Unger had spent the early part of the evening at an AA meeting and upon arriving home had been withdrawn.

"I asked him if my presence was making him uncomfortable and if he would prefer me to stay somewhere else."

"And what did he say?"

"He told me that he was not angry with me. I was not the one who was divorcing him."

Stark told of flying back to Montana and getting a call

Saturday morning from Brian Witus, telling him about Florence's death.

Then, getting a message on his cell phone from Unger, telling him to call him as soon as he could on Flo's cell phone.

"Did you speak with him?" asked Bilkovic.

"Yes, I did."

"How did he sound?"

"Very upset. I asked Mark—I was very, extremely upset and agitated—and asked Mark several times, 'What happened to her?' I kept repeating myself, 'What happened to her?'"

"What did he say?"

"He said, 'I don't know.' I asked him if she did this to herself."

"What did he say?"

"He said no. He screamed no. And then I asked him if it was a homicide investigation."

"What did he say?"

"He said no. He said, 'You're scaring me.'"

"Was he crying at this point?"

"He was very agitated. He told me he had to go and he hung up."

"Now," continued Bilkovic, and here's where it got good, "you indicated that you were close friends with Florence, correct?"

"Yes."

"How close was your relationship?"

"We were very close."

"Now, you sent her e-mails often, correct?"

"Yes."

"And some of those e-mails had intimate details. Is that correct?"

"Yes."

"Did you ever have a physically intimate relationship with Florence Unger?"

"Yes."

"How long has that gone on for?"

"Two years."

Pendergast had known what had been coming, and what the answers were going to be. She stared at Harrison and Unger to see their reaction. Harrison was stunned. Unger, impassive. Hard to read.

The question hadn't come out of the blue. The adage is: A good attorney doesn't ask a question he doesn't already know the answer to, and Bilkovic was a good attorney.

He had uncovered the affair a few days earlier, while preparing for the preliminary exam. He'd been poring over e-mails back and forth between Stark and Florence, some of them at 2 or 3 in the morning—there weren't any sexual details, but they seemed too intimate to just be between close friends—and suddenly he realized: No one had asked Stark if he and Florence had been lovers. And someone needed to.

Bilkovic immediately called Stark in Montana and started leading into it, but found himself beating around the bush.

Stark cut him off. "Mark, if you've got something to ask, ask it."

So he asked. And Stark answered, "Yes." They'd had an affair over a two-year period, and had had sex once during Stark's visit to Michigan. Stark told Bilkovic he'd told his wife about the affair the day they found out Florence had died.

After Bilkovic hung up, he'd called Pendergast. "Donna, you're not going to believe what I found out."

It was dynamite stuff. It gave Unger possible motivation. What if he'd found out on the boathouse deck that just a few days earlier his wife had had sex with his best friend? Pendergast and Bilkovic could both picture Mark trying to get romantic on the deck, Florence spurning his efforts, and an escalating scene that ended with her telling him that not only did she not want to patch things up with him, she was in love with his best friend and had been sleeping with him. And Mark, furious, hitting her, or pushing her, at the perfectly wrong spot on the deck, where she spun over the rail and down to the concrete below.

"Aproximately how many times had you been physically intimate with her?" asked Bilkovic.

"Four times."

"When was the last time?"

"The week before her death. Friday. It would have been the seventeenth."

"Did you ever speak to Mark Unger and provide him any advice about going forward?"

"Yes. At the house on Tuesday. I told Mark that he needed to picture or imagine a life for himself and the children without Florence as his wife."

"And what did he say?"

"He told me he couldn't do that. He said because he loved her too much."

"I have nothing further at this time," said Bilkovic.

Harrison stood up. "Your Honor, I know we've just had a break, but may I have a five-minute recess at this point in time?"

It was 3:29. Harrison and his client quickly left the room, went down the hall and out the door. Harrison looked livid, talking animatedly and poking his finger in Unger's chest. Asking if he'd known about it and hadn't told him. Later, Unger would deny knowing about the affair, that it had been just as much a shock to him as it had been to his attorney.

Court reconvened at 3:36.

To everyone's surprise, Harrison said: "I have no questions." Stark was excused.

Lori Silverstein attended the preliminary exam, then to satisfy her own nagging questions, drove to nearby Watervale, to look for herself at the place Flo had died and how much sense Mark's story made.

At first she'd been on Mark's side in the Did-he-or-didn't-he? debate that dominated discourse in Huntington

Woods. She'd known Mark for twenty-five years and couldn't imagine him capable of such a thing.

She walked from her car to the boathouse and when she saw the concrete apron, it hit her hard, on two levels. *That* was where Flo had suffered her horrible head injuries. The other way it hit her was its size. She remembered the previous December, when, as talk of the death continued to dominate her friends' conversation, she and Rob had finally asked Mark point blank how Flo got in the water.

Unger told them the media had it wrong. Lori remembered it vividly, Mark holding his hands up vertically, parallel to each other, six to eight inches apart. That was how big the concrete apron was, he'd said, and Flo had landed on it and rolled off.

When she looked at the apron and saw how big it was and pictured Mark with his hands in the air, it was like getting hit with a piece of concrete in the gut.

She never spoke to Mark Unger again.

BOMBS TWO AND THREE

If Harrison had been stunned by Glenn Stark's revelations on the first day of the preliminary hearing, the entire prosecution team and defense teams were about to be stunned on day two.

They had wrapped up family friends, police and witnesses from the Watervale Inn when the clerk announced during a break that lead counsel were to report to Danielson's chambers.

"We were all thinking, 'What's going on? Did somebody say something?'" said Bilkovic. It was highly unusual that the lead counsel only would be summoned, and in such tones.

Fifteen minutes later, Donna came out of chambers and told them that they wouldn't believe it, but the judge said he was going to get sick if he saw any more medical testimony.

Danielson had told them the medical testimony he'd heard so far, and the exhibits he'd seen, were more than he could handle, and if he had to hear any more—and there was a *lot* more to come, details from the autopsy report and gruesome photos to be pondered—he was going to be sick. Physically sick.

He was *not* going to be able to continue. "We'd been

holding up these exhibits in front of them. Little did we know he was about to pass out," said one of the attorneys.

They were, defense and prosecution, united. They did *not* want to start over and lose two days of testimony from fifteen witnesses. Harrison and Pendergast agreed that if Danielson could find another nearby district judge to sit in during the medical testimony, he could then review it later to determinine whether to bind the case over for trial.

"We figured Danielson could read the transcript while lying down if he had to. Keep himself calm. We didn't want to start over," said one attorney.

The reason was never put on the record. It was announced that because of scheduling difficulties with the medical witnesses, the preliminary exam would be put on hold till September.

District Judge David Hogg of Cadillac, a bustling tourist town southeast of Traverse City, agreed to clear some of his docket, and the preliminary exam was scheduled to resume on September 8.

Bomb No. 3 involved a new standard in Michigan courts for the admissibility of testimony by those proffered as expert witnesses. It was known as the *Daubert Standard*, a legal precedent set in 1993 by the U.S. Supreme Court in the case of *Daubert* v. *Merrell Dow Pharmaceuticals*.

In that case, the Supreme Court ruled that federal judges are the gatekeepers of scientific evidence and must decide whether prospective testimony is relevant and reliable. Until then, trial judges let nearly anyone offered up as an expert witness testify, no matter how thin his or her credentials, letting the jury decide how much credence to give.

The Supreme Court ruled that in federal courts, it would be fairer for judges to eliminate junk science instead of having jurors try to evaluate it. The rule was adopted by the Michigan Supreme Court on January 1, 2004, and was about to get its first big test, thanks to Harrison.

He was about to invoke the standard, and ask Judge Danielson to exclude crucial would-be testimony, not from some quack purveyor of junk science, but from one of the most experienced medical examiners in the country, Ljubisa Dragovic.

Danielson had no choice but to agree to the defense request for a *Daubert* hearing, but given that it would be filled with the medical details he wanted to avoid, the hearing would be held in front of Hogg. Later, Danielson would read the transcript and decide whether Dragovic's opinions were junk or not. If he ruled in favor of Harrison, it would eviscerate the prosecution's claim that Mark Unger was guilty of first-degree murder.

Ljubisa Jovan Dragovic is the chief medical examiner and chief forensic pathologist for Oakland County, Michigan's second largest, at 1.3 million population, which annually ranks among the top five in the country in per capita income. It is dotted with small lakes. New money lives there. Two generations ago, it was rural; today, the farms and woods have been replaced by golf courses and large, gated communities, the thoroughfares lined with strip malls and office complexes. The walls and surfaces of Dragovic's office in Oakland County's government campus are busy, all the better to keep visitors occupied in the common event that some event or another, a murder, an autopsy, a trial, has made him late for an appointment.

There is a framed saying: "Blessed are they who can laugh at themselves, for they shall inherit the earth"; a framed, 18-inch-by-12-inch diagram of all the parts of a Smith & Wesson revolver, a not-uncommon weapon of choice for the killings his staff deals with; a staff photo from 1991, early on in his stint as ME of Oakland County, with all but one of the sixteen persons in the photo wearing fake Groucho Marx mustaches in imitation of his real one; and a variety of framed posters and maps of Europe, with labels such as "Saint Tropez," "French Wine Country," "Musee Picasso Antibes," "Galeries de Papes," "Monaco Yacht Show."

Dragovic is dapper and witty. He speaks with a heavy

Serbian accent, passionately and dramatically, punctuating his statements with loud laughter and a waving of hands.

In World War II, Tito's pro-Communist partisans in Yugoslavia fought the Civil War against royalists like Dragovic's grandfather. They threw him into a mountain crevice. His father, Jovan, fought against the occupying Nazis and later won a medal for bravery. As a boy, Dragovic, who came from a family of doctors, knew he wanted to be a doctor, and he knew he wanted out of Yugoslavia.

When he was 22, he accepted an internship in San Francisco that for a semester took him away from the Unversity of Belgrade. When it was over, on the plane home, he heard a young woman say she was going to the University of Belgrade to become a doctor, and he turned around to see who was talking. She was striking. They saw each other a few times on campus, turned up at the same dinner party, started dating and were soon married. He was 24, she was 20.

Dragovic then served for a year as a regimental medical officer in the Yugoslav National Army, joined the Department of Pathology at Queen's University in Kingston, Ontario, then took a string of residencies in the U.S. He ended up in Detroit as assistant medical examiner to a politically connected boss named Bader Cassin, whom he disdained, and whom he not-so-privately referred to as "Master Bader."

"I was a sore thumb there, and constantly criticizing," he says.

Dragovic oversees a staff of thirty-five. The department does some 1,200 autopsies a year—all the suspicious and unexplained deaths, the murders, the suicides and the traffic fatalities that might later result in criminal charges. His staff also works through intergovernmental agreement to handle much of the workload from Genesee County to the north, whose biggest city, Flint, annually has one of the highest murder rates in the country.

Dragovic takes a regular turn with the bone saw and other rugged tools of the trade, cutting and sawing on the stainless steel table tops, sharing duty on holidays and weekends.

"The No. 1 rule for everybody is one spelled out by Sir Arthur Conan Doyle through the mouth of Sherlock Holmes," Dragovic frequently tells visitors. " 'You cannot advance theories before knowing facts.' If you create a theory, you fall in the trap of trying to fit the facts to your theory."

He likes to quote proverbs, too, first in their original Latin, then in his heavily accented English: "The worst truth is better than the sweetest lie," he'll say.

There's a co-equal central thought to his work. "Minutiae are not trivial," he says, repeating it in caps: "MINUTIAE ARE NOT TRIVIAL. You cannot say, 'Okay, just because they are little things, they do not mean truth. Actually, it is the little things that give you the critical sentinel positions of the jigsaw puzzle you want to piece together."

One year, in 1988, when Detroit was rightly called the Murder Capital and he worked downtown, Dragovic performed 1,200 autopsies, himself. "I think that was probably the world record."

Dragovic has his own lucrative business testifying for both defense and prosecution outside Oakland County, and he's not reluctant to testify against prosecutors and police in very-high-profile cases.

He was defense attorney Geoffrey Fieger's chief foil in the cases against Dr. Death, Jack Kevorkian, insisting that Kevorkian's so-called patients had died as a result of homicide, not suicide. Juries kept disagreeing. He was one of the few who held his own verbally against Fieger. Unable to get him to take the verbal bait in their encounters in court, out of court, Fieger played to the press, calling him "Dracula" and "the Transylvanian vampire."

Typically, Dragovic got the best of the name-calling, too. "I may be a Montenegrin vampire," Dragovic said in response, "but I regretfully must correct 'Dr.' Fieger on his geography, as I occasionally must on medicine."

Also, typically, Dragovic attended a Halloween Party afterwards dressed as—what else?—Dracula. And, now, there sits atop the front corner of his desk, nearest to where visitors sit, a fifteen-inch-high plastic Dracula with a Don King hairdo, clutching a coffin to his chest as he stands amid the skeleton and skulls of past victims.

Pendergast was enraged by the request for a hearing. "*Daubert* is supposed to keep out voodoo science," she said. "They dropped *Daubert* on me in the middle of the exam. It was another example of their sandbagging."

Dragovic was livid. The *idea* that Harrison and McGuire would have the *audacity* to impugn *him*, to try to assert for the record that what he had to say about Florence Unger's death was *junk* was . . . was . . . *flabbergasting*.

On September 8, Cohle and Dragovic, both, ironically, prosecution witnesses, squared off in the all-important hearing.

Cohle told Hogg why the cause of death was a head injury, Dragovic why it was a drowning.

Dragovic had, in recent years, according to some prosecutors who worked with him, grown increasingly likely to skimp on preparation and rely on bluster. He had become, many felt, something of a caricature of himself, Dr. Dragovic imitating Dr. Dragovic. Pendergast would remind him, "Doc, you can't just say, 'Because I said so.'"

"Because I said so," about summed up his performance during the hearing. McGuire was prepared. Dragovic wasn't. For every reason Dragovic was sure Florence had drowned, McGuire had published studies to dispute it.

Cohle was more prepared, too. "They were at each other's throats," said Bilkovic. "Dragovic got slammed."

Hogg took it in, a curious role he was playing, the designated listener whose opinion meant nothing. The transcripts were conveyed to Danielson.

On October 11, Danielson ruled that Dragovic's opinion "was neither generally accepted in the relevant scientific community or by forensic pathologists," nor was it "based on vetted research."

Dragovic, who hadn't bothered to look up any literature

to back up his findings, shrugged off the judge's withering conclusion.

"No judicial ruling can change the facts in evidence," he said.

Harrison told the press that prosecutors had been dealt "a staggering blow" and ought to dismiss the case.

Pendergast wanted to appeal Danielson's decision to Benzie County Circuit Judge James Batzer, but he told her to hold off, see if Danielson bound Unger over.

Danielson did, but without testimony that Florence had drowned, he said the charge of first-degree murder was insupportable and dismissed it. He bound Unger over on a charge of second-degree murder and released him on bond.

Pendergast then appealed to Batzer. Harrison filed several motions seeking to block an appeal and to let Danielson's ruling stand. Pendergast responded with motions of her own, with Harrison filing more in answer to hers. It went on for nearly a year. "They papered me to death," Pendergast said.

Eventually, almost a year later, in September 2005, Batzer ruled for the prosecution. He would hold another *Daubert* hearing to see if Dragovic's conclusions about the drowning could be entered into evidence.

In January 2006, Batzer held the hearing. This time, Dragovic was prepared. Batzer overturned Danielson, reinstated the charge of first-degree murder, revoked Unger's bond and ordered him to jail.

All in all, it had taken eighteen months for the preliminary exam to conclude. "Undoubtedly a world record," said Pendergast.

Batzer carved a chunk of time out of his docket and ordered the trial to start in May.

BIG BANDS, BIG CASES

This was a case that would be won or lost on arguing complicated science, and Pendergast was worried about the experts Unger's mother would be able to afford.

One day in March, Pendergast and Bilkovic were plotting strategy, particularly who would have the crucial role of handling medical witnesses. Neither of them had a medical background, though obviously each was experienced in discussing the scientific hows and whys of death.

"Mark, I can do it. I'll put everything aside the next month and do it," said Pendergast, referring to the homework she'd need to do to study the complicated science her witnesses and the rebuttal witness would testify to about Florence's brain injuries.

"If we go to Deb Carley, I bet we can get John," said Bilkovic, referring to John Skrzynski, who was head of the felony unit for the Oakland County Prosecutor's Office, a gifted trial lawyer with an expertise in cases involving medical and scientific testimony. Carley was his boss.

They asked him if he'd join their team.

"No way. I run a division," he said.

They left. Skrzynski thought about it, though, half intrigued at the prospect, half worried he'd be in trouble if he didn't at least run the idea up the flagpole with his bosses. What if they heard later that he'd turned down the offer without getting their input? You never knew what could get your career off track in the political world of the prosecutor's office.

Skrzynski asked Carley what she thought. Expecting a quick no, he got a quick yes, and was assigned on loan to the attorney general's office. The team was set.

Not only did Skrzynski have the medical expertise they needed, he was used to big cases and the glare of the media spotlight. Enjoyed it, actually, given his background as a professional entertainer.

Skrzynski, during one of his brief stints away from the prosecutor's office, had been part of the defense team that lost a highly publicized murder case against Dave Davis (the details of which, had Patricia Highsmith woven them into a novel in the vein of her *The Talented Mr. Ripley*, might have seemed like writerly excess).

And Skrzynski was the prosecutor who finally put Jack Kevorkian, Dr. Death, behind bars after he had, by his own count, helped 130 people commit suicide.

Skrzynski is a natty dresser who wears his brown hair a lot longer than might seem expedient in the buttoned-down atmosphere of the Oakland County Prosecutor's Office.

He spent his first few years in the blue-collar city of Hamtramck, a city entirely surrounded by Detroit that was then an enclave filled with Polish immigrants lured to the new world by jobs in auto factories. Skrzynski's dad, Mike, was a musician and school teacher. When Skrzynski was a boy in the mid-1950s, the family moved to East Detroit— one of the many suburbs that were filling up with tract homes in what had been corn fields, financed by cheap FHA mortgages and sold mostly to World War II vets.

Skrzynski attended the University of Michigan, working his way through college as a musician, playing the trombone in a wedding band. An English major, he graduated in 1973 and did what seemed authentic for a would-be author in those dying days of the hippie and anti-Vietnam era—he hit the road to gather life experiences.

He got as far as Houston, but after a year of making no progress on the great American novel, he returned to Michigan and a vibrant music scene, playing in a variety of well-regarded local bands, including the Johnny Trudell Big Band, the Austin-Moro Band and the Brookside Jazz Band—about as high as you got in local music circles, unless you were a Bob Seger or a Mitch Ryder.

Skrzynski also played in the house band at a club in Dearborn, backing up such visiting headliners as the Lettermen and the the Commodores.

After getting married in July 1978, Skrzynski enrolled in law school at Wayne State University, graduating in 1981 and immediately passing the bar exam.

That was a year after Shannon Davis, married just ten months, supposedly had fallen off a horse while on a ride with her husband, hit her head and died at age 24.

Dave Davis had a farm in Hillsdale County, about 100 miles southwest of Detroit, and claimed he and his wife had ridden their horses over to visit the neighbors and on the way back, riding ahead of her, heard her scream, turned around and saw her lying on the ground.

Shannon was pronounced dead at the hospital. When her parents arrived, Davis stunned them by saying he wanted his wife cremated. They strenuously objected, and Davis allowed them to take custody of their daughter's body.

Davis told police the same story. Answering an obvious question, he told them his wife didn't have life insurance.

At the scene, police found a half-buried rock that was covered with what seemed to be blood. Eight feet from the rock were Shannon's untied shoes. There was circular bruising on two small trees, the kind of bruising that comes from tethering horses. And about seven feet from each tree was a clump of horse manure, evidence the horses had been tied there awhile.

The autopsy was inconclusive—it showed that despite

her head injuries from the fall, she had died from suffocation, but what had caused *that*?

In a search of Davis' barn, police found samples of succinylcholine, a powerful horse tranquilizer and muscle relaxant, but there were no tests, then, to detect its presence in humans.

Police soon found out that Davis didn't have *a* life insurance policy on his wife, he had *two*, totaling $250,000 and paying double on accidental death. In addition to the insurance policies, Shannon was heir to the large Mohr Brothers pop bottling estate.

Police were sure Davis had killed his wife, but they didn't think they had enough, yet, to charge him.

And then one day, Davis vanished.

Several years later, after a test was developed that showed the presence of succinylcholine in human tissue, police exhumed Shannon's body. It tested positive. The horse tranquilizer had killed her, not the fall.

Davis was officially a fugitive.

On December 28, 1988, NBC's *Unsolved Mysteries* aired an episode on the case, too. It aired in American Samoa on December 29.

Acting on tips, police arrested Davis, then 44, who was using the name David Myer Bell, at the airport in Pago Pago, Samoa's capital. Davis had sailed to Samoa four years earlier and was making a living as a pilot for several island airlines.

Remarried, he had also posed as a doctor and a nurse, and had played gigs as a harpsichord player. The talented Mr. Davis, indeed.

During his trial, a number of plot twists were revealed that made the eventual movie, *Victim of Love: The Shannon Mohr Story*, which aired on the USA Network, a foregone conclusion.

Kay Kendall, one of his former girlfriends, testified that during the mid-1970s, Davis, who had spent a year pursuing a graduate degree in pharmacology at the University of Michigan before dropping out, said that you could commit the perfect crime if you killed someone using succinylcholine.

In May 1979, Davis began dating Jeanne Holman and a month later asked her to marry him.

That June, though, Davis met Shannon Mohr at a wedding, which began a whirlwind romance that culminated in their wedding in Las Vegas on September 24. On October 2, he purchased a life-insurance policy in her name for $110,000, with a double indemnity clause for accidental death.

Holman testified at his trial that a week before he married Mohr, he told her he would be disappearing soon for a year on dangerous government work that was going to pay him $250,000.

In June 1980, Holman asked him how much longer his assignment was going to last. About three or four more weeks, said Davis.

On July 23, Shannon died.

To no one's surprise, least of all Skrzynski's, Davis was convicted. It was an unwinnable case, but fascinating, looking sheer evil in the face next to you at a table when you came to work every day.

In 1993, chafing to get back to putting people in jail instead of keeping them out, Skrzynski rejoined the Oakland County Prosecutor's Office. "After you do criminal law a while, it gets in your blood," said Skrzynski. "I love trial work. You gotta think on your feet. And it gives me a chance to be a performer again."

Bilkovic, who didn't always see eye to eye with him when Skrzynski was his boss, says he is hands down the best prosecutor on the large Oakland County staff. He prowls the courtroom, flailing his arms theatrically, his voice rising and falling.

On a long trial, he is a juror's godsend.

BATTLING DR. DEATH

For a while, Skrzynski's battles against Jack Kevorkian and his high-profile attorney, Geoffrey Fieger, seemed unwinnable.

Kevorkian was a notorious champion of euthanasia, a pathologist who began a second career of sorts with advertisements in Detroit newspapers in 1987 describing himself as an expert in death counseling.

The next year he cobbled $30 worth of scrap parts from garage sales and off-the-shelf components from hardware stores and built his first suicide machine on the kitchen table of his small apartment in the northern Detroit suburb of Royal Oak. He called it a *thanatron*, or death machine.

On June 4, 1990, Kevorkian helped his first client, Janet Adkins, a 54-year-old from Oregon with Alzheimer's, die, his machine injecting her with thiopental to induce unconsciousness, then potassium chloride to stop her heart. It wasn't her death that upset people, it was the shabby surroundings of it, in a campground, inside his rusty, beat-up 1968 VW van.

Kevorkian called 911. Within hours of telling police what he had done, his Armenian name was on its way to becoming a household word.

On October 23, 1991, Kevorkian assisted in his next two

suicides, of a 58-year-old woman suffering from severe pelvic pain and a 43-year-old woman with multiple sclerosis. The first died from the suicide machine's lethal combination of drugs, the second from inhaling carbon monoxide through a face mask, a rig he called a *mercitron*.

The deaths created a media frenzy and galvanized area residents. Because there was no law against assisting in a suicide, murder charges brought by Oakland Prosecutor Richard Thompson were dismissed. In November 1992, Kevorkian began a string of ten more assisted suicides in three months.

On August 4, 1993, a 30-year-old man with ALS named Thomas Hyde was found dead in Kevorkian's van in a park in the middle of the Detroit River. On September 9, hours after a judge had ordered him to stand trial in Hyde's death, Kevorkian was present at the death of a 73-year-old cancer patient.

In May 1994, Kevorkian was acquitted of Hyde's death.

On December 13, 1994, the Michigan Supreme Court ruled that assisting a suicide was illegal under Michigan common law, and four cases against him were reinstated.

All the while, Thompson—considered by his staff as something of a religious zealot, a humorless Catholic incapable of small talk who bemoaned abortion, the end of Latin masses and, above all, Kevorkian—was beside himself.

Thompson had lost the 1994 trial. Despite his disdain for Skrzynski—a raconteur who relished a martini after work and was generally at the center of good times at the office parties Thompson reluctantly attended—Thompson assigned him as lead prosecutor for Kevorkian's next trial, scheduled for February of 1996.

In the meantime, though, Skrzynski ran afoul of Thompson over his boss's wish to prosecute a doctor accused of the mercy killing of a woman who'd had an aneurism at her grandson's Little League baseball game. A nurse claimed to have seen the doctor injecting the woman with potassium chloride.

The problem was that the patient was brain-dead at the time and being kept alive by a ventilator at the family's insistence. Under Michigan law, brain death constitutes legal death, and if the patient was legally dead, it was impossible for the doctor to kill her, again.

During a citizens' inquest, Skrzynski had the temerity to spell out for its members the state's unambiguous definition of death. They refused to bring an indictment.

Thompson was enraged.

"You can't be a true believer in guilt, you have to be a true believer in the law," Skrzynski said.

Thompson pulled Skrzynski off the Kevorkian case and gave it to another prosecutor. In February, Skrzynski and his family were on vacation in Sarasota when the phone rang. It was his immediate supervisor, Larry Bunting.

"We want you to come back and try this case," he said.

Jury selection was to start the next day, and management had had second thoughts. They wanted Skrzynski, with his medical background, on the case and they had arranged a flight back.

The case involved Merian(CQ) Frederick, a 72-year-old with ALS—Lou Gehrig's disease—who had died in 1993 of carbon monoxide poisoning in Kevorkian's apartment.

Defense attorney Geoffrey Fieger got a videotape entered into evidence that showed Frederick's suffering. "It was heart-breaking," said Skrzynski later. "It was hard to watch. I'm watching the men on the jury tearing up and I'm thinking, 'That's it. It's over.'"

He didn't need to wait for the jury to announce its verdict to know what it would be: not guilty.

On April 1, Kevorkian went on trial, again, this time with Skrzynski serving as Bunting's assistant.

On May 19, he was acquitted again. There had been more videotapes, and more weeping in the jury box. "These videotapes were so tragic. You're thinking, 'How can you force someone to live like that?'" said Skrzynski. If you're saying that as prosecutor, you know what the jury is saying.

That November, an electorate angry at Thompson for

continuing to prosecute Kevorkian, turned him out of office, voting in a young, baby-faced assistant county prosecutor named David Gorcyca, who looked more like a dorm R.A. than a prosecutor.

Skrzynski hadn't been an active booster during Gorcyca's campaign, and assumed his career in the prosecutor's office was at a dead end when the new boss was sworn in in January 1997. Not only had he not helped get Gorcyca elected, he was linked to the same Kevorkian cases that got Thompson booted.

Skrzynski was at a job interview when his pager went off. He was told to report to Gorcyca's office.

"Holy shit," he said to himself. Thinking you'll get fired doesn't necessarily prepare you for when it happens.

Skrzynski wasn't being fired, though. He was being handed another big case, a headline maker.

The previous May 16, an attractive woman named Deborah Iverson, an ophthalmologist at Beaumont Hospital, one of Michigan's best medical facilities had been kidnapped in broad daylight from a downtown parking lot in the affluent, low-crime suburb of Birmingham.

She'd had a 9 a.m. appointment with her psychiatrist, which ended at 9:45. At 10:08 a.m., a check for $1,000 on her account was cashed at the drive-up window of a nearby bank. At 11 a.m., a second check for $300 was cashed at a second branch.

The next morning, her Toyota Land Cruiser was found in a rural area. Iverson was face down on the floor in the back seat. She'd been strangled. Clutched in her hand was a photo of her two young boys, Ricky, 4, and Colin, 2.

Had her death occurred a few miles south in Detroit, it would have been headlines for a day or two. That she was kidnapped in Birmingham in a seemingly random act made it huge news. It was in the headlines and on TV for months, as leads popped up and petered out.

Her husband, Robert, also a doctor, was the prime suspect, despite passing two lie-detector tests, and his insurance company withheld payment on the $1.1 million policy on his wife.

On December 30, 1996, the case broke with a call to police from an attorney representing an anonymous client. The day before, a woman named Anitra Coomer called a friend and said her live-in boyfriend, McConnell Adams, had severely beaten her. She also told the friend that Adams was the one who had killed the doctor who had been in the news. Later, the friend called the attorney for advice.

What had happened in May was: Coomer and Adams had a 2-year-old son. They were $480 in arrears to day care and had gotten an eviction notice from their landlord.

They headed to Birmingham to look for a suitable candidate to rob. Iverson, handsomely dressed, getting into her $40,000 SUV, was perfect. After they forced her to cash the checks, they drove her to a desolate spot. Iverson told them about her kids, pleading for her life. Coomer went through Iverson's wallet, found a photo of the boys and handed it to her.

She handed the belt from her coat to Adams, who wrapped it around Iverson's neck and killed her.

Skrzynski put the punks away for life.

In April, as a reward for his work on the Iverson case, Gorcyca promoted him to chief of the felony division.

That December, Skrzynski, as was his wont, was enjoying himself at the office Christmas party. He'd had a few to drink and approached his boss with what might have seemed an unbroachable topic. This was, after all, a man who had won reelection by campaigning that it had been a waste of taxpayer expense to keep putting Kevorkian on trial.

"Dave," Skrzynski began, "if fucking Kevorkian does it again, I want to prosecute him."

In March 1998, Kevorkian tallied his 100th assisted suicide.

In November, CBS' *60 Minutes* featured Jack Kevorkian, who had long since become a national figure. Skrzynski tuned in.

Only this time what he saw wasn't assisted suicide. Kevorkian showed Mike Wallace and a national audience a video he'd shot two months earlier of the death of Thomas Youk, another ALS victim. This time, Kevorkian hadn't just hooked his client up to one of his death machines, he'd worked the controls, pushing the button that pumped a lethal cocktail into Youk's body.

"Holy shit!" said Skrzynski to himself, invoking one of his favorite epithets. "That isn't assisted suicide. That's murder."

Days later, Kevorkian was charged in Oakland County with an open charge of murder, assisting a suicide and delivery of a controlled substance.

On March 26, Kevorkian was convicted of second-degree murder and delivery of a controlled substance.

Kevorkian served 8 years and was paroled on July 1, 2007, for good behavior and poor health. He was, said those close to him, near death, a result of hepatitis contracted years earlier while doing research on blood transfusions in Vietnam.

Avoiding euthanasia himself, though, he made a dramatic recovery once out of prison and was feeling feisty enough in 2008 to announce he would run for U.S. Congress.

PART FOUR

THE TRIAL

WEEK ONE
AT LONG LAST, A TRIAL

Jury selection was scheduled to begin on Wednesday, April 26. A few days earlier, just as he was heading out the door to his son's baseball game, Bilkovic got a call from Harrison, wanting to know if Donna would consider a plea deal.

"I don't know. You'll have to talk to her," said Bilkovic.

"Would she consider manslaughter?"

"I don't know. I'll talk to her."

Bilkovic called her. Truth be told, Pendergast was sweating this one, and tempted by an easy way out. She thought they had a good case, but she knew Harrison did, too. There was the reluctance of Cohle to rule the death a murder. And a defense exhibit put together by an engineer at MIT could be powerful stuff if she was unsuccessful in barring it.

So, an offer to convict on lesser charges was intriguing. But it wasn't her decision, it was her boss', Attorney General Mike Cox. He told her any deal would have to be for far longer than the sentencing guidelines for manslaughter, and would have to be approved by Claire and Harold Stern.

On Tuesday, they met in Judge Batzer's office.

Harrison said he'd consider a manslaughter plea under standard guidelines, which were 19 to 38 months.

"The only way I'd consider taking manslaughter to Cox is if he'll agree to ten to fifteen years," said Pendergast.

"He won't take that," said Harrison. "We'll never agree to that. Never, never, never."

"In that case, I'll see you all tomorrow," said Batzer.

Harrison later would claim that Pendergast had asked about the possibility of another plea deal late in the trial. "It was cat-and-mouse on both sides. We never got anything in writing," he said. "We rejected it, not them. If he agrees, he has no chance of ever getting his kids back. It was initiated by the judge, which was another signal the judge didn't see it as a first-degree case." Pendergast and Bilkovic denied that such talks had occurred. "You have to understand Donna," said Bilkovic. "Once a trial starts, she's not one to waiver."

There had never been a jury selection like this one in the small town of Beulah. The jury pool began with a list of 350 names, all of whom filled out a fourteen-page questionnaire. Defense attorneys and prosecutors studied the questionnaires, looking for those to eliminate for cause, trying to figure out who might be sympathetic.

On Wednesday, formal jury selection began, finishing two days later with fifteen members, three of whom would be eliminated by a blind draw at the end of the trial.

It was safe to say the town had never seen a trial like this, either.

A crew from NBC *Dateline* was in town, as were local TV crews, print reporters and photographers from Detroit, and numerous friends and relatives of both Florence and Mark.

The county clerk rounded up brochures, menus and tourist guides from the Chamber of Commerce to prominently display at the courthouse.

The restaurants in town put the word out that they could use some extra help for a few weeks. Crystal Mountain, a nearby ski resort that catered to golfers in the spring and summer—northwest Michigan is dotted with world-class courses—offered reduced rates for out-of-towners attending the trial.

The sheriff's department hired a deputy to provide extra security during the trial.

Not everyone was thrilled, though. County Commissioner Mark Roper complained that the trial had cost the county $20,000 before it even started. The county had to remodel two bathrooms in the courthouse, expand a small courtroom and paint lines in the asphalt parking lot to make official parking spots. Then there was the metal detector that had to be installed at the front door, a level of security no one in the small town ever imagined.

Those at the county's Visitors and Convention Bureau were worried about the long-term effect of the alleged murder and trial. The bureau's spokesman, Michael Brougham, told the press that people were worried the area was being stigmatized unjustly by a foul deed done by a distant outsider.

"We have a beautiful area up here, a safe area," he said. "It's not pleasant being associated with a murder."

WEEK TWO
PEOPLE V. *MARK UNGER*

At 10:10 a.m. on Wednesday, May 3, 2006, Circuit Court Judge James Batzer's clerk quietly, with an air of routineness that belied the tension in the packed room, began the trial:

"*People* versus *Mark Unger*," she said.

Pendergast rose. "Good morning, Your Honor," she said, and introduced herself and her assistants, Mark Bilkovic and John Skrzynski.

Robert Harrison introduced his team, which included Tom McGuire, Matt Klakulak and Roger Wotila, and the bailiff brought in the jury.

The judge, perhaps betraying his nervousness, told Pendergast to proceed with her opening statement, then caught himself. "Oh, yes, we want to swear the jury."

Pendergast began with a theatrical burst. "I'm not going to say, 'Good morning.' It would be obscene. There's nothing good about a morning when we begin to discuss the senseless obliteration of a human life, in front of victims and the family of the deceased. So, instead, I'm going to say the opposite. The opposite of good being bad. The opposite of morning being night. And I'm going to tell you about a very bad night, which is the very reason that you're in this courtroom today.

"Picture a horrific image straight out of the worst of nightmares. A woman battered and bruised, her broken body mangled, maimed and bloody, crumpled in a heap on a hard cement slab, silenced and speechless, unseen, but still alive and breathing in the dark of night," she said.

It reads as overdone, but in the courtroom the alliterations and the sibilance were effective. The jury stared at her, brought right into the scene at the Watervale.

"Fear of the dark, and of the bad things that happen in the night, was now a stark reality as she lay unconscious and unheard in the still of the night, unknowing and unaware, as her murderer approached her in the dark . . . her body would be moved, placed face down in a cold dark lake, where she would spend the final moments of her life, staring blankly at death in the face as the very life drained from her broken body.

"What you're about to hear in this courtroom will disturb you, will horrify you, will haunt your dreams for a long time to come. Maybe the rest of your lives," said Pendergast.

Pendergast dialed back on the hyperbole and the drama, and recounted the chain of events that had led everyone to this place on this day.

She told of the Ungers' marriage in 1990, of the gambling and drugs that strained it, of Mark's rehab, of their fights, of her wish for a divorce and his efforts at reconciliation.

"Ladies and gentlemen of the jury, there is an old saying that dead men tell no tales," she said. "But in this courtroom, a dead woman will speak to you through the evidence. The evidence will scream out to you, although Florence Unger's cries have been silenced forever. The evidence that will point in one direction, and one direction only."

At 10:57, the judge declared a recess.

"Your Honor, ladies and gentlemen, GOOD MORNING," Harrison began his opening remarks, stressing the last two words. "And it IS a good morning. Not because Florence Unger is not with us, but it's a good morning because the process is starting, now, finally, to present the truth to a group of good people who will make the right decision. And so for Mark Unger and his family, for me, for the rest of the attorneys here, it is good that this is now starting."

Harrison told them they would hear no evidence of confessions, would hear from no eyewitnesses, would hear nothing about fingerprints. They would, he said, hear about a safety railing on the deck Flo Unger fell from. "The evidence will show you that the so-called safety railing . . . was so decayed, it was an accident waiting to happen," he informed the jurors, adding that it was so low, it violated building codes and offered no protection.

Moreover, the owners had removed five high-wattage bulbs on the deck to save on electricity, leaving one light fixture that left the deck in darkness, a deck covered with slippery algae.

"If there was any moisture on it at all—and we know there was moisture on it in the night in question—the algae on that old deck turned into something akin to a slippery ice rink."

He said the evidence against his client was circumstantial, the witnesses contradictory and inconclusive. Police at the scene jumped to conclusions, police technicians neglected to perform their jobs properly.

He told them that while Flo's beauty was flawless, her personality was not. She'd had a two-year affair with Mark's best friend, that until then, "Flo had lived a lifestyle that was carefree, reasonably rich and full, and it included no need to work. Her days were filled with—as I'm sure her friends will tell you—shopping, going to the gym, lunch with her girlfriends, lunch with her men friends. Life for Flo was wonderful, until Mark couldn't bring in the kind of salary that he had previously been bringing in, and he had to go into the rehabilitation center. And Flo's life changed at that point, and she had to go to work. And she didn't like it."

Harrison asked if an injury to the head suffered in the fall had killed Flo, or if she'd drowned. Pendergast had said, in making the state's case, that the only way Flo could have gotten in the water was for someone to drag her or push her or roll her into the lake.

"Why is Dragovic"—Harrison dropped the title of "Doctor"—"bending over backwards to help this prosecution team in this case? Well, as you will find out, without Dragovic's scientifically unsupported and false opinion that a drowning occurred in this case, they do not have a first-degree murder case.

"Now, you will also come to learn that Dragovic is quite well known for showing up in other pathologists' cases and leveling criticism at other very highly trained and well-regarded pathologists. And the cases where he does that are usually cases like this one, where there is a lot of press play, and where there's a good chance of him getting himself on television or in the newspapers.

"He has a very lucrative private practice, you will come to learn, and he testifies in civil cases. And there's nothing better for business than the free advertising that comes with high-profile case testimony."

Harrison spent several minutes telling the jury specific bits of testimony they would hear from the defense's witnesses that would contradict Dragovic's testimony.

Harrison finished his opening argument at 2:30 p.m. by saying, "The flimsy circumstantial evidence in this case is not what you see in a murder case. This is a murder case. It is not jaywalking. This kind of evidence does not belong in the courts of the United States. This kind of case does not belong in the courts of the United States.

"The final thing I want to tell you is, the evidence that will be presented by the prosecution in this case will be so unconvincing that you will, at the conclusion, say these charges are not proven, and not proven means not guilty. Thank you very much for your patience."

A BUS RIDE TO THE LAKE

Judge Batzer had a surprise for the jury. They would, after a brief recess, take a trip to Lower Herring Lake, to visit the scene of the alleged crime at the Inn at Watervale.

The judge and the attorneys discussed the itinerary and decided the jury would start its tour of the property at the boathouse, walk on the deck, go down to the beach, go up to the Inn and visit the inside of the Mary Ellen.

The judge told the jury not to take their note pads and when they got to the scene not to talk about the case. "I'm going to try not to say much of anything at all," he told them. "Counsel aren't going to say anything. And so just follow. Just follow us. All right? So we'll see you at the Watervale, then."

The jury walked out at 2:53 and got in the bus for the fifteen-minute drive to the southwest to see the property they'd be hearing so much about.

If any of the jurors were unfamiliar with the Inn at Watervale, it certainly must have taken them by surprise. All of them would have been familiar with resorts and inns and bed and breakfasts in the area. The area is dotted with them and they range from musty, mildewed small places well past their prime that require you to bring your own linens, to spacious, luxury destinations that not only supply the linens, but plasma TVs, satellite dishes and Jet Skis.

Watervale is unlike any of them. A sprawling resort, now, it was built as a company town for the Leo Hale Lumber Company in 1892. It included a saw mill, a post office/general store, and a boarding house for single men. The post office is now called the Casino Annex, and the boarding house is called the Inn. The lumber company built eight houses for married loggers, seven of which still stand.

The lumber industry transformed Michigan, and its lumber transformed America, supplying millions of board feet of white pine to build the homes the burgeoning population needed.

Michigan's early settlers had farming in mind, and there was plenty of good soil in the southern part of the state. By the 1840s, the copper and iron mines of the Upper Peninsula and the millions of acres of white pines, many of which were already towering when Columbus landed in 1492, were attracting a new wave of immigrants who wanted nothing to do with a plow horse or tiller.

Throughout the 1840s and 1850s, French Canadians and Scandinavians flocked to the lumber camps and mill towns of central and northern Michigan. Hardwoods like sugar maple, beech, hickory and oak flourished in southern Michigan, and were mostly seen as impediments to be cleared for planting. But north of the 43rd parallel, softwoods, primarily white pines often more than two hundred feet high and eight feet in diameter, dominated and were a cash crop to be cut and planed.

At first, the mills and the workers only kept up with local demand for finished boards. It wasn't until 1847 that the first shipment of white pine from the Saginaw Valley in mid-Michigan reached Albany, New York, by way of the Erie Canal.

Lumber dealers there declared it the equal of Maine white pine, until then the standard.

By 1854, the Saginaw Valley had twenty-nine mills with

a capacity for 100 million board feet per year. By 1860 there were seventy-two mills there, and a wholesale migration of lumbermen from the East Coast was taking place. The myth of Paul Bunyan and his blue ox, Babe, began with Saginaw Valley lumbermen telling their tales.

As the wood played out there, the industry spread north, where the Manistee and Boardman Rivers served as log highways. The heavy work was done, surprisingly, in the dead of winter. The cut logs were piled twenty or thirty feet high on massive sleds, which were pulled by teams of draft horses to the nearest river bank. When the ice melted in spring, the logs were rolled into the water and began their float to the mills.

A typical lumber camp in the woods might have six or seven yoke of oxen, twenty teams of horses and five or six buildings, including a large cooking shanty, to accommodate seventy men. If there were a number of camps in a particular area, serving their needs would require an influx of other trades and vendors. Small towns sprung up, some that would last just a few years, others that still exist.

In 1876, a new method of hauling logs allowed lumberjacks access to stands of pine that had been too far from rivers to be cut and hauled economically. Narrow-gauge rail lines starting snaking north. By 1889, eighty-nine logging railroads were in operation.

By 1880, Michigan was producing a fourth of the nation's lumber, and as much as the next three top states combined. By 1897, some 160 *billion* board feet had been cut, with plenty of trees still standing and the industry still going strong.

Thanks to one of those narrow-gauge railroads, which ran from the woods along the front of town and then on to a great pier on Lake Michigan, the Leo Hale Lumber Company—and Watervale—looked set to flourish for years. In the northwest corner of the state, there was still a seemingly infinite supply of pine yet to be logged.

But the well-planned, well-built town would have just a

brief existence. The year after it was founded, the Great Panic of 1893 hit. As quickly as the boom had come, it stopped.

The lumber company went bankrupt and the people left, creating a surreal ghost town of new buildings. Over the years they were intermittently used by independent lumber crews, hunters and squatters. The great pier, pounded by fall and winter storms rolling eastward across Lake Michigan, showed how quickly the Second Law of Thermodynamics can apply, collapsing bit by bit until only a few pilings remained.

In 1917, Dr. Oscar Kraft, an ophthalmologist from Chicago and an heir to the Kraft food fortune, bought the entire ramshackle village as a retreat for himself and his seven sisters and brothers.

In 2003, the resort received National Historic Designation, a move Kraft's descendants, including Dori Turner and Maggie Duncan, welcomed, as it would keep future developers at bay and make it easier for subsequent generations to keep in the family.

Lined up in a row facing Lower Herring are thirteen evenly spaced houses—called cottages by some, most are far too grand for the term—bearing names like Ella, Joshanna, Trish, Ursula, Margaret, Barbara, Fredericka and, of course, Mary Ellen. Included in the row is the former hotel and the former post office.

Farther west are the houses that overlook Lake Michigan and a stretch of shore known as Watervale Beach.

Watervale is one of those places families return to for generations. Children grow up remembering it as the highlight of their summer, and bring their children back to watch the sunsets over Lake Michigan or to hike nearby Mt. Baldy on the trail from the resort that leads through the woods and up a sand dune that towers 300 feet over the lake.

The resort has its own head chef, whose menu of homemade meals changes daily, and a pastry chef, and Dori often bakes fresh bread daily, too.

The place strives to be authentic. Guests are offered cherry juice, real (and incomparable) Michigan maple syrup and farm fresh eggs.

Turner prides herself on the furnishings. She brags on the resort's Web site that she "makes it her mission in life to scour every antique store, flea market and second hand shop in search of authentic furnishings for Watervale. . . . Entering a Watervale cottage is like stepping back into another era."

The Inn serves as the resort's gathering place. Meals are served in the dining room on the main floor and the two upper floors contain both single and double bedrooms. The Web site boasts that "Many rooms have their own sinks," a boast first made the day the place opened in 1892. Each floor has two common bathrooms.

Summer rates are by the week, only. Rates range from about $500 for a room in the Inn to $650 for some of the houses on Lower Herring Lake to more than $4,000 for the Gull Dune house overlooking Lake Michigan and the grand five-bedroom Margaret on Lower Herring.

Prices don't include the daily food charge for breakfast and dinner for each cottage guest 12 and over, and gradu-ated rates for younger children. Wednesday is barbecue night, served outside with arrays of salads, burgers, fried chicken and desserts, followed by hayrides for the kids.

Other nights, dinner seating is assigned and the dinner bell is rung at 6:15 p.m. and 7. It's not unusual to be served by someone on summer break from college who grew up spending his or her summers at Watervale.

Prices don't include cable TV, either. Cottages have nei-ther TVs nor phones, though most have fireplaces and porches or decks with water views.

Credit cards aren't accepted. Rowboats, kayaks and ca-noes are available for rent, but Jet Skis aren't allowed.

WATER, WATER EVERYWHERE

Lower Herring Lake is in Benzie County, the smallest county by land mass in Michigan and one of the prettiest. Founded in 1863, it has 860 square miles, of which 538 are water; in 2000, it had a population of just 15,998.

The county is homogenous, even by northern Michigan standards. Its 2000 makeup was 96.39 percent white, 1.69 percent Native American, 1.56 percent Hispanic, 0.3 percent African American and 0.26 percent Asian. Fully 97 percent spoke English as a first language, 1.9 percent spoke Spanish.

Per capita income was just $18,524, with median household income of $37,350.

Everyone in Michigan places things in a geographical context by where they are on the hand or mitten that is the Lower Peninsula of the state.

The Leelanau Peninsula that juts into Lake Michigan north of Benzie County is the little finger to the thumb that juts into Lake Huron on the eastern side of the state. Benzie, then, is the first knuckle of the little finger.

The county is dominated by water—the Crystal Lake Watershed and the Betsie River Watershed, Crystal Lake, Big Platte Lake, Little Platte Lake, Upper Herring Lake, Lower Herring Lake and Lake Michigan.

Upper Herring lies to the east of Lower Herring Lake and drains into it. Lower Herring in turn flows through a short channel into Lake Michigan.

Michigan's western shoreline is dotted with long, rectangular lakes that lie at an angle to the big lake and are separated from it by narrow strips of land. At one time, these lakes were bays on Lake Michigan, but after tens of thousands of years they became separate bodies of water as sand and dirt built natural dykes between bay and lake.

Beulah, the county seat, is a picturesque town on the southeast corner of Crystal. Crystal Lake is deep and clear, with a mean depth of nearly 71 feet and a maximum depth of 165. Its surface area of 9,854 acres makes it the ninth largest in the state. It is, as its name implies, crystal clear.

A bone-headed plan in 1873 had the unintended consequence of forming the beach that now surrounds the lake and provides the basis for the resort and vacation property that generates much of the county's tax base.

That year, entrepreneurs hoping to maximize their profits from the booming logging industry decided to connect Crystal Lake to Lake Michigan by digging a navigable channel to float logs.

Alas, they didn't realize that in the eons since Crystal Lake had been cut off from Lake Michigan, its water level had risen and it was substantially higher than the big lake.

When the last bit of earth was dug out and the two two bodies of water were connected, again Crystal Lake began pouring into Lake Michigan, its level dropping by 20 feet almost overnight and exposing the flat strip of beach that is now the lake's most valuable asset.

The breach was closed, the water stopped flowing and the lake remains some twenty feet above Lake Michigan. The event is still known as the "Tragedy of Crystal Lake," but for present-day owners of cottages, one man's tragedy is another's godsend.

It was an undisputed tragedy, though, that brought the jury, defense team, prosecution, judge, press and curious spectators to the Inn at Watervale in May of 2006. Having seen the cottage where the Ungers stayed, having stood atop the deck and looked down at the spot Florence Unger landed, and into the water where she either was placed by her husband or rolled as a result of the momentum of her fall, the jury quietly got back on the bus and rode in near silence back to Beulah.

A FATHER SPEAKS

At 9:39 Thursday morning, May 4, 2006, Harold Stern, Florence Unger's father, was sworn in.

Pendergast knew this was going to be a case argued in large measure about difficult science. What might decide it, though, would be circumstantial evidence, and so she had decided to skip, for now, the ghastly details of what Dragovic and others would describe and the conclusions those details had led them to.

She started, instead, in as circumstantial a way as possible. What, pray tell, might be the circumstances behind Florence Unger finding herself on a deck overlooking the lake at night? Pendergast asked him who he was, where he lived, when his daughter was born (March 16, 1966), and then:

"Is there any trait or characteristic of Florence's that was pronounced throughout her lifetime, something that you thought to be somewhat unusual?"

"Yes, she was afraid of the dark."

"And did that affect her behavior?"

"Yes, it did. When she was a child, she always had the light on in her room, she had the light on in the hallway, she had the light on in the bathroom. And she wouldn't go down into the basement by herself because she was afraid of the dark. When she left a room, she would never turn off the lights.

"And when she came over to visit us, at night, when she left, she always made sure that we went outside with her and saw her into the car and made sure that she got away safely."

"All right," said Pendergast.

But Stern wasn't done. "When she was a little child, she said, 'Hold me, Daddy, I'm scared of the dark.' And now, thirty years later, she's put in a place where she's going to be in the dark forever."

Point made, before the defense could object, Pendergast said, "Well, Mr. Stern, you just respond to the questions I ask."

"All right."

A cynic might have wondered if the back-and-forth had been scripted.

Stern said his daughter had told him she wanted out of her marriage. That she had come over to see him in his house in Huntington Woods the summer of 2002 and told him Mark was a drug addict and probably needed to go into rehab.

Stern said that Mark had gotten out of rehab in February and he and Flo had begun to see a marriage counselor. Apparently it didn't work, because one day Mark called the Sterns' house and asked to speak to his wife, yelling that Flo had told him she was going to file for divorce and seemed in a panic.

In August of 2003, after Flo had, indeed, filed for divorce, she stopped by the Sterns' house, upset. Mark had erupted in anger over the divorce. He had told her that he would take the house, get custody of the kids and see to it she got no more than $1,000 a month to support herself.

And she confided something to her father—she had always, she said, secretly hated the name Unger, and as soon as the divorce was final, she was changing her name back to Stern.

"Did you receive a call in the morning, Saturday, October twenty-fifth of 2003?" she asked.

Stern said he'd gotten a call from Mark at 8 a.m., he and his wife still in bed. His curiosity at who was calling that early and why morphed quickly into panic as he heard his wife's end of the conversation.

"She said, 'Where is my daughter?' And he said, 'Let me talk to Papa' . . . And my wife said, 'I want to know where my daughter is.' And the defendant said, 'Let me talk to Papa.' And then my wife said—she was angry and upset and she said, 'My God, you've killed my daughter.'

"When I finally started to talk to him, all he said was, 'She's in the water. She's in the water.'"

Stern told of the long drive to Glen Arbor, of the awkward encounter with Mark at Peter's house. Of Mark asking more than once, "Do you have any questions for me?" And of the shock they felt when Mark followed him and his wife out of the house and asked if they would let him have their daughter cremated.

"Why did you find that to be unusual?" asked Pendergast.

"Number one, cremation is contrary to the tenets of the Jewish religion. And number two, we knew that he was extremely upset when his father's fifth wife, who's a Lutheran, had him cremated. He was very upset about that. Outraged."

Harrison asked Stern if it was true that he and his daughter had had long periods of time when they were angry at each other and wouldn't talk.

"No."

"That's not true?"

"That's not true."

"If other witnesses testified about that, that would be a lie?"

"I don't know how they would know that."

Florence and Mark Unger; happier times at Watervale.

Courtesy of Mark Unger

Left, the Ungers' house. Cheryl and Ron Loeb's house is to the right. The Loebs testified that Florence Unger was so afraid of the dark that she wouldn't walk home alone from their house to hers and needed an escort.   *Photo by Tom Henderson*

A view from a kayak of the main building at the Watervale Resort.   *Photo by Tom Henderson*

The boathouse and the deck Flo fell from.
                                           Photo by Tom Henderson

Another view of the boathouse.

Courtesy of the prosecutors

Flo's body bobbed in the waves all day.

Courtesy of the prosecutors

The dive team moves Flo. *Courtesy of the prosecutors*

A broken support beam. Was dry rot to blame for Flo's fall?
Courtesy of the prosecutors

Deputy Troy Packard told the jury he was stunned to find that just hours after the discovery of his wife's body, Mark Unger had already packed up the family car. The defense argued that the peculiar behavior was a natural reaction to shock and grief.

Courtesy of the prosecutors

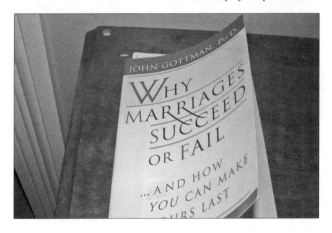

Investigators found this book in the Ungers' cottage after Flo's death, an ironic reminder of a troubled marriage.

Courtesy of the prosecutors

Wayne County medical examiner Carl Schmidt thought there was reasonable doubt for acquittal.

Photo by Tom Henderson

Kent County medical examiner Dr. Stephen Cohle said interference by Oakland County officials was unprecedented.

Photo by Tom Henderson

The prosecution (from left to right): John Skrzynski, Donna Pendergast, and Mark Bilkovic.

Photo by Tom Henderson

The defense (from left to right): Tom McGuire and Bob Harrison.

Photo by Tom Henderson

Glenn Stark tells the courtroom about his affair with Flo and anger at Mark.

Detroit News

Flamboyant Oakland County medical examiner Ljubisa Dragovic gestures during the trial. *Detroit News*

Mark Unger sheds more tears.

Detroit News

AN INNKEEPER'S TALE

Linn Duncan took the stand and was asked to describe the resort, what was owned by him and Maggie, what was owned by Dori Turner.

He described their two houses on the lake and the boathouse in between, and said that its deck was used by guests to relax on in chaise longues and beach chairs, for reading, staring out at the lake. "To sit around and do nothing," said Duncan.

Pendergast asked him if the boathouse roof looked the same when the jurors had seen it on their visit the day before as it had in October 2003.

"No. No. A month before the accident it was all wood," he said. "We made arrangements to have it updated. We knew nothing about the code."

"Accident"? The word jarred Pendergast's ear. Not good having one of your star witnesses refer to the event you're trying to prove was first-degree murder as an accident.

"You said 'a month before the accident.' You're not suggesting this is an accident, are you?"

A leading question, but Harrison left it unchallenged.

"No," said Duncan.

"All right. Now, can you tell the members of the jury, when is the last time that you took a really good look at that railing before the morning of October twenty-fifth, when you had an *unfortunate occurrence*."

Duncan told of spending Friday afternoon, the 24th, lowering all the furniture on the boathouse roof, fifteen or twenty pieces, down to the cement apron on the beach below, so it could be stored away for the season. He used a rope with a hook on it and lowered the furniture a piece at a time, putting each piece on the railing, hooking it, then lowering it while he leaned against the rail for support.

Did he notice, in all that time lowering the furniture or after, any breaks in the rail, any damage?

"Nothing. It was in good shape."

Was there any mold on the roof? Any algae? Anything to make it slippery?

No.

He told of the early morning phone call, ticked off thinking it was one of his golfing buddies come up with the idea of taking in an early round and disturbing his sleep because of it, and it being Mark Unger, instead, sobbing that his wife wasn't there, that she'd been gone all night.

Duncan recounted how he and Maggie had walked down to the boathouse, seen a body floating face down, hair floating, the water pink. Maggie had gone to call 911 and after a bit, he'd walked up the railroad bed to find Mark coming toward him.

Pendergast asked him if the foliage was the same that day as the day before, when the jury had visited the sight.

"No. In the fall, why, the bushes are up and the trees are in full bloom," referring to the color in the leaves.

"The area where you met up with the defendant, can you tell the members of the jury, could you see where Florence's body was from there, in the water?"

"Oh, no. No. You couldn't have seen it yesterday, because of the angle."

"So you're saying even without the foliage, you can't see it?"

"You're right. Couldn't be seen."

"Tell the members of the jury what happened next."

What happened next was, there's Mark walking briskly toward him and him moving more slowly toward Mark and trying to figure out what he was going to say—"it was very awkward from my standpoint, because what do you say to somebody when you know, you think you know, that it's his wife in the water and something terrible has happened?"— and they intersect and the words came out: "Mark, you're not going to like it. She is in the water."

He told the courtroom Unger "just went crazy, and crying and screaming and hollering . . . And instantly he started running down the railroad path, running to the east. And he got to the railing and went diagonally down to the water and jumped right in, right next to her."

"Had you told or given the defendant any information whatsoever about where the body was?" asked Pendergast.

"No. None."

"Did he ask you where in the water? Anything?"

"Nothing."

"Did you ever see the defendant touch Florence Unger?"

"No."

"Did you ever see him try and get her body out of the water?"

"No."

Pendergast asked him when he'd first noticed two splintered support posts on the railing of the boathouse patio. Two days after Flo's death, he said, when the police took down their yellow crime-scene tape and he went down to take some photos.

The timing was crucial. Was the damage old or new? Had to be new, said Duncan. Friday'd been the day he lowered most of the patio furniture over the railing with a rope to the concrete apron below. He'd have noticed broken support beams. The damage must have occurred Friday night or Saturday morning.

STATE OF DISREPAIR

Harrison was effective on cross-examination. He got Duncan to acknowledge that twice in the month before Flo's death, he'd met with contractors to discuss major repairs to the boathouse deck.

Harrison sprung a surprise on him. He pulled out a series of proposed exhibits, numbers 11 through 20, all pieces of wood a defense witness would later verify as having come from the railing system, and showed them to Duncan.

"Would it be fair to say, Mr. Duncan, that these are parts of pieces of the rail structure, the railing and support post structure of the deck, the way it was before you'd had the last improvements made?"

Pendergast protested, but the judge let the question stand.

"I can't say that," said Duncan. "But it looks like it."

Harrison showed Duncan Exhibit No. 12, some two-by-fours nailed together and some one-by-sixes.

"Does that appear to be dry rot?" asked Harrison.

"Yes."

"And do these pieces in Sixteen appear to be full of brown and black dry rot?"

"Yes."

"Proposed Exhibit Number Twenty, Mr. Duncan, does

that appear to be a broken, rotted part or piece from the railing system?"

"Yes."

"And Eighteen, does that appear to be a piece of the corner post of the rail system?"

"Yep."

"And proposed Nineteen . . ."

"Yep, yep, yep."

"And do these all appear to exhibit crumbled, dry-rotted wood?"

"Part of it is and part of it isn't. But they were solid enough to take my weight the day before."

"Why don't you press down on that?"

Duncan pressed into a piece of wood.

"Feels pretty, well, yeah. All right," he said, communicating clearly to the courtroom that the wood was anything but firm.

"You can break it off, can't you?"

"Yeah."

"Those posts that we're talking about, and that I was showing you there, are fifty or sixty years old, aren't they?"

"Oh, yes. Yes."

"And as a matter of fact, sir, isn't it true that you have never inspected them for dry rot?"

"Right."

"Ever?"

"Ever. I always thought they were solid. There's no reason to think otherwise."

"Mr. Duncan, after looking at those posts in that condition, breaking pieces off with your thumb and your forefinger, and thinking about this situation, do you feel that that deck was really safe for people to be up on at that time?"

Pendergast objected. "Your Honor, excuse me. Calls for an expert witness. He's not."

"He can answer. It's his deck," said the judge.

"It was perfectly safe," said Duncan.

"Perfectly safe?"

"Perfectly safe."

BLOOD AT THE SCENE

Mike Trailer, the EMS technician who had poked Florence Unger's leg to make sure she was dead, took the stand and told of his participation at Watervale that day.

He was followed by Troy Packard, a member of the Frankfort police force at that time, now a member of the Benzie County Sheriff's Department.

He told of arriving about 8:15, and being told by Trailer that it was a suspicious scene, which Packard secured with yellow crime-scene tape.

Why had he called in the sheriff and the state police?

"To me, it was very suspicious, with the large pool of blood, the cracked railing and the body in the water. I believed it definitely needed to be investigated further," he said.

When asked about the condition of the deck, he said it wasn't slippery and he hadn't noticed any algae.

Asked about Unger's behavior, he said, "The defendant was on his cell phone constantly. He received numerous calls and was making numerous calls. What was very odd in his behavior is when he would make a phone call, he would erupt in this emotion. He'd start crying and going, 'I don't know, I don't know.'

"And then he'd get call waiting and he'd click over. He would turn it off and it would be, 'Hello.' And he constantly would do this."

Packard told of noticing at one point that Unger's Ford Expedition was loaded up, the tailgate open. "I found it peculiar—here's Florence still lying face down in the water. He never asked what I thought may have happened to her. He never asked anything about what was going on. He just stated he wanted to leave, and Florence is still lying in the water."

Packard concluded his testimony by describing the search of the SUV after they got a warrant late in the day. After they'd pulled out all the stuff you'd expect a family to have on a trip, lawn chairs and kids' toys and duffel bags and luggage, they found a pile of soaked, wadded-up men's clothes—sweatpants, a sweatshirt, pair of white socks, brown slip-on shoes. It struck him as suspicious that the stuff he'd had on when he was with the body would be hidden.

Unfortunately for Harrison, that was the image the jury was left to ponder. At 4:49 p.m., the judge adjourned for the day.

Harrison began Friday's cross-examination of Packard by asking a string of seemingly harmless questions that alerted the jury and everyone else that he was setting a trap.

Is it important to be observant at a scene? Is it important to record all events and significant observations? Is it important to leave a complete record for others who might work the case? Is it important to have an open mind to all possibilities?

Yes to all.

Then, Harrison asked if the dispatcher, Nicole Lamerson, had told him that she was giving him a run and that "he was going to love it"?

"Yes, she did."

"And then, did she say to you, 'A lady just called, she lives on Watervale, I don't know how these people know each other, but she said this lady's husband called her and wanted to know if they had seen his wife because she had been talking about suicide'?"

"I recall something being mentioned about suicide."

"And so the concept, at that point, of an accident was no longer prominently in your mind, was it?"

"I wouldn't say that."

"I'm asking you if you were consciously thinking to yourself this could be an accident?"

"It could have been an accident."

"Is that what you were thinking?"

"After looking at everything, it was suspicious."

"So you weren't thinking it was an accident?"

"It was suspicious."

"Can we try it 'Yes' or 'No'?"

"Was I thinking it was an accident?"

"Yes."

"After looking at the totality of the . . ."

"That's not a 'Yes' or 'No.' Just 'Yes' or 'No.' Were you thinking it could have been an accident at that point?"

"After I looked at everything, or when I first arrived?"

"Yes."

"After I looked at everything . . ."

"Yes?"

". . . it was suspicious, and it needed to be investigated."

"So, you weren't thinking it was an accident?"

"After looking at everything, no, I did not think it was an an accident."

"Okay. That's what I wanted to know. The answer is no. Okay. You had turned that off as a possibility?"

"I did not turn it off as a possibility."

Finally, Harrison got around to the wet, wadded-up clothes in the Ford. Since Packard, Linn Duncan, the neighbors and others had seen Unger in wet clothes, what was suspicious about finding them in the back of Unger's SUV?

"Who was he concealing them from?" asked Harrison.

"That's a good question. Law enforcement? Us?"

"These wet clothes—what did you expect him to do?

Would you expect that if somebody had wet clothes and they had dry stuff, that what they ought to do is put the dry stuff in and then lay the wet stuff on top of the dry stuff, or would you expect that if someone had a bunch of wet stuff, they'd wad it up and put it in a corner so it didn't get anything else wet?"

"I know what I'd do. I would put it at the end of my Expedition off into the corner and not pile everything on top of it."

"So, his big crime here, according to you, that made it appear as if he was trying to conceal it, was that he put it up in the corner instead of back in the corner, is that what you're telling us?" asked Harrison sarcastically. "And somehow to you, that was significant, right? And as you sit here, now, as you stood there, then, and when you wrote your report, you were being objective and unbiased, right?"

THE OTHER MAN

Cheryl Loeb and then her husband, Ron, the Ungers' next-door neighbors, described their casual friendship.

Cheryl told of running into Flo two days before her death and asking her how she was. She got: "You don't want to know."

Ron told of the encounter he'd had with Florence three days before her death as they were working in their yards, and when he asked her how she was doing, she looked at him, started crying and said, "Not very well."

He'd asked if there was anything he could do for her and she told him "No," adding, "Things here are very bad."

Bilkovic asked Ron if, based on their time as neighbors, he had an opinion that Florence was afraid of the dark.

"She was very afraid of the dark. Every time she was at our house talking to my wife, when they were done, if it was dark out, she would ask me to escort her home. Or my son would."

It didn't matter that their front porches were only thirty or forty feet apart, and that all the Loebs had to do to see the Ungers' front door from their property was step a few feet off their porch, Florence wouldn't accept an offer to watch her walk home. She had to be walked home. It got to the point that if it was dark out when she was leaving, Ron or his son automatically walked her home.

At 2:52 p.m., Glenn Stark took the stand. This time, unlike at the preliminary exam, the reporters knew what was coming, were already planning their leads. Their editors wouldn't have a tough choice about whose photo to run—it would be his handsome, bearded visage.

Stark told the court that before he and his wife, Kathy, and their two kids moved to Bozeman, Montana, in August 2003 to open up a delicatessen, they had lived in Huntington Woods for ten years, a block and a half from the Ungers.

The Ungers and Starks were friends. They went out to dinner, attended synagogue together and had gone on vacations together. While Mark was in rehab, Florence had confided to him that she wanted a divorce.

"She gave several reasons in several different conversations about incompatibility, characteristics that Mark possessed that she found intolerable," he said. "Such as not telling the truth, addictions to gambling and drugs, and a general state of, you know, unhappiness between the two of them."

Bilkovic asked him about the week before Florence's death.

"I was in town to finish up some business of my financial services career. And I was also meeting with some suppliers of my new business," said Stark.

"And while you were here during that eight- to nine-day stay, did you see Florence Unger?"

"Yes."

"How often?"

"Many times. Every day."

"And did you speak with her on the telephone?"

"Yes."

"How often?"

"Every day."

"Did she ever discuss any concerns that she had with you?"

"Yes. There were financial concerns, there were ownership of the house concerns. There were custody concerns."

"Did she mention anything to you about how his behavior had been in that week?"

"Yes. She said Mark had become increasingly erratic, and unpredictable, withdrawn. She told me she was very upset and spent a lot of time crying, and being very concerned about her future. She said she spent a great deal of time locked in the bathroom, sitting on the floor crying."

Stark told the court that Florence described Mark's behavior as "Dr. Jekyll and Mr. Hyde behavior." And he told of the Tuesday night before Florence's death that he had spent with the Ungers, where Mark was withdrawn and angry.

"Did he engage you in conversation?" asked Bilkovic.

"Not very much."

"How did that make you feel?"

"Uncomfortable."

"Why?"

"Well, because historically, you know, we were conversational, and I had felt like I was a presence that he was uncomfortable with in the home. I asked Mark if he was uncomfortable with me being there and if he'd prefer that I stay somewhere else. He replied, no, he wasn't angry with me being there, I wasn't the one who was divorcing him."

"Do you know whether or not the Ungers, during the period of time leading up to October of 2003, were sharing the same bedroom?" asked Bilkovic.

"They were not."

"Now, you and Florence Unger had a very close friendship, did you not, is that fair to say?"

"Yes."

"And did that friendship ever turn physical?"

"Yes, it did."

"Over what period of time?"

"A few times over a two-year period, approximately."

"And when was the last time that you were physically intimate with Mrs. Unger?"

"The Friday before the Wednesday that I left."

"How did you find out about Florence's death?" Bilkovic asked.

"I was called on the phone by Brian Witus. It was approximately ten a.m. Mountain Time on the twenty-fifth of October."

"Noon here. After you found out what happened, did you attempt to call the defendant?"

"Yes."

"And were you able to reach him?"

"Yes. I had a phone call message from him on our answering service that was from earlier, from prior to my call from Brian Witus. And I listened to that after I spoke to Brian. It was Mark. And he said, 'Call me as soon as you get this message, on Flo's cell phone.'"

"And did you do that?"

"I did. It was within an hour after the call from Brian. He picked up the phone, and I was extremely emotional, and I asked him what happened to her. And he responded that he didn't know. I kept asking him, 'What happened to her?' And then I asked him 'Did you let her go for a walk by herself?' And he said, 'No.'"

Stark said he'd asked Mark if it could be a suicide and Mark had been emphatic that it wasn't. "And then I asked him if this was a homicide investigation. He said, 'No.' And then he responded, 'You're scaring me.' And said he had to go immediately, and hung up."

Bilkovic asked him about Florence's fear of the dark.

"She is absolutely afraid of the dark. Florence wouldn't even sit out on the back deck by herself in the dark. She would call Kathy or myself and say, 'It's a beautiful night, I'd really like to sit out back. Could one of you come over? Because I don't feel comfortable sitting outside by myself.'"

Stark told of being at her funeral, of him and his wife

being the last to toss a bit of dirt on Florence's casket and
Mark walking up to them and giving them both a hug.

He told of stiffening up, not hugging Mark back, of
Mark demanding he look in his eyes.

" 'Look at me, damn it,' " Stark quoted him, putting some
emotion into it, mimicking anger.

"He said it in that tone of voice?"

"He said it in an angry, loud tone of voice."

"And what did you do?"

"I did not look at him," said Stark.

"Did you ever have any contact with him after that
day?"

"Never."

Bilkovic was done. It was 3:18. The judge called for a
recess. At 3:43, Harrison began his cross-examination, asking Stark if the quick time-line between putting his house
up for sale in March 2003 and moving that August had
anything to do with Florence Unger.

"It did not."

"Did it have anything to do with Kathy Jo Stark, your
wife?"

"Yes."

"And did it have anything to do with Kathy Jo Stark's
view of what was going on between you and Florence Unger?"

"No. It did not."

"During your trip to Michigan, you and Florence Unger
had sex together, correct?"

"Yes."

"Did you have sex in the Unger home?"

"No."

"Did you go somewhere and have sex?"

"Yes."

"Did you go to a hotel or motel?"

"No."

"Where did you go?"

"To the home where I was staying."

"Somebody else's home? Whose home was that?"

"Do I need to disclose that information?"

"I'd like to know."

"A friend of mine from work."

"Who was that?"

"Howard Rosen."

"You went to Harold Rosen's house and had sex with Florence Unger?"

"That's correct."

"Do you know where Mark was at the time that you took his wife to have sex with her?"

"I do not."

Harrison went over the telephone exchange Mark Unger and Glenn Stark had had the morning Flo's body was found. There was a line of dialogue Stark hadn't recounted which had a bearing on the conversation the two had at the funeral.

"Did you say to him, 'What happened to her?'" asked Harrison.

"Yes."

"And did he say, 'I don't know'?"

"Yes."

"And you said, 'Is this a homicide investigation?' And Mark said, 'No. You're scaring me'?"

"Yes."

"And then, Mr. Stark, did you say to Mark, 'Mark, I'll look into your eyes, and I'll know'?"

"Yes, I did."

"And then he said to you, 'Look at me, look at me, damn it. Look at me.' Right?"

"That's correct."

"He invited it, he asked it, he implored you, begged you to look at him, and you wouldn't, right?"

"I did not."

"That's all."

Big point scored for Harrison. His client wasn't angry or confrontational. He was, it would seem, confident that if Stark looked into his eyes, he *wouldn't* see guilt.

A BEST FRIEND

Bilkovic called Laurie Glass, Florence Unger's best friend since the age of 10, to the stand at 4 p.m.

Florence, she told the court, had a large circle of close women friends—her, Susan Witus, Lori Silverstein, Joan Frank and Kathy Stark. And she and Florence had talked every day, often in person since they only lived half a block apart, but at least on the phone.

She told of Mark growing increasingly unhappy, of his desperate, tear-filled calls to her to please step up to the plate for him, to convince Flo not to go through with this, that it would crush their kids.

Instead of counseling Flo to stop the divorce, though, Glass told her to stop sending Mark mixed signals, to quit doing things socially with him, to quit worrying so much about trying to get out of this as friends.

In September of 2003, Glass told Flo that she wouldn't call her at home anymore, she was too worried about Mark answering the phone and having to hear him cry and plead for her help. Their daily calls became intermittent.

Glass told of getting a call from a friend at 10 a.m. on Saturday, October 25, telling her that Florence had died, of driving over to the Sterns' to console them, and of getting a call at 6 a.m. Sunday from Mark.

"He was crying. He didn't speak at first. I spoke first. I said I wouldn't believe it was true until he called me and told me himself," she said.

"He began telling me the story . . . He said they were on a deck, and Flo had turned to him and said, 'Go check on the kids.' He cried, again, then he said, 'That's the last time I saw her.' "

"And what did he say happened when he got up?"

"He said that he had realized Flo was not there and had not been there, and he realized it right away. He said nothing had been touched, nothing. He ran downstairs and looked outside. But the car was there. He said at least if the car were gone, he would have known what she had done."

"Did he say what happened next?" asked Bilkovic.

"He said he looked to the Inn, but it was dark. He said he didn't want to leave the cottage."

"Did he say why he didn't want to leave the cottage?"

"He said someone may have still been lurking around. Then he called over to Linn and said, 'Have you seen Flo?' "

"What did he tell you happened next?"

" 'The next thing I know,' he said, 'Linn is at my door, and he said, "Mark, something terrible has happened." ' " Mark said, " 'What? What?' He said, 'It's bad. It's really bad. Flo has jumped and killed herself.' "

"Did Mark tell you what he did?"

"He said he ran right down there. She was in the water. I believe he said face down. He said he tried to pull her out, but she was so heavy. And there was blood everywhere."

Bilkovic asked her if Florence had a fear of the dark.

"Yes."

Bilkovic asked if Glass had ever been to Watervale and she said she had, the day before, that she'd wanted to see the scene for herself.

"Do you think it was consistent or inconsistent with what you knew about her that she would go out on that deck at night by herself, alone in the dark?" asked Bilkovic.

"I was struck by how far the boathouse deck was from

the cottage, and I thought that she would not be out there alone, as fearful as she was of the nighttime and the dark."

"I have nothing further," said Bilkovic.

At 4:52, they adjourned. The court, as it would throughout the trial, had other business scheduled for Monday and Tuesday, so they would reconvene on Wednesday, May 10.

"A EUREKA MOMENT"

The attorneys tried to head home for weekends, if possible. Skrzynski had to delay his trip after court adjourned Friday to meet with Dr. Cohle on Saturday to go over his testimony the next week. Skrzynski stayed in Frankfort Friday night, then drove down to Grand Rapids in the morning for a breakfast meeting at Cohle's house.

Cohle was a crucial witness. He was a prosecution witness, but his opinion that head injuries had caused Florence Unger's death, and not drowning, potentially made him more valuable to the defense.

At some point, during a discussion of Florence's head injuries, Cohle mentioned axonal injuries and the staining techniques required to define them.

"Axonal" refers to axons, very large nerve cells, so large that a single motor-nerve axon can stretch more than two feet, from the spinal cord all the way down to the muscles in the leg.

But for all their length, they are exceedingly thin, about thirty microns wide, which is about a third the thickness of the average human hair.

Axonal injuries can't be seen by the naked eye during autopsy. If they are suspected, a tissue sample must be sliced from the brain and stained. Almost in passing, Cohle mentioned that the staining only works if the person in question was alive for a period of time before death.

"How long?" asked Skrzynski, his heart jumping, his brain making a leap as well.

"Thirty minutes, I suppose," said Cohle. "You could follow it up with your neuropath."

"Your neuropath" referred to Dr. Paul McKeever, a neuropathologist at the University of Michigan, a tenured professor and physician who was also a stem-cell researcher whose work was funded by the National Institutes of Health. As Pendergast described McKeever, "His credentials are over the moon."

McKeever had been hired by the prosecution and his testimony would help buttress the contention that Florence had not died as a result of her brain injuries. He had looked at autopsy results and done his own staining on tissue samples and had concluded that while Florence had axonal injuries, they were likely not fatal.

No one on the prosecution team had thought to ask, How does the staining process work? Or, more important, How long does it take?

If, in fact, a victim had to be alive for half an hour before axonal tears would later be revealed by stains, then they just might be on the verge of blowing Mark Unger's defense to smithereens, eliminating the possibility that she'd fallen in an accident and rolled immediately into the water. If she'd lain there on the concrete apron of the boathouse awhile, how did she get into the water? It would be a big hurdle for the defense to explain, with her injuries, how she'd gotten into the lake on her own.

And an easy surmise for the prosecution to make that Mark had put her there.

Skrzynski realized all of that the instant Cohle said, "Thirty minutes."

"It was a eureka moment," said Skrzynski, who managed to keep his emotions in check during the rest of the breakfast meeting with Cohle.

Skrzynski drove back to his home in Royal Oak, a suburb adjacent to Huntington Woods, and called McKeever to pin down the time element.

It wasn't thirty minutes. It was, he said, ninety minutes that a person would have to remain alive in order for axonal injuries to appear on tissue stains.

Bingo!

Skrzynski decided to share his good news in person. He drove back to Beulah Tuesday and reported his findings to Pendergast and Bilkovic.

"Will McKeever testify to that?" she asked.

"Hell, yes," said Skrzynski.

"We all had a shit fit," was how he would describe it later.

The testimony would, said Skrzynski, if it held up under cross-examination, "blow their whole defense."

WEEK THREE
GREAT SHAPE, NEVER CLUMSY

Flo's brother, Peter Stern, started things Wednesday by recounting his part in the events of October 25 and telling the court about his sister's abiding fear of the dark.

Kate Ostrove told the court that she and Florence Unger had been fast friends since they'd met while working at a suburban Detroit shopping mall in 1992. And of Flo's resolve to get a divorce, of wanting to hold off filing for it until Mark got out of rehab because "I'm not going to kick a dog while it's down."

According to Flo, the Ungers hadn't shared a bedroom for the two and a half years before her death. She had tried to talk Flo out of the weekend in Watervale, but Flo said she was going because she wanted to show her kids that their parents could be amicable despite their break-up.

Bilkovic asked her if Flo exercised.

"Yes."

"Infrequently? Frequently."

"Frequently."

"Good shape or great shape?"

"Great shape."

"Clumsy or non-clumsy?" Getting at a possible defense contention that her death might have been a slip and fall.

"Totally non-clumsy."

On cross-examination, Harrison asked her if there was ever any violence from Mark towards his wife. No. Had she ever seen any signs of anger in Mark? No. Had she told police after Flo's death that Flo had told her during a call on the way north that she was very happy?

"Yes."

Joan Frank, who, with her husband Steven, had taken two vacations with the Ungers and who had been hired by Mark to help market him as a mortgage banker before he'd gone into rehabilitation, took the stand next.

She told of being with Flo the first time she'd gone through the bills after Mark went into rehab, and being shocked by how much they owed. She told of trying to help promote Mark, again, after he got home in February, but he had no interest in resuming his career. That Flo grew increasingly angry over his perceived laziness, of having to work at a job she didn't like, that Flo had pleaded unsuccessfully with her to come with them to Watervale.

She told of calling Mark the Monday after Flo's death and telling him she needed to talk. They'd sat down in his bedroom upstairs, and Mark told her of the drive up Friday, the charming cottage and how much Flo loved it, of their dinner in Frankfort, what a really nice time it was.

"They got back from dinner and they went for a walk," Joan told the court, recounting Mark's version of events as they sat in the bedroom. "And he said, 'You know, she even let me put my arm around her.'"

"When he told you that 'she even let me put my arm around her,' did that strike you as unusual?" asked Bilkovic.

"Bells went off, like flags. Just absolutely."

"Why?"

"Flo had said to me that she was repulsed by Mark. They did not have an intimate relationship in a very long time. Over the past several months, when I was in their company, I never once saw them holding hands or kiss or hug, or even be really near each other."

"So, when he told you that, what happened at that point?"

"I remember saying to him, 'I need to know what happened. I mean, I can't be at peace, and she can't be at peace, and I need to know.' And at that point, he thought I was accusing him of doing something, and he became hysterical . . . I had to say to him, 'No, that's not what I'm saying.'"

Frank said she spoke to Mark thirty or forty times after that in the subsequent months, but he never offered up a theory of what happened.

Harrison had a good cross-examination. An image had been painted of Mark sitting idly at home, while the bills piled up and his poor wife was forced to take a job she hated. Harrison got Frank to admit she knew he had disability insurance policies that paid him $10,000 a month, tax-free.

"Is it accurate that up until the point in time that Mark was in rehab, Flo had nothing to do with the paying of the bills, that Mark took care of that?" he asked.

"That was the impression I got."

"And then when she opened the bills, she was, like, shocked at paying these large bills? The whole concept of paying monthly expenses in an affluent lifestyle was a shock to her?" he asked sarcastically.

"Amongst your circle of friends, was Flo described as a shopaholic?" he asked, without waiting for an answer to the previous question.

"Flo loved to shop, but Flo was also great at finding great deals."

"She loved going out to all of the stores in Birmingham and Troy and Bloomfield Hills and go shopping, right?"

"Yeah. She shopped."

At 2 p.m., Jim Ryan took the stand. He was the neighbor down the road from the Watervale resort whom Dori Turner had called early in the morning.

He told of spending the morning shepherding Unger around, being with him when Mark told the kids their mother had died and calling Peter Stern to tell him his sister had died.

"During the course of the time that you're at the cottage that morning, did the defendant ever once, you know, express any concern as to what had happened to his wife, or ask you what you thought might have happened, anything of that nature?" asked Pendergast.

"No. He did not."

In cross, Harrison asked him, "Can you think of any reason why you would be the person that Mr. Unger would come to, to find out what would have happened to his wife? There wouldn't be any particular or special reason why you would have special insight into what happened to his wife, is there?"

"No."

Harrison should have cut him off there.

"But I guess I was surprised that he didn't seem to want to ask Officer Packard or myself, or didn't seem to have any questions about what had happened," Ryan continued. "I guess if I had been told to stay away from the scene, I wouldn't go to the scene, but I would sure be asking somebody, I would be trying to ask somebody what had happened."

On redirect, Pendergast asked one question. "Did the defendant ever, during the course of the time that morning that you had contact with him, wonder out loud, or express any concern in your presence as to what had happened to his wife?"

"No. And he didn't ask me to go to anybody else to find out."

DRY ROT

Frances D'Angela, the forensic scientist with the state police crime lab in Grayling, took the stand at 9:45 a.m. to begin Thursday's proceedings.

She told of arriving at the Watervale at 2:25 p.m. with her crew of three and shooting photos of the area with her 35-millimeter camera.

Pendergast asked her if the boathouse deck was slippery as she did her work.

"No. It was not slippery."

"Did you see any kind of moss or algae growing all over the surface of that deck?"

"Nothing obvious."

"During the course of the time that you were in contact with the defendant, did you observe anything unusual about his demeanor?" asked Pendergast.

"Right before the DNA swabs were collected, Mark Unger asked if Flo was still in the water, and when we said yes, he got noticeably upset, sobbing very loudly, but I never noticed any tears."

Harrison asked about the condition of the boathouse deck. There was a big screen set up where photos could be shown. Harrison used a laser pointer to indicate an area on one of the photos she'd shot.

"What is the condition of the deck here, these— what appear to be rough and dark spots all over? What are those?" he asked.

"I think it was just discoloration of the wood."

"Was it water staining, water spots, water damage?"

"I don't recall anything unusual about the deck."

"Okay, let me ask it again. Does it look like water damage or water stains?"

"It could be stains."

"Okay."

"Do you see a green color all along here underneath the rail on the deck surface?" he asked, red laser point circling an area on the photo.

"Yes, I do."

"What do you suppose that is?"

"I don't know."

"Did you see that when you were out there?"

"I don't recall. Could be part of the weathering of the wood."

"Do you know what algae is?"

"Yes."

"Do you know what moss is?"

"Yes."

"Could that be moss or algae on that deck surface?"

"That's a possibility."

Harrison asked her what time it was when Mark Unger had asked her if Florence's body was still in the water, needing to undo the damage she might have caused his client by saying he'd sobbed but without tears.

"It was around four forty-five."

"And you told him yes?"

"Yes."

"And he became visibly upset?"

"Yes."

"And you were aware at that time that Mrs. Unger's body was found and seen by Mr. Unger at some time in the neighborhood of eight a.m. that day?"

"Yes."

"So we're talking about eight and a half hours later when he asked you if her body was still in the water?"

"Right."

"And you said he became visibly upset?"

"Yes, there was sobbing, but no tears."

"He was sobbing but he wasn't tearing?"

"No."

"And do you know how many times he cried and sobbed during that eight-and-a-half-hour period while his wife's body remained in the water?" .

"No, I do not."

They broke for lunch at 12:25 p.m. The judge told the jury the staff at the Brookside Inn was expecting them.

Jennifer Patchin, another state police technician, took the stand at 2:10 p.m. and recounted her participation.

On cross, Harrison showed her Exhibit No. 37, a photo of the broken railing on the boathouse roof.

"Did you consider those support posts were fragile and rotted?"

"Whether or not they were rotted wouldn't really be my area of expertise."

"So you didn't?"

"That's correct."

"If you had taken some of that wood material that had been splintered out and taken it back to the laboratory, isn't it possible to conduct tests on that wood to determine whether there was any plant material growing in it, like algae or moss?"

"At our laboratory, we don't have anybody that specifically does that."

"Isn't it common that police departments, even if they have a scientific laboratory, will frequently send things to specialized places to be able to do specialized kinds of testing that you don't do at your own laboratory?"

"That is an option with an investigation, yes."

"And there are a number of places around the country

where specialized testing can be done, including the FBI laboratory, isn't that true?"

"I would believe that to be correct."

Harrison showed her three other photos of the broken railing, which showed differences in color in and around the various breaks, and pointed out one specific piece.

"Does that look to you perhaps like dry rot, both brown and black dry rot?" he asked.

"I really don't know the proper description for dry rot."

"What's the green stuff over there on it?"

"Um, maybe algae. I really don't know."

"Would that generally be associated? Algae with a rotted, wet surface?"

"You know, I really don't know."

"Have you seen wood crumble like this before because of dry rot?"

"I'm not an expert in dry rot and wood, so I really don't know what to expect from dry rot."

The judge called it a day when Patchin stepped down, a day Harrison thought had ended well.

NOT A DEATH BY DROWNING

Stephen Cohle took the stand at 9:30 Friday morning, May 12.

Skrzynski did the direct examination. He would handle the medical and scientific exams. (Skrzynski's other value to the prosecution was to serve as out-of-court jester. The prosecution team was staying at the Harbor Lights resort in Frankfort, and Skrzynski and Bilkovic ate breakfast every morning at Celia's on the bay. "He'd sense I was stressed out and he'd calm me down," said Bilkovic. After work, it was Skrzynski's joking and storytelling at dinner or over a drink that erased the stress of the day.)

Cohle told the court of studying police reports before he'd conducted the autopsy on Florence's body on October 27, two days after her death. Determining a death by drowning is one thing, but labeling it an accident or murder requires context, which is where the police reports came in.

"It's not a typical uncomplicated drowning, because people don't drown in shallow water, unless they are incapacitated," he said. "It may not be a drowning at all. But it if is, if she drowned in that depth of water, then she had to be disabled, because she's an otherwise healthy woman, and there's no reason that she would, you know, just lay [sic] face down and drown."

He described the autopsy, from inventorying her clothes to looking for superficial cuts and bruises to cutting her chest open and removing her organs, to pulling back her scalp, removing her brain and finding a morass of fractures in her skull.

Responding to questions from Skrzynski, he mixed in a detailed biology lesson that covered in mind-numbing detail the various structures of the brain and their Latin names, which part did what, which axions controlled what limb.

He described the physics and chemistry of injury and physical changes in the body after injury, both before and after death.

He talked of cribriform plates and cranial fossa and olfactory nerve roots and the calvarium, of the tympanic membrane and the subarachnoid space and the superior sagittal sinus, demonstrating with a model of the brain and with autopsy photos.

Mercifully, at 10:49, the judge called a recess.

They resumed at 11:14, with more of the same. Short questions. Long, detailed answers that seemed more like classroom lectures.

Finally, at 12:10, after Cohle described weighing Florence Unger's saturated lungs, Skrzynski asked, "Eventually, you say that the cause of death is the craniocerebral trauma, all the brain injury you've been talking of?"

"That's correct."

"All right. Can you rule out in this case that she drowned?"

In his fashion, Cohle responded, "I would say this: It is possible that drowning contributed to her death. Drowning may have been the final event. Because I say that, I don't think it would be fair to say that it's a pure drowning, because she has significant head injury. And then, of course, she is found in the water. So the question is, well, could she have drowned after receiving the head injury? My answer is, it is possible."

And that led to the reason why everyone was in this courtroom on this day.

"Now, Doctor, you said also that you have to determine the manner of death?"

"That's correct."

"And you said that there are those five categories, and in this particular case, you chose the category, what?" Skrzynski asked inelegantly.

"Homicide."

"You said homicide. Okay. Doctor, explain your reasoning to us. Why, in your opinion, was this a homicide?"

"Well, my reasoning was as follows: It's clear that she fell or somehow went over the edge. It may have been an accidental fall, I don't know. But she falls from the top of this boathouse onto the concrete slab twelve feet below. She was there, laying there for some time, long enough to bleed, and to stain the concrete slab."

"So, in your opinion, how long do you think she might have had to be there to accumulate that much blood?"

"Maybe twenty, thirty [minutes] or so. It would make sense to me. So to answer, to continue with your original question that you asked, which is why did I call this a homicide, or why did I consider it a homicide, I have a hard time figuring out how she got into the water."

"Why is that, Doctor?"

"Well, it seems to me that if one lands on, basically, from twelve feet above onto a flat concrete surface, pretty much straight down, at least, I don't think that her momentum would carry her into the water, that she would continue to roll. She has a very significant head injury. I think it's very unlikely that she would be able to get up on her own volition and continue into that water."

And then: "*I mean, anything is possible.*"

Having made Skrzynski's point, that the sheer presence of her body in the water after a fall like that was enough to make this a homicide, Cohle made the defense case, too: Anything could have happened.

How sweet and unexpected *that* must have sounded at Unger's table.

"In this case, there was another pathologist that got involved, is that correct?" asked Skrzynski.

"There was one early on."

"Right. And who was it?"

"Dr. Dragovic."

"And Dr. Dragovic is the chief medical examiner in Oakland County, is that correct?"

"Yes. He and Ms. Pendergast and Mr. Bilkovic and Detective Armstrong, and I believe there's another officer or two, came to visit me at my office several months after this autopsy to discuss the case. Basically, Mr. Dragovic had the opinion that this is a drowning. He's much more definite than I am that this is a drowning. And the idea was to see if, upon talking with him and hearing his reasoning for drowning, would I be able to form a stronger opinion myself that it was drowning?"

"Now, Dr. Dragovic has a way about him, would you say?"

"He has a certain, yes, way of presenting himself. He's very definite."

"Dr. Dragovic is trying to, he's trying to talk to you about his opinion? Let me ask you this: Was Dr. Dragovic trying to get you to change your opinion?"

It seemed an odd line of questioning, more fitting for a cross-examination. Dragovic would testify soon, and the defense would try to paint him as implacable and coercive, trying to have an undue influence on Cohle. Skrzynski was heading them off.

"Well, you know, I wasn't at gunpoint, but I think he is a person who does have strong opinions, and believes, I guess, that others should agree with him. And he is . . . he's forceful."

"As a result of listening to him, did you change your opinion?"

"No."

"You've never changed your opinion about this matter at any time?"

"I have not."

It was 12:28 p.m. They broke for lunch.

The defense team had to feel good about the morning as they walked out. The death had come from a fall. As to how Florence Unger had gotten into the water, well, as Cohle testified, you never know, anything could have happened. And as to how they would begin their afternoon attack, Skrzynski gave them their perfect starting point: Cohle's office in Grand Rapids, the day the forceful Dr. Dragovic and Donna Pendergast came calling.

It'd be a fun place to start, a rare chance to impeach at length one of the state's star witnesses and noted court-room performer before he ever got on the stand.

A MEETING OF THE MINDS

Court reconvened at 1:50. Tom McGuire had the honors. "When the prosecutor left off, he was asking you some questions about a meeting that occurred in your office in Grand Rapids."

"Yes."

"Do you recall when that meeting was?"

"Well, I think it was probably November or December of 2003."

"You knew Dr. Dragovic by reputation?"

"I've known him personally for quite a few years."

"Have you ever been the subject of criticism by him?"

"Well, I might have been. I'm trying to think. I don't remember if I've seen anything in print. I mean, usually when he and I meet in person, you know, it's reasonably cordial. I know his deputy has been critical of some of my testimony, and I know he had a verbal disagreement with my partner on a case."

"He criticized your partner in a deposition that he gave?"

"The case I'm thinking of is, there was a case where my partner did an autopsy, I think it was the Upper Peninsula or at least the northern part of the Lower Peninsula. A woman was accused of shooting her husband, who was either a current or former police officer, and my partner testified for the prosecution. Dr. Dragovic testified for the defense and subsequently said something to the effect of he wouldn't hire my partner to work for him because he wasn't skilled enough."

"And did he also say something like that about your wife?"

"He probably did. My ex-wife." She was also a forensic pathologist.

"Your ex-wife. I'm sorry. Don't want to get you in trouble while you're here. Do you recall the circumstances of that?"

"I know she has testified at least a couple of times in cases where he was involved. And I do have the recollection of her saying he said some uncomplimentary things about her, but I do not remember the specifics."

"Anyway," said McGuire, "on this particular date, you get a visit by these people from Oakland County?"

"Yes. As the meeting evolved, it seemed the main idea of the meeting was that Dr. Dragovic had some opinions about this case. And, basically, he stated those opinions. And I think the idea was whether I was able to agree with those opinions or not."

"Let me go back for just a moment. You conducted the autopsy on Florence Unger and as a result of the autopsy, you prepared a report? You produced an opinion about the cause of death, but you had not reached an opinion about manner of death?"

"Correct."

"And then you get this visit by folks?"

"Yes."

"Who want to talk to you about the manner-of-death opinion."

"Well, yes. I think that was part of it. Also, the issue that was discussed that mainly sticks in my mind was whether drowning played a role in her death."

"That's right. Cause-of-death issue, as well?"

"Yes."

"Who did most of the talking at this meeting?"

"Dr. Dragovic."

"Did he express to you some reason why he would be in a better position to make a judgment about this matter than you were?"

"I believe he implied it's because he's a neuropathologist or has training in neuropathology."

"Are most forensic pathologists also neuropathologists?"

"No."

"Pretty uncommon?"

"Correct."

"I understand from Dr. Dragovic that there may be only half a dozen such people in the country."

"That's probably true."

"So the great bulk of forensic work in pathology in this county, ninety-nine-plus percent of it, is done by people who are not neuropathologists, but simply pathologists?"

"That's true."

"You do brains in your work?"

"Yes, I do."

"About how many do you do in a month?"

"Probably, I would say twenty to twenty-five a month."

"Did Dr. Dragovic bring to your attention some argument that came from deep within the recesses on neuropathology inaccessible to you?"

"Well, it's hard for me to characterize where he got the argument, exactly. But he had a reason for why he believed that drowning was a factor in this woman's death."

"In fact, he opined to you that he believed she drowned and did not die from the head injuries that you said she died from?"

"True."

"And he was trying to sell that point of view to you?"

"Yes."

"To get to the question of whether she drowned, you would have to rule out head injury as the cause of death. And you couldn't do that?"

"Well, I didn't feel I could, no."

"You finished your determination about cause of death, and then you went into an inquiry concerning the manner of death?"

"Yes."

"What was your view, Dr. Cohle, about whether this was a homicide? What degree of certainty do you have to attach to it?"

"Well, as I indicated earlier, because I could not understand how she could have gotten herself into the water—and anything is possible—but it seemed quite unlikely that she could have. That's why I called it a homicide . . . I think it's more likely homicide, for the reason I've described about her entry into the water, but that's as far as I can go."

"Fifty-one percent?"

"At least that. Fifty-one or so."

"So you're basically coming down to a preponderance of evidence?"

"Yes."

The prosecution had to be jolted. The medical examiner who had conducted the autopsy and ruled on the manner of death had in effect said the chances Florence Unger had been murdered were "fifty-one percent or so." Which left forty-nine percent, and that was reasonable doubt in anyone's book.

"Thank you, Dr. Cohle," said McGuire.

Skrzynski needed to undo the damage, try to salvage his own witness and nearly a day of testimony that had turned devastating.

"Doctor, you are not aware of all the evidence that will be presented in this case in support of the allegation, or in support of the accusation that this is a homicide, isn't that correct?" he asked.

"Correct. That's right."

"So, you don't know everything that even this jury will know by the end of this trial?"

"Exactly."

"But your support for it is based on what you could glean from the body and the surrounding . . ."

"That's right."

"Okay. So, again, that does not include all the evidence that the jury will hear?"

"That's true."

"And, yet, even knowing that, you are still willing to say that the manner of death in this case is homicide?"

"Correct."

"And that's not changing?"

"Correct."

Skrzynski was done.

McGuire, happy the crucial "fifty-one" was still the number of record, was done, too. "Dr. Cohle, I don't have any further questions. Thank you, sir. Have a good trip back to Grand Rapids."

It was 3:49. The court recessed.

A TRAUMA EXPERT

Dr. Brian Zink, a former medevac flight physician and professor of emergency medicine at the University of Michigan, where he ran a lab studying brain injuries through funding from the National Institutes of Health, took the stand next.

He had reviewed the autopsy and studied the autopsy photos and told the court that Florence Unger's brain injury would have left her comatose and incapable of purposeful movement.

Skrzynski asked him if it was possible Unger had suffered a seizure after her fall that might have led to her rolling into the water.

Zink said seizures following such injuries occurred in fewer than 1 percent of victims, and that such seizures would involve tensing movements, typically directed toward the center of the body and not likely to result in the body's moving.

"It's not a wild flailing about that you sometimes see on TV or something, where a patient is moving, you know, all over," he said.

"Doctor, have you seen patients with this degree of brain injury before, the kind that Mrs. Unger had?"

"Yes. Many times."

"Are you able to give us a prognosis for a person with a condition like this, based on your experience?"

"Based on my personal experience and knowledge of the literature, with her degree of brain injury, I believe she would have had about a twenty-five to thirty percent chance of dying in the first few days of the injury."

You could feel a jolt in the courtroom, see reporters reflexively respond; now, *this* was news.

"So, that's a seventy to seventy-five percent chance of survival?"

"Right. Let's look at the other end. So, twenty-five percent chance of dying, twenty-five percent chance of a reasonable outcome of returning to relatively normal function, and about a fifty percent chance of being disabled to the point of not being able to return to previous activities."

"Doctor, when you're talking about the survival rate, does that include the patient having access to medical treatment as soon as possible after the injury?"

"Yes, certainly."

On cross, McGuire had serious damage that needed to be undone.

"As I understand it, the basis for the opinions in this case is the photographs that you've looked at that were taken at an autopsy?" he began.

"Yes. And also the autopsy report of the brain findings."

"Don't you think that's pretty thin stuff on which to make the opinions that you've given here?"

"I don't think so."

"Did you talk to the pathologist?"

"No."

"Any reason why not?"

"I did not have access to the pathologist."

"He was here this afternoon. He was here all day."

"Right."

"You knew that, right?"

"Yes, I did."

"You could have called him. You're in Ann Arbor, he's in Grand Rapids. You've been on this case for over a couple of years. Why didn't you call him?"

"I didn't think I needed to talk with him. I had his written report."

"If there were some magical way that some patient could walk into the emergency room with pictures of their injuries like this, I guess they could just hand you the pictures and you could work with them. You wouldn't have to look at the patient, is that fair?" said McGuire sarcastically.

Veteran courtroom watchers took that as a sign: If a defense attorney drips sarcasm on the messenger, it's because he can't attack the message.

"In a clinical setting, no, that's not how it would work."

"Because it's a whole lot better to take the patient into consideration and look at the actual patient, isn't it?"

"I'm sorry?"

"It's a whole lot better to look at the human being than it is to look at the pictures?"

"I can't agree with that. I'm sorry."

They were through for the day. There had been big moments for both sides. Cohle's testimony had taken up most of the day and had gone resoundingly for the defense. But Zink's testimony was a great way for the prosecution to end the week.

WEEK FOUR
MAGGIE'S TURN

On Wednesdsay, the 17th, two weeks after her husband had testified, Maggie Duncan took the stand. Pendergast wanted her to buttress some points made by her husband, and she recounted the day they'd found Florence floating face down.

Mainly, Pendergast wanted her to go over the condition of the boathouse roof, and she said she didn't recall any algae or patches of moss.

Robert Harrison handled her cross-examination.

"You told us that the flooring was fine on the deck?" he asked.

"Yes."

"Do you remember a conversation you had with an insurance man from the Westfield Insurance group that was recorded?"

"In Florida."

"Right."

Harrison had a transcript of a deposition he'd arranged, to get on the record conversations they had with their insurance agent following Florence Unger's death.

Harrison told the court he was going to read a quote from her near the bottom of page 39 of the transcript: " 'Referring to the railings, yeah. We noticed the paint started chipping on it this year and it's time we brought this thing up to code.' Do you remember that?"

"No."

"Do you want to see it?"

"No."

"Do you remember your husband saying, 'It's starting to look a little ratty?'"

"No."

"Do you remember you saying, 'The floorboards were starting to warp, you know'? Did you say that to the insurance man?"

"If it's written down, I said it, I guess. But I don't remember it."

"And did your husband say, 'They were pulling nails up and warping,' and you said, 'So, it was just time'? Did you say that?"

"Whatever you say I said."

"You said you were going to bring it up to code. How did you know it wasn't up to code? Do you remember whether you learned or determined that your deck was not up to code?"

"No, I did not know it was not to code. I knew that we wanted to redo it."

Harrison asked her if she and her husband had an attorney representing them at the deposition. When a customer falls to her death from the top of your boathouse and you know the defense is going to claim the railing was old, decaying and faulty—and you know, yourself, that it wasn't up to code—it's not a bad idea to get an attorney to help prepare for any possible civil suits.

"No. Not that I can remember."

"Did you have an attorney named Matthew T. Tompkins, from Cardelli, Hebert and Lanfear?"

"No. Not that I'm aware of."

"Okay."

The transcript he held was clear about who attended the deposition. There was, indeed, a Matthew with a T.

On re-direct, Pendergast asked Duncan what she had

testified to at the deposition regarding why they'd decided to redo the deck.

"Our son had said it was time. Our deck is the focal point, everybody spends a lot of time on our boathouse, morning, noon, night, whatever. And our son said, 'You know, it's been a while. We should redo it.' You know, make it a little prettier. A little nicer."

"And the fact is, you testified, 'The only reason we were going to do it is to make it look prettier'?"

"Right."

Harrison countered, "You don't recall your own words, saying that it was ratty?"

"No. I never said it was ratty."

"That the floorboards were warped, that the nails were popping out?"

"So, we went down and hammered some of the nails down. The nails were never popping up to the point where somebody would hurt themselves."

"Mrs. Duncan, are you concerned about perhaps your own responsibility in an accidental death by Florence Unger?"

"No."

"Are you concerned about a lawsuit?"

"No."

"Okay. Thanks, Mrs. Duncan."

Dori Turner took the stand at 10:32. She told of going out with her cousins and friends the night before Florence's body was discovered, getting in about 9:30 and Maggie calling her to ask a question.

It was misting, and she told of looking out a window of her house toward the lake and the Duncans' boathouse. The light bulb on the deck had burned out and there was nothing she could see.

"It was pitch black. And if you live in a city, or a town, you have no idea what darkness really is. It was very dark," she said.

At 8 the next morning, she heard screaming and looked

out her bedroom window. It was Mark, and he took off running toward the boathouse.

She recounted her take on the rest of the morning's events.

"Did you observe something unusual about the defendant's demeanor that you told the police about?" Pendergast asked.

"Well, it was a fairly high level of hysteria. I mean, for all of us. And he was crying, but there were no tears."

On cross, Harrison asked, "Have you, in your years, Ms. Turner, seen someone so overcome with sorrow and unhappiness that they sobbed until they either ran out of tears, or they sobbed without tearing?"

"I have seen people sob till they run out of tears."

"Okay. So, the answer is yes, you have?"

"Yes."

Dr. Paul McKeever, the neuropathologist from the University of Michigan, took the stand at 11:44. He told Skrzynski that Dr. Zink had enlisted his help on the case, to help determine the extent of Florence Unger's brain injury, in particular to look for evidence of axonal damage and to assess whether there was what is called herniation, where the brain stem pushes down into the hole at the base of the brain that opens up to the spinal cord.

As McKeever explained it, "As I was stuck in traffic and wondering if I'd make it here, today, I was thinking of sort of like a freeway. If there's an accident somewhere along the freeway, that doesn't necessarily cut the freeway in half. Usually it doesn't. Unless it's an earthquake. But, instead, you have a lane or two blocked, and everything slows down that was normally going down there. And unlike the freeway, the axon can swell, and it gets constipated with all that stuff that should have been going down to the tip and feeding the axon, but no longer is."

Looking for sheared or damaged axons, McKeever worked from autopsy photos, from slices of brain tissue

Dr. Cohle had taken, and from additional sections taken from what he termed her "wet-tissue stock."

McKeever said he found no evidence of herniation, which causes hemorrhaging and other damage to the brain stem that usually is enough to cause death. What he did see was swollen axons, a process he said stops immediately upon death.

"It takes at least an hour and a half for the axon to swell the way I saw the axonal swelling," he said.

McGuire handled the cross-examination. He asked McKeever how much he gets paid for his expert testimony, a common practice by both prosecution and defense attorneys. They'll ask the question, sneeringly, the implication that the witness is a say-whatever-for-hire, never mind their own expert witnesses are being paid, too.

"Five hundred dollars an hour," said McKeever.

Then they discussed at length the injuries McKeever observed, including left temporal lobe contusions, right soft tissue contusions and cerebral edema.

"Are you familiar with the work of a well-known person by the name of Geddes, from London?" asked McGuire. "Who, I understand, has written the most that anybody has written on the subject of diffuse axonal injury. Let me show you the paper. Do you recognize the name?"

"Yes."

"Who is that?"

"He's in the Royal London School, I believe. And he studied axonal injury a lot."

"Let me ask you a question from there, if I might. I'll just ask you if you agree with this statement: 'In summary, the diagnosis of diffuse axonal injury is not always easy . . . Early axonal injury detected by immunostaining should be interpreted with caution. Even with immuncytochemistry, precise dating of histological changes may not be possible.' Would you agree with that, sir?"

"Right."

Pendergast was very happy with McKeever's testimony. She had worried for months that two highly respected medical examiners, both prosecution witnesses, disagreed about what had killed Florence Unger. One said brain trauma, the other said drowning. The jury could believe Cohle and still come back with second-degree or manslaughter. If it believed Dragovic, that was the path to first-degree.

She needed a tie-breaker, and after hearing what McKeever had said, she thought she had it.

RILING THE JUDGE

They broke for recess. For much of the last two days, the jury had sat through hours of complicated, at times mind-numbing, sleep-inducing testimony about the physiology of the brain and examples of brain injury.

The next few minutes would prove to be some of the most charged and entertaining of the trial. Alas, the jury would hear none of it.

The star witness, Dr. Dragovic, was about to make his long-awaited appearance. The verdict likely would hinge on what he said and whether or not the jury liked him and believed him. McGuire had fireworks in store. Skrzynski wanted to make sure they never got lit.

"Need to argue something before you bring the jury back," said McGuire after the judge had entered the room.

The issue they were about to raise had come up in pre-trial discussions.

"Your Honor," Skrzynski began, "I wanted to, before we get started with the testimony of Dr. Dragovic, who's going to be the next witness, I wanted to bring a motion *in limine*. My understanding is that the defense intends to impeach Dr. Dragovic, impeach his credibility, apparently, with a letter, in part with a letter that was taken from a case called *State* against *Mark McCracken*, and it's issued by a district judge in the state of New Mexico, David Bonem."

A motion *in limine* asks a judge to decide, absent a jury, whether certain evidence may be presented under the premise that arguing the issue in front of the jury would be prejudicial.

"We heard about this before," said the judge.

"Yes. And my motion is to preclude them from cross-examining Dr. Dragovic on this letter . . . It's hearsay and I'm questioning the relevance of this letter. This is a ruling that was made by a district court judge on a case whose facts we are not familiar with, on findings that Dr. Dragovic made, and we don't know exactly what the findings were or how they applied to the case. So, I would ask that the court issue an order indicating that they cannot cross-examine quoting the letter or putting the letter into evidence."

Batzer inquired, "Are you going to be seeking to . . ."

"Absolutely," McGuire interrupted.

". . . get that into the record?"

"Yes. We think this should have been raised at a motion *in limine* before the trial. We've already used it as part of our opening statement. So now we're really prejudiced if he gets to do this at this point in time. This could have been done much earlier."

"You used it as part of your opening argument?"

"Yes. We are entitled to have some notice on this, and now is not the time to do it."

"Well, how is it admissible?" asked the judge.

"It's a document that tends to show the witness, that one of his opinions was rejected by another court," said McGuire.

"Oh, there's no way you can get that into the evidence. Absolutely no way is that admissible evidence," said the judge. "It's an opinion about a case we know nothing about. We don't know any of the facts of the case. We don't know what his opinion was in the case. We don't know why the court rejected it."

"We do know why the court rejected it. The court says why it rejected it. The court said it was rejected because it wasn't credible nor was it plausible."

"But that's in a factual vacuum."

"There's no requirement that I litigate a whole case as part of an evidentiary foundation."

"Well, you're not going to litigate that case. It's simply not admissible. It has nothing to do with this case. It's wholly and completely irrelevant, and there is no way, under God's green earth, that that is admissible into evidence."

Hard to state it more firmly. McGuire, though, wasn't taking no for an answer, yet. "It bears on his credibility as a witness," he said.

"No, it doesn't."

"When another judge finds a witness to be incredible?"

"It has nothing to do with this case."

"It does have something to do with this case."

"No, it doesn't."

"It does, too! He's coming into this court as an expert witness, proffered as an expert witness, and the fact that some other judge has listened to him and found his opinions to be not credible is relevant to his credibility, Judge. That's an elementary proposition of law. And I am stymied that you would not think this admissible."

"What are we going to do? Call in that judge, subpoena that judge in and say, 'Okay, why did you find him not credible?' No," said Batzer, saying it more calmly, more quietly, than one might have expected.

"There's a four-page opinion, here, and it goes into some detail about it," McGuire persisted.

"No."

"What would I have to have in order to make it admissible?"

"It would have to be relevant to this proceeding. It would have to not be on a collateral issue."

"His credibility is always an issue in a case. Every witness' credibility is an issue."

"It has nothing to do with this case."

"It does, too, have something to do with this case!"

"My ruling is it doesn't."

"Oh, I'm sorry. I would like to have that opinion marked for the record, so that we know what we're talking about in the future," said McGuire, letting all know this was an appealable issue. "Are you saying I can't even ask him about it? I can't ask him if another judge has said he's not credible? Is that part of your ruling, or just the paper?"

"No, you can't ask him about it. You can't ask him about that case. You can't."

"Period?"

"Period."

"That just doesn't make any sense to me at all, Your Honor."

"Thank you very much. It doesn't make sense to you. It makes sense to me. I'm not frequently called senseless. And if you do it, again, I'll have something more to say on it," said Batzer—still quietly, though.

McGuire, treading closely to a contempt citation, kept on. "I have to say this, Your Honor. For thirty years of dealing with expert witnesses as a lawyer, I have heard lawyers ask, 'Has your opinion ever been rejected by a judge anywhere? Have you ever been held not qualified to testify?' That's a rather routine question of an expert witness. And to be disallowed to ask that question I think is— Well, I've said what I've said about it."

"Well, I say that case has nothing to do with this case. It's immaterial."

Skrzynski interrupted their fight for the last word. "Your Honor, Dr. Dragovic is here from Pontiac, and I don't know if he was prepared to stay overnight. We had hoped to get his testimony finished today. I just ask that we be allowed, if we could just get started, again, if the court has made its ruling."

The jury was brought in. It was 3:27.

Had Batzer ruled in McGuire's favor, the jury would have heard that on December 28, 2004, Judge Bonem had written a letter to special prosecutor Randall Harris in the matter of the *State* v. *Mark McCracken*.

The letter served as Bonem's ruling on testimony by Dragovic and whether or not probable cause had been established to proceed with a murder case against Mc-Cracken:

> ... the credibility of witnesses at a preliminary hearing is a proper consideration for the Judge or Magistrate in determining probable cause [and] the credibility of witnesses at the preliminary examination is a question of fact within the province of the committing magistrate to determine ... I determine that the testimony of Dr. Dragovic is not plausible or credible. The only factual support ... for the testimony of Dr. Dragovic ... was negligible. ... The finding by Dr. Dragovic of "homicidal asphyxiation" stands alone among the three testifying pathologists ... and the two additional reporting pathologists ... Dragovic's opinion is based upon speculation and cannot form the basis for a probable cause finding related to manner of death.

Instead, what those in the court heard was Judge Batzer saying, "Call your next witness."

Dr. Dragovic was sworn in at 3:28 p.m. and spoke of his training, the various posts he'd served in a long career and his three board certifications, in anatomical pathology, neuropathology and forensic pathology.

When asked by Skrzynski how many autopsies he'd conducted in his career, he said, "Thousands. Last weekend I performed nine."

"So, over a thousand?"

"Oh, no, no no. Many thousands."

And how many involved drowning?

"I really do not keep track of that. But, unfortunately, it's a frequent occurrence. There are close to four hundred lakes in Oakland County. And then there's a major body of water next to Southeast Michigan, which is Lake Saint Clair. And the Detroit River. And back in Baltimore, I practiced at the shores of Chesapeake Bay. I actually had one drowning last weekend, it was a drowning in a bathtub. Of course, that's another situation," said Dragovic, ever entertaining.

He told of the mysterious beginning of his involvement in the Unger case, when in November 2003 a member of the Oakland County Sheriff's Department showed up at his office and asked him to look at two photos.

"Did you ask to get involved in this case?" asked Skrzynski.

"No. I never do that. I wouldn't even begin to do that, because I have enough workload of my own."

Dragovic told of the drive to Watervale on January 8, 2004, on what he said was the coldest day of the year, and examining the scene for forty-five minutes, the wind howling off the lake and everyone freezing.

And then driving down from there to visit Stephen Cohle in Grand Rapids. "I commented on my concerns and consideration that drowning would be the mechanism that superseded death in this individual, even though the head trauma was of such magnitude that would have resulted in death . . . if she had no treatment. If she had some treatment, there was a chance of some survival, potentially."

"What do you mean by superseding?"

"Something that happened faster, that actually interrupted the process of brain reaction to that injury. And looking at the scene, at the fact that she was found in water, the fastest mechanism that can create waterlogged lungs is the mechanism of drowning."

"Dr. Cohle had already made a pronouncement regarding the cause of death, and he said that it was the head injury that caused the death, correct?"

"Sure."

"What was it that made you think that it was drowning instead of a head injury?"

"There was no logical relationship between the degree of brain reaction [and] the findings in the lungs. So that was the discrepancy, and we talked about that briefly. Taking into consideration that a body was found in the water, and the fact that the body showed waterlogged lungs. That was the critical connecting the dots." Dragovic didn't mention, of course, that the dots hadn't been connected in Cohle's mind during that crucial visit. That, in fact, Cohle was so opposed to Dragovic's conclusion that he would tell those who asked that Dragovic had no scientific basis for concluding that Florence had drowned, drowning being a diagnosis of conclusion that requires all other possibilities of death to be excluded, first.

"So, you had ruled out the head injury as a cause of death?"

"Not as *a* cause of death. Head injury is the proximate cause. Without head injury, death would not have occurred."

"Why is that?"

"Well, number one, without this head injury, this individual would not have been unconscious. As a result of that, this individual would not have drowned in shallow water. However, a person that is unconscious is capable of drowning in a bowl of soup.

"If you're placed in shallow water, you drown as a result. You don't hold your breath. You don't fight. You inhale water directly, and that water goes in, and within a minute, you're out. You're dead."

"Did you come to a conclusion about what the cause of death was in this case?"

"Yes. The immediate cause of death was drowning. The proximate cause of death was major head trauma that made that drowning possible."

"Dr. Cohle, his opinion regarding manner of death was that this was a homicide. Do you agree with him on that?" asked Skrzynski.

"Sure."

"Why is that? What about this case supports your conclusions that this is a homicide?"

"In defining 'homicide,' it had to have been a purposeful act involved. This is why I went to the scene in the first place. I looked at that railing, the way it was broken. It was clear that some violent event occurred there, took place there, that would have propelled the body of the deceased over."

"Your Honor, I object! He has no qualifications to offer this kind of opinion, whatsoever. He's talking outside the purview of a pathologist," said McGuire.

The judge called the attorneys forward for a bench conference, then announced that they would continue in the morning. Court recessed at 5:06. For the defense, it was a disastrous place to stop, the last words of testimony the jury heard having been about a body being propelled over the railing.

WAITING FOR THE DOCTOR

Because of a scheduling conflict—Dragovic had to be in Oakland County early in the morning and wouldn't be able to get back to Beulah till 1 p.m.—the prosecution had several other witnesses ready to go on Thursday.

Fred Oeflein, the co-owner of Camp Lookout on the north end of Lower Herring Lake, took the stand first. He told of his encounter with the Ungers Friday night, that they chatted briefly before he said he needed to get going in his boat to the camp.

He said a gust of wind had blown out the candle and they were standing there in pitch dark and, he recounted, "She said, 'I could never do that, I'm afraid of the dark.'"

Chris Wooten, the head of the Benzie County volunteer dive team, was next. He told of being called by the sheriff and told to gather his crew, that a body had been found in the lake. Of arriving about 9:30 and being asked to hang around while the scene was processed. And at 6 p.m., the team finally entering the water in their wet suits to take measurements and bring her out.

Pendergast started to show him a photo and was interrupted by Harrison, who objected that the defense had not been given the photo ahead of time. Pendergast was furious.

"I do resent that Mr. Harrison would stand up here and

say, 'I don't have this photo.' I don't know what he did with it. I don't know all the photos were on the same disk. I do know that we provided Mr. Klakulak, several times, the same photos," she said. "I take umbrage at that. I'm very thorough. I'm meticulous and make sure discovery is turned over."

"I find Ms. Pendergast's umbrage entirely unpersuasive," said Harrison.

"You take umbrage at her umbrage?" asked the judge.

"No. I just find it silly."

"All right. We'll take a recess," said the judge. The photo was entered into evidence.

After the trial, Pendergast admitted that Harrison got under her skin. She accused him of being patronizing, of talking over her objections, of sandbagging her repeatedly in court with issues that should have been resolved privately. He'd reply that it was nothing personal, you had to understand Pendergast. "She can't help herself. For her it's a battle to the death every time."

At 11:40, Susan Witus took the stand. As had Flo's other friends, Witus recounted Flo's unhappiness in the marriage, her shock when the bills started coming in while Mark was in rehab and realizing how much his gambling and drugs had cost.

She told of Mark begging her on the phone to go to bat for him and try to talk Flo out of the divorce, and how she stopped calling Flo at home so she wouldn't have to talk to Mark.

And she told of Flo's fear of the dark, that Flo had told her one time about how dark it could get up north. "She said, 'You know, it's really beautiful, but I have to tell you, at night it gets really dark. I won't go outside. I'm scared to go outside at night,'" Witus said. "When she was alone, she just stayed in by herself."

She told, too, of talking to Flo on Friday morning, October 24, just before the Ungers began their drive north, that Flo told her it had been the worst week of her life, she'd spent two nights crying on the bathroom floor, that she and Mark had spent the week warring.

On cross-examination, Harrison asked, "They had been warring all week?"

"Yes."

"You didn't take that to be anything violent, did you?"

"No. I didn't."

"And you're personally unaware of any violence by Mark Unger, isn't that true?"

"I've never seen him be violent."

Witus was excused at 12:25 p.m. The judge dismissed the jury, telling them to make their way to downtown Beulah. "The Hungry Tummy will be expecting you," he said.

Most days the defense ate in, sharing lunch with Mark in a conference room at the courthouse. Often, the food was from L'Chaym, excellent, absolutely first-rate Jewish food, which they all thought was a hoot. Here was this Jewish guy on trial in about the most Gentile place in Michigan, with a place called L'Chaym just down the road.

"Pretty funny in Beulah, a Jewish joint," said Harrison.

Being able to eat good Jewish food was a comfort to Unger.

Before the attorneys and judge broke for lunch, though, they had to pick up where they'd left off regarding Dragovic, and his claim the day before that some violent action had "propelled the body of the deceased over" the broken railing.

"Well, what are we going to fight about, now?" asked the judge after the jury left.

"Well," said McGuire, "the testimony that was in progress and to which I made objection was that in his opinion, the deceased was violently kicked and/or punched, an act which apparently sent her over the railing. And I objected on the basis that, number one, he has no expertise to say that, that's outside the boundaries of a forensic pathologist or a neuropathologist. He's just wildly speculating about what happened."

"Part of the job of a forensic pathologist is to determine

the manner of death. That includes how wounds were in-
flicted, how injuries occurred on the person," countered
Skrzynski. "I think that's part of the testimony that we've
reached, now, where he's going to start giving his theory of
the manner of death.

"I'm going to allow Dr. Dragovic to state his opinion
on the manner of death," said Batzer. "But he's going to
have to tie it to the physical evidence. If it's wholly specu-
lative, I'll strike his opinion."

"IF I WERE A CARPENTER . . ."

Dr. Dragovic took his seat in the witness chair at 2 p.m.

Skrzynski had Dragovic briefly go back over the nature of Florence's head injuries and that they'd rendered her unconscious and unable to get into the water through her own efforts, voluntary or otherwise.

He also said that Cohle's autopsy showed bleeding in the belly cavity. "We're talking about trauma that is rendered by a punch or a kick," he said.

Skrzynski put a photo taken during the autopsy in the projector, which showed the right side of Florence's head and what appeared to be bruises and small scrapes. Dragovic said some of it could have happened in the fall, but "some of it is indication of surface injury, where the skin is pushed over a rough surface."

"Is that injury consistent with Mrs. Unger's head having been dragged along the concrete?"

"Sure."

Skrzynski showed him another photo, of her hip area, which showed bruising on the left side. Dragovic told him the bruising was consistent with a blow to the abdomen, and that the fracture of her pelvis could have happened either by being propelled backwards against the railing, or upon landing on the cement.

"Is there anything else that we have not spoken about that led you to the conclusion that this was a homicide?" asked Skrzynski.

"The visit to the scene and examination of the railing by myself, by actually touching it and asking to review the part that was removed, showing evidence of force being applied. And that did not match the idea of someone just falling over a railing. That's where I considered that the body had to have been propelled in the direction of the railing to cause the fracture of the railing."

"And how do you propose that it was propelled?"

"Objection, Your Honor!" said McGuire. "Same objection as before."

"Overruled."

"There are findings in the body, but there is common sense," said Dragovic. "And if you look at it, you have to apply common sense. If you see that the railing is broken, why would the railing be broken in such a fashion? There has to be some logical explanation for that. How does the body flip over, breaking and striking that railing? It has to be propelled, by pushing, by shoving, by kicking, or punching, by physical force, being applied to the body."

McGuire had Dragovic recount his standard workday with the county—8 a.m. to 4 p.m.—and his workload. He told McGuire that if he did work before 4 p.m. for other counties, they reimbursed Oakland County $250 an hour, none of which went to him.

"But if you work on non–Oakland County business after 4, that's money that goes to you?"

"Absolutely."

"That's the American way, I believe you said. That's the reason you came here, to practice American capitalism. Isn't that right?"

"That's true. I believe in it."

"When you testify in a civil case—and you testify quite often in civil cases, do you not?—how much do you charge for a deposition?"

"It's a standard four hundred dollars per hour."

"As a matter of fact, don't you charge a minimum fee of twelve hundred dollars for a deposition, because you require that lawyers pay you for a minimum of three hours of your time?"

"That's the standard approach."

"You charge twelve hundred dollars for a deposition that may take fifteen minutes?"

"A minimum of three hours, yes."

Dragovic confirmed that in the last five years, his consulting had taken him around the state of Michigan and around the U.S., including Norfolk, Virginia, Indian River, Florida, and New York.

"Whoever requests my presence," said Dragovic. "Last week, or two weeks ago, I was in Cherokee County down in Georgia, on behalf of the district attorney there. On Saturday, I fly to California on behalf of a defense witness in a case that involves brain injury."

"You gravitate toward cases where you can get your name in the paper?"

"No."

"Get your face before the cameras?"

"No, sir."

"Is that a fair statement, sir?"

"No. It's not a fair statement. It's very much a nuisance. The fact is, the cases come to me. I don't go after cases. And I cannot prevent that. I'm a public worker. I'm a public pathologist, sir."

"Dr. Dragovic, would it be fair to say that by getting your name in the news media frequently on high-profile cases, it's free publicity for your private work? That's the American way, too?"

"Well, it may be, but not in my case. I'm, myself, in the position of being exposed because the jurisdiction that I serve is the center of interest not only countrywide, but worldwide."

"So, it doesn't help you to get private business that your name gets in the paper a lot?"

"Not that I notice."

"Do you like that, when your name gets in the paper? Is that important to you personally?"

"I don't care about it, because it does not provide me with any benefits. It does not pay the tuitions of my children."

McGuire was determined to get something on the record about the New Mexico case in 2004.

"You went down to New Mexico to testify in a case?" he asked.

"I went down to New Mexico on a number of cases, sir."

"I'm talking about the McCracken case."

"Yes."

Skrzynski jumped to his feet. "I object, Your Honor. I think we had a ruling on this."

"Not going to disobey the ruling. Not going to do that," said McGuire. "Not going to do what he thinks I'm going to do."

"Well, why don't you come up and tell me what you're going to do?" said the judge, summoning them forward for a bench conference.

When it was over, McGuire was allowed to resume. "Do you recall the case I'm talking about?" he asked.

"Yes, sir. I was involved in the investigation for the attorney general's office in that case."

"There were a total of five pathologists in that case who offered opinions, is that correct?"

"I don't remember. The case was reinvestigated by me."

"About five people?"

"Possibly, yeah, Maybe even more."

"Fair to say that you contradicted all of them?"

"Sure."

They moved on to Dragovic's involvement in the Unger case.

"You're not the pathologist for Benzie County?" asked McGuire.

"No, sir."

"Dr. Cohle does the work for Benzie County?"

"I understand that's the contract, yes."

"You know Dr. Cohle?"

"Sure."

"And he's a good, competent pathologist?"

"He's among the leading forensic pathologists in Michigan, sir. Among the three top forensic pathologists in the State of Michigan."

"He is a graduate of the Baylor University medical school, one of the best medical schools in the world?"

"Sure, yes."

"So, here you have a situation where a woman has died, you have an autopsy by a guy, Steve Cohle, who you know by reputations, maybe even you know him a bit socially?"

"I know him both socially and by reputation, yes."

"And you have a matter that occurs outside of Oakland County, and here you have in your office all these people from Oakland County, they're Oakland County detectives, Oakland prosecutors, the question must occur to you: 'What the dickens is going on here? Why am I, the Oakland County medical examiner, being asked by Oakland prosecutors and Oakland detectives about a situation that occurred in Benzie County?'"

"No, sir."

"You weren't even curious about it?"

"No, because it's common practice."

"Oh, yes, I'm sure it is," McGuire sneered.

(Later, McGuire would say, "The real story is how they enlisted the Oakland County coroner, who had nothing to do with this case and had no investigative powers in that jurisdiction." Harrison would say, "Oakland County's involvement makes no sense at all. It was a big publicity-seeking power trip. They wanted to be in on a big case." Though others speculated that Harold Stern had exerted political influence to get Oakland involved, Harrison discounted the theory, saying, "There was a lot of talk about that, a lot of speculation, but I don't have any evidence of that.")

"Dr. Dragovic, do you regard yourself as the medical examiner for the world?" asked McGuire.

"No, sir."

"You don't like it when your side of the case loses, do you?"

"I'm not in the business of winning or losing. I'm in the business of interpreting facts for the courts. I understand that there is an adversary situation in every court in this country, and I respect that."

"That's not what I asked you. All I asked you was a simple question: You don't like to lose, and you want your side of the case to win, correct?"

Dragovic shook his head from side to side.

McGuire asked him about a recent case in Wayne County, where a defendant named Timothy Ray Null was convicted despite Dragovic's testimony for the defense. "And you got angry afterwards, didn't you?" he asked.

"Me?"

"Yes, you."

"With whom?"

"Didn't you write a letter and send copies of it to the Wayne County Prosecutor's Office, to lawyers there, to Brian Zubel of the state attorney general's office?"

When McGuire moved to enter the letter into evidence, Skrzynski objected, and the judge told the jury and Dragovic to leave the courtroom while they discussed it. They missed a good show.

"My objection to this is in the nature of the same objections that I made to the previous specific case. It's irrelevant to the issues here," said Skrzynski.

"I think we have a witness who has a very strong opinion of himself, who doesn't seem to agree with most other pathologists that he comes in contact with. Here is recently, in a case where his side of the case was not victorious, and he takes a shotgun blast at the Wayne County Medical Examiner's Office," said McGuire, who read an excerpt from the letter to the judge.

" 'In consideration of these findings and the circumstance surrounding this death, the manner of death should have been appropriately classified as suicide. The grave confusion in this matter is like the result of inadequate death

investigation, incomplete premortem and postmortem physical findings and lack of professional responsibility and
common sense.'

"Dr. Dragovic has a history of getting himself into
cases and contradicting all the other professional pathologists. That's what's going on in this case. He's contradicting two other pathologists that the prosecution has called
here. He's going to contradict the defense pathologists.
And I think this is additional evidence of that, that I'm
entitled to have the jury see. I think it's very strong evidence of bias."

"No. It's impeachment on a collateral issue you're offering," said the judge.

"This is not a collateral issue. When we are talking
about the bias of the witness, that's always a material issue."

"That's a collateral issue," the judge said forcefully.

"When you're dealing with credibility, it's never a collateral matter, ever," said Harrison, entering the fray and
lecturing the judge on the law. "What you're doing here is,
I say to you respectfully, is preventing us from even getting
into the area at all."

"The rule says plainly you can't impeach on a collateral
matter using extrinsic evidence," said Skrzynski. "If they
don't understand what those words mean, then they should
look it up."

"I want to thank Mr. Skrzynski for being insulting, but
he's just plain wrong," said Harrison.

"My ruling is no," said the judge.

"Judge, I would just like to point out that this is something he authored. This isn't like the judge in McCracken's
case. This is a writing of Dr. Dragovic, himself," said Mc-
Guire.

"It's collateral," said the judge.

"It's not collateral," said McGuire.

"I've made my ruling."

The letter was marked as Defendant's Exhibit B, to be
put into the record, for the appealable record, but not in
evidence.

McGuire wasn't going to let it go. He picked up the *Michigan Evidence Courtroom Manual* and read from page 613. " 'A matter is not collateral if the fact inquired into . . . reveals a bias or interest on the part of the witness.' I think that's clear. A bias on the part of the witness."

"He's trying to make him look bad in front of the jury," said Skrzynski.

"He deserves to look bad in front of the jury," said McGuire.

"We're not going into that in this trial," said the judge.

"That doesn't make any sense," said McGuire, treading thin ice, again. "Come on, Judge. This is a serious case. This is a murder case."

"I appreciate it's a serious case, and I'd like to get on with continuing the trial," said the judge.

At 4:13, the jury and Dragovic reentered the courtroom.

McGuire put a photo of Florence's skull up on the projector and asked Dragovic about the nature of the fractures and contusions.

"Serious brain injury?" asked McGuire, following a technical description from Dragovic about "mild subarachnoid hemorrhage which was diffuse over the left surface of the left hemisphere."

"Devastating."

"So, you have this autopsy in hand, you're in your third meeting with people from Oakland County. Have you yet formed some curiosity about why it is they're asking the Oakland County Medical Examiner to come to the north, to Benzie County? Any curiosity about that?"

"They asked me to go to evaluate the scene, of course."

"My question was if you had any curiosity about it?"

"Obviously, I was to assist them. So . . ."

"That's not my question, Doctor. Listen to my question, please. Did you form any curiosity at that time about why they were asking you, as an Oakland County official, to come here?"

"I don't form curiosities, sir. I just listen to what I'm asked, and make a decision on whether I can help or not."

"So, you're going to go to Benzie County, a trip of about two hundred and fifty miles, and you'd also planned to go down to Grand Rapids to see Dr. Cohle. This was an all-day trip, right?"

"Sure."

"A lot of driving. It's going to involve six, seven hundred miles before you're done, isn't it?"

"I wasn't driving, so I didn't care."

(McGuire, from his line of questioning, may have gotten word from someone in the prosecutor's office or attorney general's office that Dragovic, indeed, had chafed at the idea of the long drive north and back. Pendergast and Bilkovic had gone back and forth with each other over who would tell Dragovic. "You tell him," the one would say. "Oh, no, you tell him.")

"So, you went to the scene. What did you need to have answered that you could find out by going to the scene?"

"The three-dimensional feeling that one gets, getting to the scene and looking physically at that railing there, looking at the cement slab, looking at the sea wall."

"So, you went to get a feeling? And that's what you got, a feeling?"

"I think you are mischaracterizing my statement, sir."

"I'm only using your words. You don't go to the scene of all your autopsies, do you?" During one of the depositions before trial, Dragovic had admitted he couldn't remember the last time he'd been at a crime scene, he had underlings to do such work.

"Not unless there is an issue."

"You only go to the scene of autopsies when there's newspaper play, isn't that true?"

"No."

"When was the last time before today that you went to the scene of a death?"

"My office can possibly provide that information."

"But you can't?"

"Not off the top of my head, exactly. But I've been to the scenes of homicides that I've handled that the media did not know about until later."

At one point, McGuire made mention of "the accident," a classic defense ploy.

"What accident?" asked Dragovic.

"Mrs. Unger's accident, that's what I'm referring to, but I'll talk to you about it in terms of her death," said McGuire.

"Excuse me, sir. You're referring to an accident, where I do not agree with your concept."

McGuire asked about Dragovic's examination of the rails during his visit and grilled him about photos showing where rails had been removed by police for examination and photos that showed cracking and deterioration.

"And you satisfied yourself that it was sturdy and accomplished its task as a safety railing, was that true?"

"That's not true. I wasn't there to accomplish the assessment of safety railing purposes. I was there to accomplish the viewing, physical viewing of the rail, itself."

"Are you capable of making a determination about whether wood is rotten or not?" asked McGuire.

"I'm not a wood expert, sir. If it's falling apart, to me it's rotten. If it's not falling apart, it's not. But I'm not the wood expert."

"You made no judgments about it at all?"

"That's correct."

"You didn't even test it for that purpose?"

"I'm not a carpenter, unfortunately. I wish I was."

"So, for your limited purpose of investigating homicide, you moved the vertical posts and satisfied yourself as to something. What was it you satisfied yourself of?"

"The top railing showed clearly that it was shoved by force in an outward direction."

It was not a good place for things to stop, but they were out of time. The judge adjourned at 4:54 p.m.

SATISFYING HER DOUBTS

McGuire would have to wait till the next week to get another crack at Dragovic, who had to be in Oakland County on Friday, scheduled to be a short day because the Batzers' daughter was getting married Saturday.

On the docket for the prosecution were four more Unger family friends, beginning with Lori Silverstein. She was long-time friends with both Ungers, and her husband, Robert, had gotten Mark the job he'd hated so much at the mortgage company.

Unlike many of Flo's friends, she considered herself close to Mark, too, and thought him innocent when word shot around Huntington Woods of Flo's death.

She told the court that on the Thursday after Flo's death, she finally had a chance to talk to Mark about what had happened, and that Mark had told her about sharing a laugh with Flo about some odd boatman they'd met Friday night who insisted on heading out across the dark lake in the rain, and of Flo's insistence on his going in to check on the kids. When he'd come back, Flo was gone.

He told her he'd assumed Flo was visiting Maggie Duncan—the light in her house had been off earlier, but was on when Mark returned to the boathouse—and he went back to his cottage and fell asleep. He told her he woke up at 7:30 a.m. and realized Flo had never come back.

Over the next six or seven weeks, as talk of that weekend's events reverberated through Huntington Woods, she became increasingly dubious of his tale.

"I was frustrated," she said, "because I was wondering why Mark—if everybody is saying this wasn't an accident, why he wasn't more angry about who may have been involved in this. And when I questioned him, he told me that the media and everybody had it wrong, that it was the wrong information. And so I outright asked him to tell me what happened, and how Flo got in the water."

"And what did he tell you?" asked Bilkovic.

"He told me that it had been misinformation . . . everybody thinks it was a large piece of concrete from the deck to the water, but it was actually—and he showed me with his hands, about a six-inch-wide area—and he thinks that she fell on that, hit it, and then landed in the water, is what he told me."

"And he showed you that with his hands?"

"He showed me with his hands, the amount of space. He said she went in the water, and then he said to me, 'Can't you just see her? I can picture her wrapped in a blanket, pulling this lounge chair backward on this deck.' That she must have just gotten too far and fallen over the fence."

Bilkovic asked her if she had attended the preliminary exam in 2004. She had. While she was there, she drove to Watervale and went down to the lake.

"Was there anything about that that struck you as odd?" asked Bilkovic.

"Yes. Because now I could visualize just the amount of space there was from the deck to the water, and it looked to be about three or four feet," she said. "And in my conversations with him I visualized this smaller area . . . the six-inch-wide thing, as he put it."

On cross-examination, she said she had never seen the Ungers scream or yell at each other, or any physical confrontations.

Of the width of the apron, Harrison asked, "Is it possible that Mark was saying, 'She was this far from the water,' not that 'the concrete landing area was this wide,' but that she got in the water because she landed 'this far from the edge'?"

"I clearly remember him standing in my house, holding his hands at that space as I demonstrated, described it as a six-inch-wide thing."

"But we know, of course, that that concrete apron is way, way wider than this, right? . . . You've seen films of the dock area on television. The media was playing video of that very dock area within the first week of the incident. Did you see any of the films on the news showing the spot, and where the blood was, and all of that?"

"It wasn't clear in the films or the newspapers that I saw, the amount of space."

"It would certainly be stupid to try to tell somebody that she fell on a piece of concrete that's this wide, wouldn't it? You would have to be pretty stupid to try to tell somebody that, right?"

"Who was I to question? As I told you, I didn't see the space, so I didn't know the area. This is the story he's telling me."

Harrison asked her if Florence had been afraid of the dark.

"Not to my knowledge. No."

"Have you previously described Mark Unger as a sensitive guy, just a big teddy bear kind of guy?"

"Yes."

"Who's emotional, sensitive, and sweet?"

"Yes."

"Very sweet and very nice?"

"Yes."

"Did you ever think Mark was capable of harming Flo?"

"No."

Robert Silverstein took the stand at 11:44 and buttressed his wife's account.

"Did he say anything about the cement slab that Florence Unger had fallen on?" asked Bilkovic.

"Only the reference to the length of space to the water. That it was a short slab. The conversation we had was inconsistent to what we had read about, so we were questioning from his viewpoint what was the distance of the slab."

"And what did he tell you? Do you remember him showing you with his hands?"

"I do." Silverstein held his hands up, about six inches apart.

Harrison asked him if, in all the months of media coverage, he had seen pictures or film of the cement slab.

"I recall some pictures, yes."

"I mean, it's a very obvious thing, when you look at it, to see that in fact it's certainly not six inches wide or eight inches wide, isn't it?" asked Harrison.

"Yes."

"In terms of the context, Mr. Silverstein, of what Mark was talking about, do you think it's possible that there was a misunderstanding here, and he was referencing how close to the edge of the water she was where she hit, and that's how she got in the water?"

"We were questioning the portrayal from the media as to the amount of space. And in our conversation, the reference was that there was not as much space as was being conveyed on the media and in the news."

Kathy Stark took the stand at noon, which must have been extremely painful, knowing that her husband had told the same packed courtroom earlier about his affair with her good friend.

Even so, when asked by Bilkovic what Florence was like, she answered, "Flo was lovely. She was funny and kind and generous, and as warmhearted a person as can be.

He asked her if Flo was afraid of the dark.

"She was. Yes."

"How do you know?"

"Countless incidents. Being that we lived close to her,

she used to call myself or my husband at times when she needed to retrieve something from her car and it was dark. If it was dark out and if the lights weren't on in the neighbor's house, she wouldn't go outside. I would go over and knock on her door, and she'd come out and we'd get the bag out of her car.

"She would call and say that she would want to sit on the porch but it was very dark outside and she would want us to come over . . .

"She'd hear noises."

Harrison had an alternative explanation for the frequent calls to the Starks. He asked, "Mrs. Stark, did Florence ever tell you that she was having an affair with your husband?"

"No."

"Looking back at what has occurred here in this case and these kinds of calls to come over and get something out of her car, have you ever questioned your judgment about what those were all about?"

"No."

"Have you ever thought to yourself that maybe when she called your home all of those times over and over again, she was attempting to reach your husband, to see if he could come over, and maybe she got you some of the times?"

"It's possible."

"And perhaps she was trying to talk to him?"

"No. He was her friend, as well as I was. She felt strongly about both of us."

The court adjourned at 12:36.

WEEK FIVE
RETURN OF THE VAMPIRE

Dragovic took the stand on Wednesday, May 24, at 10:10 a.m. He'd last been in this court the previous Thursday. In the meantime, he'd flown out to Riverside, California, and testified in Superior Court there.

McGuire showed Dragovic a magnified photo of the railing from the Duncans' boathouse deck. It showed what looked to be dry rot.

"Did you see this kind of thing when you were there?" asked McGuire.

"At that magnification, no."

It was going to be one of those days.

"I didn't ask at what magnification. Did you just see what's represented here?"

"I'm not sure what you're showing to me. It's a detail of something. Detail of a wooden structure."

"See the railing here across the top? Does this look like the railing on the top?"

"Only if you tell me that it is."

McGuire handed Dragovic another photo, which showed more of the deck, including the piece of rail that was in the magnified photo.

"Did you see that when you were there?" asked McGuire, referring to the splintering, rotting wood.

"I don't remember that particular detail. I don't know."

"If you saw it, would that be important to you? Would that strike you as something important in this case?"

"If I considered it important, I would have taken it into consideration and made an attempt to memorize . . ."

"But you see nothing particularly important about what's represented in that photograph, right?" said McGuire, cutting him off.

"Not for my purposes. For someone else's, I'm sure there might be an issue of some repair needed or some damage being there."

McGuire showed him another photo.

"This photograph also contains some damaged posts, see that?"

"Yes, sir."

"Did you see those when you were there?"

"Oh, yes."

"Were they important to you?"

"Not when I was there."

"And you made no notes about it, correct?"

"Written notes?"

"Yes."

"No."

McGuire then handed him a piece of wood, marked as Exhibit 12, a piece of the deck railing.

"I want you to touch the wood with your hand, give me some idea of whether you can determine if the wood is solid or whether it shows evidence of rot," he said.

"Well, this piece of wood is damaged. How extensively damaged, I cannot tell. I'm not a wood expert, certainly. But the rest of it feels solid. The bottom part feels solid."

"Are you able to compress the wood when you touch it?"

"In this upper part, yes."

"That's pretty rotten, isn't it?"

"I would say it's damaged. I can't use the proper technical word, because I'm not an expert in that area."

"Dr. Dragovic, would it be true that pathologists such as

yourself very rarely go to the scene of an accident or death? That's something you have investigators to do for you, isn't it?"

" 'Seldom' is a statistical term. When there is a need to assess and reassess a scene, it's done. That's the answer."

"Do you remember if you went to the scene of some death at all last year?"

"I'm pretty sure I went to some. But exactly to which one, only my office can track that."

They moved from the tactile world of rotting wood to a long and technical discussion of brain- and lung-tissue slides that had jurors badly in need of the recess the judge declared at 11.

After recess, McGuire returned to Dragovic's visit to Cohle.

"What was the status of your opinions about the cause of death by the time you arrived there?" asked McGuire.

"Well, I knew that Mrs. Unger sustained severe brain trauma. Head trauma. And I knew that Mrs. Unger was recovered from the body of water. And I had my suspicions that Mrs. Unger drowned in that body of water."

"Well, had you pretty much made up your mind?"

"I don't quite understand your question. This is not about making the mind up. The process of analysis in death investigation is not about making up the mind."

"You tried to talk Dr. Cohle into entertaining the proposition that you were advancing, that she drowned?"

"Into considering it."

"You had this opinion by the time you got to Dr. Cohle's office."

"I had the idea, sir, yes."

"Do you remember testifying in a deposition in this case back in the fall of last year?"

"Yes."

"Do you remember being asked the question, 'Before you got to Dr. Cohle's office, had you formed an opinion about this woman's cause of death?' And giving the answer, 'No, sir'?"

"That is correct."

"You just told me that you pretty much had an opinion."

"No, no, no, no. I explained very carefully that I had the ideas about the mechanism of death and the causes of death. But I did not form an opinion. Forming an opinion means putting something in writing. Formulating something as an opinion. That's what it is. You don't float around theories just like that. You have to have something formulated. You cannot keep opinions in your pocket. You put opinion on paper. I had not done that at that time. I issued my opinion on May seventeenth, 2004."

"Dr. Dragovic, are you just making this up as you go, sir? Are you just making this up as you go?"

No one in the court was fighting sleep, now. All eyes were focused on the good doctor.

"Excuse me?" he asked.

"Just what I said. Are you just making this testimony up as you go? That's my question."

"I don't think so," said Dragovic, hardly the answer Skrzynski wanted to hear.

Pendergast had to stifle a laugh. She was enjoying the back-and-forth between McGuire and Dragovic.

"So you don't have an opinion unless they're written down?"

"That is correct. A forensic opinion is written-down opinion."

The timing of that written opinion, said Dragovic, was a result of the long lag between visiting Dr. Cohle's office on January 8 and getting slides from Cohle's office in May for further examination.

McGuire pointed out that Cohle had finally decided on December 23, 2003, to amend his autopsy report to say that the manner of death was homicide, rather than what he'd written originally, "pending investigation." Why had the prosecutor's office waited five months after Cohle decided it was murder to file charges, but only four days after Dragovic filed his report?

"I don't work in that sphere."

"Did anyone tell you, Dr. Dragovic, that they weren't going to file charges based on Dr. Cohle's report, because they needed you to come up with this drowning theory in order to make a first-degree murder case out of this?"

"No one said anything like that. No one inferred [sic] anything like that, sir. I do not work for any prosecutor. In particular, I don't work for the attorney general's office of the state of Michigan."

After a break for lunch, McGuire resumed his cross, asking, "You testified on one occasion that you once testified seven times in one day in different courts?"

"That was back when I worked for Wayne County, Detroit."

"Did you actually testify in seven different cases in one day?"

"Yes, some of them at the Thirty-sixth District Court, and others at the Frank Murphy Hall of Justice. I actually testified in four cases in three different cities in the state of Michigan one time. And Swedish professors were with me visiting, seeing how the work was done," said Dragovic proudly.

McGuire asked about testimony by Dragovic that Florence could have been alive on the concrete slab for an hour or an hour and a half before she died.

"I indicated many minutes to an hour, maybe even longer . . .

"That's what I testified about."

McGuire, picking up a transcript, referred to testimony Dragovic had made during the *Daubert* hearings before Judge Batzer the previous January: "I asked you, on page one hundred and forty-six, 'Do you have an opinion about the length of time that she may have lain on the cement concrete surface before she went in the water?'"

McGuire read Dragovic's answer: " 'That would be measured in minutes. How many minutes I cannot tell. We are using the highest, most measurable unit of time that is considered. So "minutes" may mean five minutes, eight minutes, ten minutes, fifteen minutes. I don't believe that she was there for an hour. Had I thought that she was there for an hour, I would have indicated so. I don't believe— I don't have any evidence to say so.'

"Now, that's what you said when you testified under oath?"

"Sure."

"Now, which is true, Doctor? The evidence that you gave in January, or the evidence that you gave from that witness stand? Both of them were under oath."

"Both of them are true," said Dragovic.

"Both of them are true?" asked McGuire.

"Of course."

"Of course," repeated McGuire, to comic effect.

"Yes, if you want me to explain. Yes. On the basis of examination, just gross examination, and examination of the circumstances, one can project minutes of survival on the basis of more specific information that is provided through specific stains. And the references that indicate how long you need for those stains to become positive. You have to factor that in. So it extends the time, which is obviously—you see, in science, in scientific evaluation, every new bit of information . . ."

McGuire cut him off. "There's no question to you about that, sir?"

"I'm sorry?"

"I just asked you which was true."

"Both are true."

Again, McGuire asked, "Are you just making this up as you go, Dr. Dragovic?"

"No, sir."

"There is a man on trial for murder, here. Do you understand that, sir?"

"I perfectly understand that, sir."

"I'm not sure you do. I have no further questions."

But he did, following Skrzynski's redirect. Skrzynski went over some of the technical issues regarding drowning— such as the kind of regurgitated foam that indicates drowning—and Dragovic's often frenetic load as an expert witness.

"You testified earlier that at some point you testified in seven cases in one day, is that correct?" asked Skrzynski.

"Yes."

"You mentioned the Thirty-sixth District Court. How many courtrooms are in the Thirty-sixth District Court?"

"I wouldn't even begin to guess, but it is the busiest district court in the nation, I believe."

"Would you say there are more than forty courtrooms in that courthouse?"

"Very likely, yes."

"You also said you went to the Frank Murphy Hall of Justice?"

"Sure, that is two blocks down."

"And that houses all the circuit court courtrooms that hear criminal matters?"

"Yes, sir."

"And there are maybe forty additional courtrooms in that building, is that right?"

"There are altogether twelve floors, I think, in the building. And courtrooms are everything below the eleventh and twelfth floors, as my memory serves me."

"So, testifying in seven different courts in one day, were you doing that because there were high-publicity cases that you had an opportunity to show your face and get publicity for?"

"For the most part, there would be no one in the courtroom in those cases, even in the circuit court proceedings."

"Do you remember there being twelve floors to the Frank Murphy Hall of Justice?" countered McGuire.

"I believe eleventh and twelfth floors are prosecutor's office."

"You wouldn't be surprised if I told you that I did a little work in that building, myself, and may have some personal knowledge of it? The tallest floor is the ninth floor, isn't it? It's where the cafeteria and the clerk's office are located. And the courtrooms don't start till the fourth floor, correct?"

"Oh, no," said Dragovic.

Here's where it got funny.

"Judge, that's not true," interceded Skrzynski.

"I worked in Wayne County," chimed in Pendergast.

"This is what we can do," said a sarcastic Judge Batzer. "We can let the doctor step down and we can put all the attorneys here who have worked . . ."

"I've been waiting for that chance," interrupted McGuire.

"And they can testify as to how many floors there are in the Frank Murphy Hall of Justice," finished the judge.

It was Harrison's turn. "I was in there when the building first opened. I was there, too."

"Some more testimony," piped in Dragovic.

The only thing keeping it from being a *Monty Python* skit was that no one was doing any funny walking.

McGuire got back to the cross. "I believe there are only fifteen to twenty district judges. I don't know how there can be forty courtrooms. Can you explain that?" he asked.

"To me—and my memory might be skewed because I was always so busy there—I would have bet that there were more than forty judges there, but you can check. I don't know. This is not an expert definition," said Dragovic.

McGuire put a photo up on the screen, a shot of something pink. Dragovic said it was a mixture of blood and hemorrhagic foam.

"Would you be surprised if I told you that Dr. Cohle looked at the same photograph and said there was no evidence of foam in that photograph, at all? That it was just dried blood?"

"If he said so, that's fine."

"Dr. Dragovic, can you offer me an explanation for why two experienced pathologists, yourself and Steve Cohle, could look at a picture of a woman, and one man say that's evidence of foam and the other man say it's evidence of dried blood? Can you give me a reason for that?"

"No, I cannot. There is one correct answer, though."

It was 3 p.m. Dragovic was done.

Later, Harrison would say of the day's star witness: "Frequently wrong, but never in doubt. He's an egomaniac who loves the spotlight. He says this stuff and he gets away with it because he's so smart, it's hard to pin him down. But Tom wouldn't let him get away with it."

"WHAT KIND OF A QUESTION
IS THAT?"

At 3:33, Tom Kelley, the sergeant in charge of the detective bureau at the Benzie County Sheriff's Department, took the stand.

Kelley had since retired, on January 1, 2005.

He told Pendergast of his work at the scene, then driving Unger back to the station for his formal interview.

He read aloud Unger's terse account of the weekend's events, which ran to just over a page. "Walked to the deck. She wasn't there. Went back to the cabin. Fell asleep, watching DVD . . . Woke up in the morning, no Flo. Called Linn and Maggie. Linn told me he found her."

Read by Kelley, it seemed all the stranger for its staccato brevity and missing nouns and articles.

"I ran down there. I tried to get her out, but blood started coming out. Started crying," it ended.

He told of Unger making cell phone calls throughout the half hour he'd spent in the detective's office, and getting so upset at one point at not being able to get a call through that Kelley halted the questioning and led him outside so he could get better reception.

He said that after Unger told him that as far as he knew, he was the last person to have seen her alive, he read him his rights.

Pendergast asked him about Unger's emotions.

"Mark was in and out of his emotions. He would be crying and sobbing, and I would offer him tissues, like this box of tissues here, and there was no tears. And then he would get matter-of-fact with me, and speak very calm, and very concise," said Kelley.

"Finally he said to me, says, 'If you got something to say to me, if you got something to ask me, then ask me.'"

"I said, 'Okay. Did you push her off the deck?' He answered by saying, 'What kind of a question is that?' At this point, he wanted to go back to the cottage. He was done talking to me."

"You said, 'Okay. Did you push your wife off that deck?' And he said, 'What kind of question is that?'" asked Harrison on cross.

"That's correct."

"And that was a way, a manner of speech of saying, 'I didn't push my wife off the deck'?"

"What it meant to me is, he wasn't giving me an answer. That's a yes or no question."

"Pardon me?"

"That's a yes or no question."

"We've had a lot of those in this trial, and we haven't gotten a lot of yesses and nos," snapped Harrison.

"You pushed her or you didn't. You're pregnant or you're not," said Kelley, firing back.

"And did you ask him this: 'Your kids will have to carry this for the rest of their lives. Why don't you just tell the truth about what happened and make it easier on your kids and everybody?'"

"I might have said that."

"And did you say to him that he was free to go at any time, but then you wouldn't let him go because you said, 'The big boss said no'?"

"No. It did not happen."

"Would you agree with me, Mr. Kelley, that different people deal with deep emotions in different ways?"

"In my thirty-three years in police work, I have never seen anything quite as disingenuous as . . ."

Harrison cut off the damage. "I guess you didn't hear my question. Have you, in your experience, seen people deal with emotion or trauma in widely different ways?"

"Yes. Never like that, but yes."

"You want to throw that in there like that, that's okay. And would you also agree with me that sometimes people deal or react to death in a stunned or blank or emotionless manner, and sometimes people can't stop crying, sometimes for days? You've seen that, too, haven't you?"

"Yes, sir."

"You've seen the gamut, okay? And would you agree with me that there is no set of rules and regulations about how somebody should act in a terribly upsetting situation? Their wife found face down in the lake, for example?"

"To a point."

At 4:43 p.m., court adjourned.

Connie Wolberg walked out, steaming, Jerry at her side. They had been at the trial throughout. Harrison had consistently taken a hard line with the police who'd been at the scene, a tried-and-true tactic in Wayne County, where he'd learned his trade and where an antipathy for decades between black Detroit residents and what had been a mostly white police force had made attacking cops' ability a can't-miss strategy. But here? She thought it was dumb. She'd told Jerry it was dumb, that these cops aren't the enemy, they're friends and neighbors. Harrison was acting like they were all Barney from *Mayberry RFD*, and they weren't, and she had a gut feeling their neighbors on the jury didn't like it.

Connie was convinced of Mark's innocence, and convinced even more that Harrison was going about trying to prove it in the worst way possible. He needed to stick to facts, argue science and avoid the innuendos of prejudice and incompetence. She figured if she wasn't buying it, the jury certainly wasn't.

ASKING FOR THE MOON

The highlight Thursday came after the jury was excused at 5:01 p.m. Ironically, of all the hours of testimony they would hear over the weeks, one of the most important exchanges occurred out of their hearing, over a period of two days.

Pendergast was worried about a proposed defense witness, Igor Paul, a retired engineering professor at Massachusetts Institute of Technology and an expert in biomechanics. Or, more precisely, about a series of animations he'd made purporting to show how Florence Unger could have fallen over the boathouse railing onto the cement apron and then rolled into the lake, without human intercession.

The prosecution had gotten copies of the animation in March. "This could really hurt us. This is really high-tech stuff," Pendergast had said then.

But the sequence couldn't hurt it if they kept it from getting admitted.

Pendergast wanted the judge to hold a *Daubert* hearing on whether the animations were admissible. The prosecution was close to resting, and the defense was scheduled the next Wednesday, when trial resumed after the long holiday weekend, to call engineer John Zarzecki and Wayne County Medical Examiner Carl Schmidt before calling

Paul. Pendergast wanted to hold the hearing before the defense began, while Harrison wanted it after his first two witnesses.

"How does it make a difference?" asked the judge.

"How it makes a difference is, whether or not Mr. Paul is going to be allowed to testify to certain things is going to affect how I cross-examine other witnesses, on many different factors," said Pendergast.

McGuire said there were logistical problems if they scheduled things the way Pendergast wanted. His first two witnesses could only get off work one day, and if Paul went first, they likely would be held over for a second day. And Paul was flying in Wednesday, which meant he wouldn't be able to get to Beulah till Thursday. There was no way to know, now, if he could get his ticket changed.

"My understanding was, we discussed this in your office," McGuire continued, "and I suggested that it would make more sense for everybody's benefit if there was a little predicate testimony laid first, then it would be easier to make judgments about Dr. Paul's testimony, and it was my understanding that was what was agreed to."

"It was not agreed to," said Pendergast forcefully.

"I just don't believe that—and I say this respectfully—there's no way it would change how she would cross-examine those people," said Harrison, disrespectfully. "And we did mention doing this in chambers with you. I thought everyone agreed . . ."

"Judge, first of all, it was never discussed," said Pendergast.

"What she's saying is just nonsense," said McGuire.

"Judge, I don't want to, once again, get into an arguing match," argued Pendergast. "I just consulted with Mr. Bilkovic on the off-chance that I'm in the early stages of Alzheimer's, and he remembers the same thing as me."

"Oh, come on. That is not true. Come on, Donna," said McGuire.

"Well, I don't remember it, Mr. Bilkovic doesn't remember it. But to require us to cross-examine two critical witnesses without knowing if this animation testimony is coming in . . ."

"Her paranoia is going beyond belief," said Harrison.

"We don't need the ad hominems about people's mental conditions. The attorneys are not on trial here," said the judge.

"She has no right to do this *Daubert* hearing when she wants to," said McGuire angrily. "There's no inherent right to do that. She's just asking for the moon here. I don't see why we can't do this in a way that we have settled on."

"Well, I thought we had settled it," said the judge. He said he, too, thought they'd agreed the *Daubert* hearing would come at the beginning of the defense case. He told McGuire and Harrison to try to get Paul in a day earlier just in case, but for now they should all plan on the defense starting with the two other witnesses, then putting Paul on.

If Pendergast needed to ask the first two follow-up questions based on Paul's testimony, they could always be summoned back for recross.

"Fair enough?" asked Batzer.

"Fair enough," said Pendergast.

A FINAL WITNESS FOR
THE PROSECUTION

After the jury entered the courtroom at 9:40 a.m. on Friday, May 26, Lieutenant Steven Rains took the stand. On November 21, 2003, he had been assigned to the Lansing headquarters, overseeing eight officers across the state who specialized in traffic-crash reconstruction.

He told the court of being asked to bring his equipment, primarily something called the Sokkia Total Station, a device surveyors, road crews and cops use to measure angles and distances, to the Watervale Inn to help prepare a scaled diagram of the entire area.

Rains told of walking out on the wood planking of the roof of the boathouse, and said the roof was sound, that he didn't see any moss or vegetation, and that the surface wasn't slippery.

He and State Police Trooper Jerry Hillborn conducted a loadcell test on a section of railing to see how much weight it could stand if someone leaned against it.

"We reached one hundred and ninety-eight pounds, which was about one and a half times the weight of the individual," he said, referring to Florence. "Based on that, we said that's far enough."

Rains said he then conducted another test on the rail,

what he described as a layman's test, conducted without equipment or measuring tools.

"What I did was—and I weighed about one hundred and eighty-five pounds at the time—I walked up to it, got in a comfortable position, and aggressively went at it and kicked it, struck it with my left foot, right in the same area that we had applied a steady force," he said. "It actually popped the nails out."

McGuire did the cross. "You did these tests that Mr. Bilkovic has referred to on that afternoon that you were there in November? At the end of all that, tell us what your opinions were," he said.

Bilkovic interrupted, arguing, oddly enough, that Rains, who only moments earlier had been his expert witness, was now just a lay person, knowing where McGuire was heading. "Judge, I'm not placing an objection. I just want to make this clear that obviously this is a lay opinion that you're offering at this time," he said.

"I would like to know what your opinions were that you put in your report," said McGuire.

"As long as this is being accepted as a lay opinion, I have no objection," said Bilkovic.

"Would you like me to just read it from my report?" asked Rains.

"Judge, I don't think it's proper to have him read his report," interrupted Bilkovic, again. "I think he can ask him what . . ."

"I'll be happy to do that. That's fine with me," said Mc-Guire. "I believe that one of the things that you felt was that the height of the rail was such that it was an inviting place to sit down onto, is that fair? You noted that that was a comfortable height that allows for individuals to back up and rest against the railing rather than support themselves by placing their hands on the railing. This is what people would do, or tend to do, given the height of the rail?"

"Yes."

"And it was also your opinion that this body position that we've just talked about was the most plausible, given the testing done—that for some reason Mrs. Unger lost her balance, and in an effort to recover, grabbed the rail. She continued to fall backwards over the rail, with most of her body acting as a rotational lever against the top rail, resulting in the damage to the support posts and her subsequent loss of grip. That was your opinion?"

"That was my third scenario, that that might be something that could have happened."

Someone had snapped a photo of Rains and Hillborn at the railing, with Rains sitting down as he imagined Florence Unger might have done, and McGuire had it entered into evidence.

"I would call that an accident, wouldn't you?" asked McGuire.

"I would not call it an accident. I don't formulate an opinion as to whether it was an accident or whether it was purposely done," said Rains.

Tesha Lee Hankes, a hairdresser for seventeen years at the Palazzolo Salon in Royal Oak, took the stand. She said she'd styled Florence's hair for ten years, almost on a weekly basis, and even Saturdays when she wasn't having anything done, Flo'd stop in to say hi. Hankes had also cut the boys' hair, since Tyler was born and Max was two.

She'd invited Flo to a couple of parties over the years, the most recent a sterling-silver jewelry party the month before she died. Flo had confided in her, telling her about her marriage and impending divorce.

She said that on the night of October 24, 2003, she was at a pumpkin-carving party and a mutual friend of hers and Flo's had called her to tell her she'd heard Flo had died.

The next morning, Tesha drove to the salon to find Flo's cell phone number and give her a call. "I didn't believe that she was dead. It wasn't on the news," she told the court.

She called Flo's phone. Mark answered.

"I said, 'Is Flo there?' He said, 'Who is this?' I identified myself as Tesha. He immediately started crying. I said, 'So, it's true?' He cried harder. I said, 'What the hell happened, Mark?' He started to calm down. 'Well, we were on the deck together, everything was good, everything was fine. I went up to the house to check on the boys. I came back down, Flo was still there, she was fine, so I just went back up to the house.'

"I said, 'Well, what happened?' He goes, 'She must have tripped or fallen.'"

"He told you he went back to check on the boys, and he returned back to the deck and Florence Unger was still there and she was fine?" asked Bilkovic.

"Yes."

Harrison did the cross. "You didn't consider him to be a friend of yours?" he asked, of Mark.

"No, sir."

"Did you tell police that you felt Mark was a habitual liar?"

"Yes."

"And did you tell police that in your opinion, you think Mark's first instinct would be to cover it up?"

"Yes."

"And did you also indicate at your prior testimony that you hardly ever talked to Mark?"

"That is correct."

"Okay. So, he wasn't a client, he wasn't your friend, you hardly ever talked to him, but you decided that he was a habitual liar, and that his first instinct would be to cover it up?"

"Yes, sir."

"Let's talk about what you said he said. The prosecution is making a big deal out of the fact that you claim that Mark told you that he came down to the deck a second time, and that Flo was there and fine and he left, okay?"

"Yes."

"Did they tell you that a whole bunch of people have come in here and testified and not one of them has ever said that Mark said that she was back on the deck a second time?"

"No, sir."

"Did they tell you that's going to be a great way of trying to argue that Mark's story was somehow inconsistent?"

"No, sir."

On re-direct, Bilkovic asked Hankes, "Now, you had some conversations with some other people immediately after you talked to Mr. Unger, didn't you?"

"Yes, I did."

"And during those conversations, did you tell the people the version that Mark Unger gave you that you told this jury today?"

"Yes."

He asked her with whom. With Jimmy Palazzolo, her boss. Her sister. Lori Karbel, who was the one who had told her Flo had died—told her at the Sunday flea market in Royal Oak, and Kate Ostrove, who was at the market, too. And Joanne Pintar, who owned a decorating store called Home, where Flo hung her photographs for sale. She'd told them all on Sunday, right after she got off the phone with Mark.

"It wasn't until George Cantor wrote the article in *The Detroit News* that I realized that his official story did not match the story that he had told me," she said.

There was one more prosecution witness, Detective Sergeant Walter Armstrong of the Michigan State Police, assigned to Manistee, a port town on Lake Michigan, south of Frankfort.

Armstrong told of his first involvement in the case, helping out at Watervale the day Rains and Hillborn conducted their load tests on the boathouse railing. He went back to Watervale on October 27, 2004, during the preliminary exam, to make a video "that might give an idea of what could be seen walking down the roadway, the old roadbed in front of the Watervale Inn cottages, back on October 25 of 2003," he said, referring to the path Linn Duncan and Mark Unger had used going back and forth to the boathouse.

The request to make a video came from Bilkovic, who

got the idea when the preliminary exam had taken a bad turn for the prosecution in October 2004 when District Judge Danielson had ruled out Dragovic's testimony during a *Daubert* hearing.

Armstrong showed up at the scene in a business suit and Bilkovic was in khakis, so the prosecutor was the one who rolled up his pantlegs and waded into the lake to help set the scene. Armstrong had taken a first-aid CPR training dummy, called a Resusci Anne, to the scene, and before he began filming, Bilkovic placed "Anne" in the water, angled the way Florence had been when she was found, and secured her in place with two stakes pounded into the shoreline.

Armstong told the court he'd taken his camera and walked back up the path to just west of the Mary Ellen before turning around and, while filming, retracing his steps to the boathouse, up the boathouse steps and across to the edge of the roof, where he could see the concrete apron below and Anne bobbing in the waves.

The video was then played for the jury. It and his accompanying narration took six minutes.

Pendergast thanked him. What was important was not what was seen, but what wasn't. As Armstrong had walked down the old railroad bed toward Anne, nothing was visible of her until he was almost on top of her, on the boathouse deck. How would you know to run straight to her unless you already knew where she was?

At 2:59, Pendergast announced: "The People at this point would rest."

The jury was released at 3:02 and told by the judge to enjoy their holiday and be back on Wednesday, May 31, at 9:15 a.m.

WEEK SIX
A MOTION TO ACQUIT

The jury entered the court at 9:40 a.m. on Wednesday, May 31, only to be told by Judge Batzer that he had a funeral to go to and they were being dismissed until 1:30 p.m.

After the jury left, Harrison made a motion he'd worked on much of the holiday weekend. "I would like to argue a motion for directed verdict," he said.

"Certainly," said Batzer.

"Your Honor, I'm not going to belabor this record for a number of reasons, the most important of which is that I know how on top of the evidence you are, and have been. I know that you understand it extremely well, and I don't need to instruct you on what has been testified, and I mean that in a sincere way," he began.

"As I think we all know, when ruling on a motion for directed verdict, you, as the trial judge, must view the evidence and consider the evidence presented by the prosecution, up to the point in time when this motion is made, and that view of the evidence must be in a light most favorable to the prosecution.

"In our view, the prosecution has failed in its burden . . . The prosecution relies very heavily on the testimony of Dr. Dragovic. And if there is any evidence that we have heard in this case, or any case, it is probably as equivocal and subject to a variety of interpretations like no other."

A sentence like the last one showed that while he might be a fine lawyer, he wasn't a wordsmith, as was made even clearer by the next sentence, of 109 words and numerous clauses and commas.

"Now, I understand that is not a tradition, but it is not uncommon that any kind of differing testimony is frequently said to present a question of fact, and therefore, taking one interpretation because you must take the evidence in the light most favorable to the prosecution means that you are required, some judges say, to take that interpretation, leave the opposite interpretations or other testimony even from the same witness, and set it aside and say that there is sufficient evidence for a rational trier of fact seizing upon that morsel, and saying, okay, we have met the burden for purposes of a motion for a directed verdict," he said.

"Everyone who has ever viewed this evidence, from the district judge on up, I believe, and I certainly don't mean to speak for you, but everyone has remarked, in their own way of saying it, that if you look at this evidence, and you look at it from one perspective, or one point of view, it is strongly suggestive of involvement in the death of Florence Unger," he said, raising a huh?-what'd-he-say? response from those in attendance.

"On the other hand, if you were to look at this evidence, and your perspective or your point of view, or where you are coming from, wasn't to accuse Mark Unger of a crime, these circumstances point to nothing whatsoever in terms of criminal responsibility or culpability. That kind of evidence is not the kind of evidence that is sufficient to take a case, a murder case, any kind of murder case.

"The bottom line is that if the prosecution's linchpin is that Mr. Unger placed her in the water in order to conceal a crime, which of course is what we have heard, it is not only illogical, but it defies common sense. Because as both Cohle and Dragovic have testified, that's the reason that they made the call that this was a homicide, in Cohle's view, to the point of fifty-one percent assurance in his mind, barely enough to get it over the hump. It would defy common sense for the prosecution to say, 'That's the linchpin of our case, that he put her body in the water—how he did it, we, of course, still don't know.' And that, in fact, it is nonsensical, because if he put her body in the water, and that is what tips it to homicide, why would he do that and tip it off, and tip it off onto himself?"

If one could penetrate that paragraph, it tied its logic in a circle. You'd have to be stupid to think dragging a body into the water would cover up the crime, since the body in the water is what made people think it was a crime, and Mark Unger isn't stupid, therefore he wouldn't have done it, and no crime was committed.

Pendergast responded at length. Harrison responded. She responded. He responded. It was all for nothing. Any potential drama had all been sucked out by Harrison's first salvo. No one who heard it doubted where it had gone. Nowhere. Batzer denied the motion and left for the funeral.

TO THE DEFENSE

Court reconvened at 1:55, with McGuire calling John Zar-zecki to the stand. Zarzecki was the engineer who had been hired by Dave Ruby to assess the boathouse and the integrity of its roof and railing.

Zarzecki said he and Ruby had been told to stay off the deck until the others were done with their work, and then weren't allowed to conduct any tests other than pushing and pulling at the railing and support posts.

The first three posts they pushed were solid. The fourth, in the middle of the front of the deck, had a lot of give. "Five or six inches by hand pressure, just back and forth quite easily," he told the court.

"And if you put a lot of pressure into it, what would happen?" asked McGuire.

"I imagine it would have probably broken off."

Zarzecki said he'd seen large icicles hanging down, later measured between twenty-four and thirty-six inches long, a sure sign, he said, of an ice dam.

"It's when the slope of the roof and the amount of run-off is not sufficient to get the water off the roof before it refreezes," he said. "It does a lot of damage to the structure underneath, gets it saturated with water, basically causing mold and decay to start in the spring."

On April 2, 2004, Zarzecki had gone back to Watervale without Ruby to inspect the deck more closely.

The Exponent crew was there and after everyone had gathered on the deck, the Exponent folks had told him to wait for them to finish their work before he did any of his own.

Though it had been early in the season, the deck was slippery with algae, Zarzecki told the court. "It was greasy, as we would call it. If you walked with a leather-bottom shoe, you would be slipping on it."

The Exponent team had gone to work with a chain saw, cutting the railing into pieces. Zarzecki said their work revealed appalling craftsmanship.

"They would cut the horizontal rail members and simply pick the [vertical] post up. It wasn't even really a post. It had only been sitting on top of the deck. It didn't even penetrate all the way through," he said.

When Exponent was done, he said, he'd gone to the number four post, the site of the ice damming in February, reached down and with his bare hands was able to rip off the wood at the edge of the deck. "There was mold growth and decay on all that wood underneath that deck. And some moss growing on the vertical surfaces," he said.

Photos that he took that day were entered into evidence, showing damage and decay in various of the vertical posts. "This kind of damage can't occur over a three- or four-month period. It takes years for it to occur," he said.

McGuire asked about the railing's height, twenty-six to twenty-seven inches. "The building codes in the state of Michigan for the last twenty years have required a thirty-six-inch height," he said.

"If someone leaned against this railing, would it prevent them from falling over?" McGuire asked.

"It would not. Your center of gravity is off. And the railing did not have the capacity to hold the amount of weight required. The entire railing along the lakeside was completely rotted."

He said he'd gathered bits of wood left behind by the Exponent crew, which were admitted into evidence.

"You can see that the wood is completely disintegrating. There's nothing left of it. It doesn't take any effort to break it apart into little crumbs," he said. "You can simply grab the wood and it turns to powder."

Bilkovic handled the cross-examination, but wasn't able to undo the damage. A string of prosecution witnesses, most of them police officers or lab technicians, had repeatedly said they hadn't seen any moss, or sign of algae, hadn't noticed anything slippery or dangerous about the deck.

Zarzecki convincingly painted a far different picture of a deck in the late stages of decay, rotten, algae and mold feasting. And he'd had the post segments and photos to prove it.

LOSING THE BATTLE

Dave Ruby began things on Thursday. He buttressed everything Zarzecki had said. "In the condition that timber was, it was an accident waiting to happen," he said.

At 10:38, Dr. Carl Schmidt, potentially a pivotal witness in the case, took the stand. He was the chief medical examiner in Wayne County, training ground for some of the most colorful MEs in the country, including Dragovic and Werner Spitz, a frequent expert witness who saw his free-lance work decline after he told a reporter for a magazine profile that he'd dance naked on a table for cash.

Schmidt had been a forensic pathologist for twenty-one years. He was raised in Mexico and got his medical degree from Universidad Anáhuac in Mexico City in 1981.

After a stint at general surgery in Pennsylvania, Schmidt served a residency in anatomic and clinical pathology in Ohio and in 1985 was hired as assistant medical examiner in Wayne County.

In 1989 he took a concurrent post as chief ME of Monroe County, just to the south of Wayne County, and in 1993 was named chief ME in Wayne County, as well.

Schmidt had served in Guatemala, Nicaragua, Colombia, El Salvador and Honduras as a consultant for the U.S. State Department in a program teaching forensic science and death investigation techniques to law-enforcement and medical practitioners.

He wasted no time disputing the conclusions of his predecessor in Wayne County.

To say Schmidt had a rocky history with Dragovic would be putting it mildly. Schmidt thought him egotistical, deceitful and self-serving. Earlier in the year, they had been on opposite sides of a case in Wayne County, with Dragovic testifying on behalf of the defendant, Timothy Roy Null, who had been charged with the strangulation death of his girlfriend, Alicia Gyomory, a case McGuire had referred to earlier, when unsuccessfully trying to get a letter Dragovic had written admitted into evidence.

The prosecution claimed Gyomory was in the process of committing suicide, having ingested a deadly dose of prescription drugs, when her boyfriend entered the house and, in a rage, strangled her.

Dragovic testified that she'd died of the overdose. Schmidt said that severe bruising on her neck and burst blood vessels in her eyes proved she'd been murdered.

On January 18, 2006, on Oakland County letterhead, Dragovic both faxed and mailed a letter to Null's attorneys and sent copies to the Michigan Office of the Attorney General and the Wayne County prosecutor, Kym Worthy.

The letter read, in part:

It is obvious that Alicia Marie Gyomory died of a self-inflicted overdose of Bupropion [Wellbutrin] . . . In consideration of these findings and the circumstances surrounding this death, the manner of death should have been appropriately classified as suicide.

The grave confusion in this matter is largely the result of an inadequate death investigation, an erroneous interpretation of the pre-mortem and post-mortem physical findings and a lack of professional responsibility and common sense. The facts in evidence have been minimized in favor of a theory that is completely devoid of substantiation by physical evidence.

Dragovic testified to that effect in the subsequent trial. The jury believed Schmidt, and Null was sentenced to life without parole.

Dragovic wasn't content to leave it there. He forwarded the letter, or claimed to, to the National Association of Medical Examiners and the American Academy of Forensic Sciences.

Dragovic could, it seemed, hold a grudge. Years earlier, a security guard at a suburban Detroit shopping mall was charged in the choking death of a shoplifter who had been apprehended in the parking lot. It was, said Schmidt, homicide, perhaps justified, perhaps not.

Without examining the body, Dragovic came to a different conclusion and testified for the defense. The autopsy showed that the alleged victim had suffered from heart disease, and Dragovic said it was the heart disease that had killed him, not strangulation.

The prosecution won the case, and Schmidt wrote a scathing letter about Dragovic's work for the defense that was published in *The Detroit News*.

Schmidt, busy enough on his day job, rarely testifies apart from his duties with Wayne County, once or twice a year. He oversees eight pathologists, three shifts of investigators and a staff of fifty. The department is called out on some 12,000 deaths a year, bringing about 2,400 bodies back for autopsies.

Schmidt agreed to review the file on the Unger case as a favor to McGuire, whom he'd gotten to know years earlier and had developed a close friendship with. Schmidt says they see eye to eye on politics (Democratic), issues of the day and literature. "We both read the same magazines— *The New Yorker, New Republic, New York Review of Books, Atlantic Monthly,* all the left-wing pinko magazines," he jokes.

Schmidt has a reputation for coming to trial prepared, unlike Dragovic's for sometimes winging it. He had worked with Pendergast before and knew she'd expect him to come ready.

"My initial impression was that she died from her head injury . . . that even though she'd been found in the water, the major injuries, especially the head injury, were sufficient to explain her death," Schmidt testified.

"Did you know that Dr. Dragovic has opined here that she didn't die from head injury, she died from drowning?"

"Yes."

"Do you disagree with that?"

"I do."

(Schmidt had reviewed transcripts of Dragovic's testimony. Decorum required a degree of civility in court. Outside the courtroom, after the trial, Schmidt savaged Dragovic's testimony. "Where he said she had to have drowned because her brain had not swollen enough to account for her death was unmitigated bullshit. There are a number of textbook citations where there is minimal swelling of the brain, and death occurred. When I think of him testifying that her brain hadn't swollen enough, my temperature rises. He's a brilliant man who has a razor-sharp wit. Instead of spending time coming up with these tortuous arguments he thinks bolster his image, he'd be more productive if he'd just do forensic science.")

"Now, he has said that having heavy lungs, waterlogged lungs, pulmonary edema is evidence of drowning," McGuire continued. "Is that true?"

"No. That's not true."

"Why not?"

"Because heavy lungs can appear for a number of reasons," he said, explaining that severe head injury often leads to a leaking of fluids that fills the lungs.

"When a pathologist tries to make a diagnosis of drowning in a person that's deceased, it's necessary to first exclude all other potential causes of death. That's the standard operating procedure among pathologists, is that fair?" asked McGuire.

"That's correct."

"And in this case, are you able to exclude traumatic brain injury as a cause of death?"

"No."

"You would agree with Dr. Cohle in that regard?"

"Yes."

"The cause of death in this case is what?"

"Blunt trauma to the head."

McGuire asked Schmidt if he'd made an assessment of the manner of death.

"In this case, I would have classified it as indeterminate."

"Why?"

"Because there is not enough information to assess whether this woman actually fell or if she was pushed."

"Dr. Dragovic, I'd like to ask you some questions about . . ." McGuire began, catching himself. "What did I say?"

"Dragovic," offered Skrzynski.

"Oh, my God! I better take a break here. I need to be punished," said McGuire, eliciting snickers in the courtroom. "Holy moly. Dr. Schmidt, I've lost my train of thought."

McGuire started to put a photo up on the projector. "This is a particularly brutal picture, and there may be people who don't want to see this, so I have to warn people about that," he said.

It was the right side of Florence Unger's head, where it had impacted the cement. It had been shaved.

"If you look at that photograph, does it give you an opportunity to make a judgment about whether there was any drag marks on her face anywhere?"

"There are no drag marks on her face anywhere."

"Is there any evidence her face was dragged in any fashion?"

"No."

"If this person's face was dragged, and she was a limp body, would you likely expect to find evidence of dragging on the cheek bone, as well?"

"Correct."

McGuire asked him about Florence's fractured hip.

"There was testimony in this case that Ms. Unger's hip could have been fractured had she been thrown against the railing. Do you think it's possible to fracture a hip if someone is thrown against a railing like that?"

"No."

"Why not?"

"Because hip fractures are really hard to cause. The hip is actually a fairly massive bone. It's difficult to fracture a hip, especially in a younger person like her, in whom the bones still have a relatively high water content."

"Let me ask you about the question of seizures," said McGuire. "Is it possible that Ms. Unger had a seizure once she laid on the concrete?"

"That's possible."

"What can you tell us about traumatic brain injury seizures?"

"Well, I think it's well described that you can have seizures after trauma. They can happen moments after trauma."

"If Florence Unger had fallen from the deck and landed on the concrete, and she was laying somewhere near the edge, is it possible that she could put herself into the water as a result of movements occurring during a seizure?"

"Sure. That's possible."

McGuire was done. The direct had gone very well. Schmidt had come off as credible, calm and reasoned.

Skrzynski got Schmidt to admit he was not a neuropathologist and that the pathology of a nervous system having suffered severe trauma was not his specialty.

"Mr. McGuire asked you at one point if heavy lungs were evidence of drowning, and you said no. Isn't that what you testified to?" asked Skrzynski.

"No. What I said was, in the context of head injury, it's likely due to the head injury."

"You didn't mean to say that fluid in the lungs is not evidence of drowning, correct?"

"Correct."

"And the fact that this woman was found face down in a body of water, that can also be evidence of drowning, correct?"

"Sure."

"As a matter of fact, Doctor, you cannot rule out the fact that this woman may have drowned, can you?"

"Not completely."

"Okay. So, she may have drowned?"

"I think a better way to state that is that she died from her head trauma because it was pretty severe. But that there may be a component of drowning."

"Now, isn't that like there may be a component of pregnancy in a pregnant woman? If mean, if you're lying in a body of water, face down in the water, trying to breathe, and you suck in water instead of air, is that drowning?"

"You don't know if she sucked in water. In fact, there is no reason to think that she did," said Schmidt.

"Well, Doctor, her lungs are heavy, are they not?"

"Right."

"Do you know what the weights of her lungs were?"

"I think they were about six hundred grams each. But I can look it up."

"Wasn't the right lung about eight hundred and eighty grams?"

"That's right."

"And normal being about three hundred?"

"Three fifty."

"Okay. And the left lung was about six hundred and seventy grams?"

"Right."

"And normal is about two hundred and fifty?"

"Right."

"That's two and a half and three times heavier than normal. You would agree with that?"

"I agree."

"So, there's considerable edema in the lungs, correct?"

"Correct."

"Now, you said you thought that maybe this fluid in her lungs was a result of what you called neurogenic pulmonary edema, right?"

"Correct."

"What would be the mechanism of that?"

"No one knows. There are a variety of mechanisms that have been postulated to try to explain a neurogenic pulmonary edema. But it's been well described in association with either brain injury or seizures."

"Now, Doctor, is it safe to say that you believe that she died immediately upon impact?"

"Or very shortly thereafter, yes."

"Now, Doctor, you said, by your slides here, that there was blood in the lungs, right?"

"Correct."

"And that was an indication she had inhaled blood, right?"

"Correct."

"All right. One of the lungs—I believe it was the left lung—ten percent of the volume of the left lung was blood, right?"

"That's what the autopsy report says."

"And two percent of the volume of the right lung is blood, too?"

"Correct."

"Now, Doctor, I mean, are you saying that she took one gigantic inhalation of blood which filled the lungs to that capacity and died?"

"That's possible," said Schmidt.

"That this was done in one inhalation of blood?" asked Skrzynski.

"If you're in an agonal state, you can have a very deep inhalation, or even a couple of them."

"An agonal state? What does that mean, Doctor?"

"It means that as you're dying, in other words, as the final terminal effects of your injuries are exerting their effects on your body, you can take a deep breath."

"In addition to that, in addition to being able to fill ten percent of her one lung with blood and two percent with the other, not only that, but there would have had to have been enough blood blowing out of her initially to cause the bloodstain that was on the concrete, is that right?"

"Sure."

"Now, since you said this was indeterminate, that means not only did she die instantly, not only did the lungs fill instantly, not only did the stain occur instantly, not only did the fluid occur instantly, but she also go into the water instantly, right?"

"No, she fell into the water, well, as part of the same falling event."

"That's right. Instantly, right?"

"Whatever time it took, yes," said Schmidt.

"All right. Doctor, we hear testimony from Dr. Zink that it would in fact have been highly unlikely that Mrs. Unger suffered a seizure following this . . . Do you have any kind of evidence that would contradict that testimony from Dr. Zink?"

"There is literature that says you can suffer seizures immediately after a severe head injury. I think it would be, off the top of my head I think the number is something like ten percent."

"What's the literature you're talking about?"

"Well, I have some literature right here, a review of posttraumatic seizure disorders that talks about post-concussive seizures."

"You're talking about severely injured, traumatic brain-injured patients who are comatose?"

"I think it talks in general about all kinds of head injury, it doesn't make a distinction between comatose and non-comatose patients."

"So, you really have nothing to overthrow Dr. Zink's testimony that, based on his own experience with three or four hundred patients, that it doesn't happen?"

"But I have literature that says it does."

"Doctor, when she hit the cement, she would have had to have expelled the blood that ended up on the cement, is that correct?"

"Yes."

"And then she rolled away from that into the water. Can you explain, Doctor, how it came to be that when Linn Duncan the next morning found the comforter, that it was on top of the blood, which she would have had to expel on the cement. How did the blanket get on top of the blood?"

"I don't know."

"You don't have any explanation for that?"

"No one has offered one."

"Well, I'm asking you to offer one for the scenario for hitting and rolling into the water immediately on her own."

"I don't have one."

Skrzynski was done. It was a strong cross.

It was McGuire's turn at repair.

"Let me ask you a question this way: If Dr. Cohle told you in a conversation that, 'Well, I've come to the opinion that this was a homicide, but I got there only by a preponderance of the evidence,' what would that mean to you?" he asked.

"Well, I would take it to mean that you're not completely sure."

"What degree of certitude do you have when you issue an opinion like that?"

"Normally, you have a great deal of certitude. Sometimes the body has the information you need, and sometimes it doesn't. Sometimes you don't have all the information you want. And that's why, in this case, I would have certified this as indeterminate."

"You were asked some questions about how quickly the pulmonary edema can occur when it has a neurogenic origin, when it's caused by brain injury."

"Right."

"Are you aware of any studies that have been done that relate to injuries to Vietnam soldiers, concerning that phenomenon in relation to head injuries?"

"Yes."

"Can you tell us what it said?"

"It said that you could get neurogenic pulmonary edema even in individuals who die practically instantaneously."

"Relating to this particular case, if, upon impact, that process began immediately, or almost immediately after the impact, and yet Mrs. Unger rolled into the water, and let's say she wasn't immediately dead, she survived in the water for a few seconds, for a brief period of time, would that process continue until her death actually occurred?"

"Yes, because the heart doesn't stop beating. Although death is very quick, almost instantaneous, the fact is that with head injury, your heart does continue beating for a short time, until the rest of your body starts decompensating."

"Do you consider yourself as having expertise in this subject of brain injuries?"

"I think by definition all forensic pathologists have expertise in injuries to the brain."

"If you took a quick mental survey of all the souls that passed in front of you in the course of a month, what proportion of those people would have come to you as a result of a brain injury?"

"At least twenty to thirty percent."

Schmidt was excused at 4:11, and the jury was excused for the day. Schmidt's testimony had contradicted Dragovic's. Had it raised enough doubt to rise to the legal standard of reasonable?

AN ANIMATED HEARING

The jury was done, but the other participants were not. It was time for the crucial *Daubert* hearing that had been discussed at length the week before about the admissibility of Dr. Igor Paul's animations . . .

Paul took the stand at 4:22 and told the court he lived in New Hampshire and had retired in 2003 after thirty-nine years in the mechanical engineering department at the Massachusetts Institute of Technology, where he'd taught undergraduate and graduate courses in mechanical engineering and product design, and done research in bioengineering and biomechanics.

He was, he said, an expert in the application of forces and the law of physics on the human body, in particular what forces and motions cause what kinds of injuries, and the biomechanics of breaking bones and of head trauma.

Paul said he had served as a consultant to the Children's Hospital in Boston, the Mass General Hospital for Children and Harvard Medical School.

He had testified as an expert witness at least one hundred times in forty years and had published more than eighty papers in peer-reviewed journals.

Paul said he'd gotten involved in June 2004 when the defense asked him to determine what scenarios could have led to Flo's fall, the blood on the cement and her final resting place in the water *without* the intercession of a third person.

Paul said that by applying the laws of physics, it wasn't difficult. From that height, he said, her body would have hit the ground with 1,800 foot pounds of force. Some of that energy would have been absorbed by her injuries, 200 foot pounds or so for the head injuries, 100 to 150 foot pounds for her fractured pelvis, another 100 pounds by soft tissue damage.

"The rest of that energy goes into the motion of the body. If you take those energies and subtract them out, there is more than twice the available energy for the body to roll directly into the water," he said.

Pendergast must have been wondering what the jury would think, hearing what she was hearing. If this didn't seem to amount to reasonable doubt, what would?

Paul said he could account for the blood where it was, too, having worked out calculations on the amount of pressure that would have built up in the nasal membranes and ears upon impact, pressure so high it would have required the immediate release of fluid from the nose, mouth and ears.

He said that after making his calculations, he came up with five separate scenarios involving falls over various spots on the railing where Florence could have ended up in the water.

Paul said he made rough sketches, then hired an artist in Sutton, Massachusetts, Joel Howe of FrameWork Media, Inc., to make computer-animations of each scenario, thirty frames a second showing a trajectory, a landing and a roll into the water. (The company is so proud of its animation in the case that it brags about it on its Web site and shows a cartoon animation of a body falling to the ground and tumbling into water.)

Pendergast went quickly on the attack. "Dr. Paul, is it fair to say that over the course of your career, you've done a great deal of testifying?"

"Yes."

"And, in fact, you have somewhat of a reputation for being a person who comes into a case at the last minute, isn't that fair?"

"No."

"Well . . ."

"Just the opposite."

"Let's start with *Johnson* versus *Webster Incorporated*. Do you remember that case?" No one ever accused Pendergast of being underprepared.

"No."

"Contacted as an expert one week before trial and your testimony was excluded. Do you remember that?"

"No. I don't think my testimony was ever excluded."

"Well, what about *Baker Valley Lumber* versus *Ingersoll Rand*? Do you recall that case?"

"Yes."

"And, in fact, in that case the court found that your theory of the case was insufficient to meet the scientific standards of *Daubert*. Do you recall that?"

"I do recall it."

"Do you recall a case of *Olson* versus *Bell Helmets*?"

"Yes."

"Testimony excluded there?"

"I was not allowed to testify on the medical aspects. I was allowed on the biomechanical aspects."

"But the re-creation was found to be inadmissible, is that correct?"

"No. That's not correct."

"Would you like to see a copy of the summary of the opinion?

"How many cases have you testified in—I couldn't find any on Lexis—where you were testifying to the free fall of a body in a criminal case?" she asked.

"I've only testified in two criminal cases, so if it's a question of criminal cases, no."

"How many cases have you testified in total as to the mechanics of a body in a fall?"

"About six. The last one was a deposition given where a

girl was killed accidentally falling over a low railing. While she was kissing her boyfriend."

"When did you first go to the crime scene?" she asked.

"I never went to the crime scene."

"You've never been there to this date?"

"That's right."

"That includes this date," said McGuire sarcastically, referring to the redundancy of the last three words of Pendergast's sentence.

"Thank you for the clarification, Mr. McGuire," she said.

This had long ago become personal for them.

At 6:16 p.m., Pendergast said she needed about fifteen minutes more before turning things back over to McGuire.

"Save it for another day," said the judge.

Paul had an 11:30 flight out of Traverse City the next morning, so there would be no time in the morning to wrap up the hearing. Paul said he could be back the following Wednesday.

At 6:19, court was recessed, with potentially the largest issue in the trial left unresolved. Would the jury see his animations, showing a body falling, hitting concrete and rolling into the lake, no one else in sight?

NOT IN THEIR POOL

Court reconvened at 10:30 a.m. Friday, starting late because Harrison and Pendergast had talked earlier in the morning to Max Unger in preparation for his scheduled appearance. There was, though, a change in plan.

"My client, Mark Unger, out of concern for his son's emotional well-being, has directed and instructed me not to call him," said Harrison.

"Is that correct, Mr. Unger?" asked the judge.

"That's correct."

And so, Marci Zussman was called to the stand, instead.

Mark was her first cousin on her father's side. She had met Florence Unger at a holiday dinner at her parents' house fourteen years earlier, when Mark brought her and introduced her as his future wife.

She and Flo became fast friends, seeing each other almost daily and talking on the phone daily without fail. They went antiquing around Southeast Michigan. Most Sundays they prowled the Royal Oak antique and flea markets for treasures.

They had their manicures together, their kids played together, their families took vacations together, including one at Watervale in 2002.

Harrison asked her if she was familiar with the boat-house.

"The boathouse deck and the area around it is the gath-ering place," she said. "It's like the central focus of the re-sort. Families would all gather on the deck and visit, and the kids would play on the grass behind the boathouse, or along the water."

"Did Florence Unger ever go out on the boathouse deck at night when it was dark?"

"Yes."

"How do you know that?"

"Because we would agree to meet there after the kids were asleep, or after I put my kids to sleep, since I was there with no spouse."

"Had you ever known her to be there alone on the deck at night in the dark without anyone there?"

"Absolutely. She would tell me, 'I was out there last night looking at the stars, thinking about things.'"

"Did you ever go out to the deck and she was already there?"

"Yes. Waiting for me."

"Were you aware of Florence having any kind of sig-nificant fear of the dark?"

"No, I wasn't."

Zussman told Harrison she had heard rumors some-thing was going on between Flo and Glenn Stark, and once asked her pointblank if she were having an affair with him.

"I can remember standing in the kitchen, and she looked at me and said, 'No.'"

Harrison asked her about Florence's shopping habits.

"That was Flo's thing, shopping. If she was mad at Mark, she would go shopping. Kind of like an addiction, in a way. It was something that she was into. She was very knowledgeable about antiques."

It had been brought up earlier that Florence and her fa-ther had been feuding before her death. Stern had denied any trouble, and Harrison asked her if she had been involved in a rift.

She told the court that in the summer of 2003, the recreation center told parents they could no longer bring outside teachers or coaches to give swimming lessons to their kids. Zussman wanted to keep her twins' coach.

"So, I asked Flo if she thought we could use her parents' pool, you know, a half hour twice a week, to bring the teacher and the twins to learn to swim."

"Were you permitted to bring your children to the Sterns' house?" asked Harrison.

"No, I wasn't."

"And did Florence Unger tell you anything in terms of how she felt about that?"

"She was appalled and shocked and hurt that her father would do that."

"And do you have any knowledge of whether or not they spoke for a long period of time after that?"

"To my knowledge, they did not speak hardly at all after this pool incident."

Harrison finished by asking her if she knew about a trip the Ungers were planning over Christmas of 2003—she did, to his mother's place—and if Florence had ever indicated a change of mind about the divorce.

"Wendy and Jeff are two very good friends of mine who had two small children, and got divorced when their kids were like four and two. And a few years later, they got remarried, and they're still married today, and their kids are grown," said Zussman. "And Flo called it a Wendy and Jeff. Like she had to do this right now, but that possibly they would be able to get back together at some point and remarry."

Pendergast came out swinging. "Mrs. Zussman, you're telling this jury under oath that Florence Unger would sit on that deck in Watervale in the dark?" she asked, turning a question into a statement. "You know that Florence's fear of the dark is an issue in this trial, don't you?"

"Yes."

"Tell the members of the jury who Joan Frank is."

"Joan Frank is a friend of Flo's."

"And you're aware that Joan Frank has testified in this trial, is that right?"

"Yes."

"And in fact, you've bad-mouthed her around Huntington Woods in the Jewish community for testifying in this trial, didn't you?"

"No, I have not. She has bad-mouthed me all around town."

"Who have you discussed this case with since the case started?" asked Pendergast.

"My family and my closest friends."

"Who have you discussed Joan Frank's testimony with?"

"Nobody. My friends and I discussed what she said about Mark on that TV show. We discussed that. 'Did you see Joan Frank on the news? It was really sad what she said.'"

"Do you know Kate Ostrove?"

"Kate Ostrove, she hasn't talked to me since this happened. Kate Ostrove does not talk to me, because she has also bad-mouthed me."

"So, everybody bad-mouths you."

"I object," said Harrison. "I don't even think it's interesting about whether women are bad-mouthing each other. I don't think it has anything to do with this trial."

"She can cross-exam," said Batzer. "The objection is overruled."

"What is your relationship with Laurie Glass?"

"We were friends through Flo. We are mothers in the same school, our kids go to the same school. We are polite, but not friends."

"Why is that?"

"Because we are on different sides. The sides have been created by Flo's parents."

"That's my point. You would agree with me that you're related to the defendant?"

"Yes."

"And you, out of your own mouth, right now, have just said you're on the other side, is that correct?"

"That is how it has been developed since this happened."

"Isn't it in fact true that after Flo decided that she was going through with the divorce, you, basically, for lack of a better term, sided with Mark?"

"No. That's not true at all. Flo and I were closer. I mean, I was going through problems, marriage problems at the same time. And we were very bonded with our marriage problems."

On redirect, Harrison asked on question, "You said the sides were created by Flo's parents. What did you mean by that?"

"In our neighborhood, if you want to be able to see Max and Tyler, you cannot talk to anybody that has an Unger in their name. So, people that I've known my whole life, because they are permitted in the Stern circle of life, if they know that they talked to me or my family, the Sterns won't let them have access to the boys. So, nobody wants to be known for communicating with myself or my brother's family."

NO FEAR OF THE DARK

At 11:19, Lyle Wolberg, Mark's nephew, took the stand.

A successful money manager while still in his mid-30s, he had recently co-founded his own firm, Telemus Capital Partners, LLC, which had opened its doors the previous summer in the Detroit suburb of Southfield with $1.2 billion in assets, news that created big headlines in the local business community.

(In 2007, *Crain's Detroit Business* would name Wolberg to its list of the forty most influential business leaders in Southeast Michigan under the age of 40. His sister, Amy Butte, had been named to *Crain's New York Business* 40 Under 40 list in 2003 and was named by *The Wall Street Journal* as one of its 50 Women to Watch in 2004, when she was chief financial officer of the New York Stock Exchange. In 2006, she was named CFO of MF Global, the world largest futures and options brokerage.)

"Did you have any knowledge or awareness that Florence Unger had a fear of the dark?" asked Harrison.

"I was not aware of that," said Wolberg, who said that Florence frequently walked the five or six blocks to their house to visit and walked home in the dark, alone.

"The last time I saw her, a Wednesday night, she walked over and came to be with my newborn and hang out, and walked home by herself," he said. "I have twins that were three at the time, and we put them down, so it had to be after eight, and she stayed for a few hours." There was nothing so dramatic as a murmuring in the court, but it was testimony that snapped some observers to attention, strong unambiguous testimony that seemed to say that all the previous talk about Florence's phobia was overblown. Wolberg told of hearing about Flo's death that Saturday morning and calling Mark.

"He was just crying," said Wolberg. "It was just constant crying. And after about four or five minutes, I asked him was he okay? And what happened? And he just kept crying. My immediate concern was obviously for him, but also for Max and Tyler. And so I asked him where Max and Tyler were. And he just kept crying.

"I went back to a recent experience that I had, which was that my wife's father passed away, and it was so important for her to have family around her. I said, 'Mark, you've got to get the boys and you've got to come home.'"

"What did he say?"

"He said, 'Okay. Okay.'"

Wolberg told of the drive north. When they got to Watervale, they found Mark in the Duncans'. "I've never had a man, in my adult life, hug me or cry as much. It must have been ten minutes of him and I just holding and embracing, and tears from both of us," he said.

Bilkovic handled the cross and rattled off the names of the witnesses who'd said Florence was afraid of the dark.

"Are you in any way offering an opinion to this jury today as to whether or not you thought Florence Unger was afraid of the dark?" he asked.

"I never saw her express to me a fear of the dark."

"Do you have any reason or explanation why she would tell a complete stranger, on the last night of her life, that she was afraid of the dark?"

"I don't know."

Bilkovic asked him if his father, Jerry, a constant spectator at the trial, had kept him updated.

"I've asked him not to. I tried to say, 'Look, I don't want to know specifics.'"

"You and Mark Unger were very close, correct? And you still are?"

"Correct."

"You look up to him?"

"I do."

"Hope to be the type of father he is?"

"Yes."

"Hope to be the type of person he is?"

"I hope."

"After this incident happened, you ended up living in Mark Unger's house with him for a period of time, correct? While your house was being remodeled?"

"Correct."

"You consider your relationship with him to be as close as brothers, correct?"

"Correct."

The court had other business in the afternoon. At 12:07, the jury was excused and told to return on Wednesday, June 7.

WEEK SEVEN
SETTING THE TRAP

The *Daubert* hearing with Paul resumed Wednesday.

I got Paul to say the animations had cost about $10,000. Two of them showed Florence having what appeared to be seizures as she slid off the cement apron and into the water, and Pendergast asked him if that was the correct interpretation.

"Yes."

"Can you explain to the court, then, why in these two portrayals of types of seizures Florence Unger would have, you have her vibrating on the edge of that seawall or breakwall?"

"Actually, my initial animation was movement of the limbs without precursor of a tremor. And I think, after that, I had discussions with Mr. McGuire and we agreed that one should include, in terms of illustration, a tremor-like seizure, as well as a gross movement-of-the-limbs seizure."

"You didn't have deposition testimony from Dr. Zink, is that correct?"

"I did not."

"You didn't have the deposition testimony of Dr. McKeever, is that correct?"

"That's correct."

"You didn't have the deposition testimony of Dr. Dragovic or Dr. Cohle, is that correct?"

"That's correct."

"So then you, in turn, tell somebody who has no familiarity with this case, based on some representations to you by Mr. McGuire, how to portray the seizures in the video, is that your testimony?"

"Yes."

Pendergast was ready to spring a trap.

She marked what she said was a frame-by-frame slowdown of Paul's animations as People's Exhibit No. 267, and asked that it be entered into evidence. And that defense counsel stipulate to what it was.

McGuire refused. "You're going to have to verify it. I mean, you've got something that I don't know if it's the same or not, and I don't know if the witness is able to know."

"Then we'll go through it frame by frame, and this *Daubert* hearing will not be done today. It's a thousand frames," said Pendergast.

"That's up to the court whether we go through a thousand frames," said McGuire.

"The bottom line is, this is their animation slowed down frame by frame. We're certainly entitled to slow it down," said Pendergast.

"I agree," said the judge. "Go ahead."

Pendergast started asking Paul about his knowledge of seizures, but Batzer interrupted. Paul was not qualified, he said, to know whether animations two and four depicted seizures accurately. Absent a medical expert testifying to their authenticity, he would not allow the jury to see the portions of the animations that showed her seizing.

Harrison, McGuire and, speaking for the first time in the case, defense attorney Roger Wotila of the prominent northern Michigan law firm of McCurdy & Wotila P.C., argued vociferously that the judge was wrong. (Wotila was considered a star in the northern Michigan legal firmament.

He helped with jury selection but except for arguing two motions was on the sidelines during proceedings.)

Batzer was adamant.

Pendergast asked him to exclude all the animations, but he ruled the jury could see them. The defense hadn't lost much. They were still left with two complete, animated scenarios by an acknowledged expert in biomechanics that showed, backed by what he claimed were the laws of physics, how Florence could have ended up in the water without any help by Mark.

The jury was brought in at 12:03 p.m.

Harrison, McGuire and Wotila knew they had won a huge, potentially case-changing victory.

Pendergast had lost the battle. Or had she?

Paul repeated his credentials for the jury.

"You're not here to tell the jury in your opinion that there was or was not a criminal act?" asked McGuire.

"No."

"You're only saying that there are other means by which this whole event can be explained, besides the involvement of a second party?"

"Yes. There are various scenarios of her having accidentally gone over a long railing and wound up where she wound up, without any other person involved," he said.

Paul explained that the key to his scenarios was that the railing on the boathouse deck was nine to ten inches below the center of gravity for someone the height and weight of Florence Unger.

And he told how, based on where she'd landed, three feet out from what would have been a vertical fall, she must have had a modest movement toward the lake of three feet per second when she went over the rail.

He said that with her weight of 150 pounds falling a distance of twelve feet, a force of 1,800 foot pounds would have built up by the time she hit. Had she hit in a purely vertical fall, all 1,800 pounds would have been absorbed by her body, which would have produced far worse head injuries than she'd endured, which only required 200 to 250 pounds.

"The rest of the energy, some of it went into the fracture of her pelvis," he said. "Some of it went into just tissue deformation, without injury, contusions and such. The rest of the energy went into an energy of roll. She hit, and part of the energy was absorbed by her head and her pelvis, and then she rolled into the water."

"Maybe we can play these animations, now," said McGuire.

The first showed a woman standing on a deck, her back to a railing. She leaned back, either to sit on the railing or to brace herself against it, misjudged where the rail was and began to fall backwards as the rail caught her mid-thigh. Her hand grabbed the rail and body rotated so she was facing down the length of the rail and went over it sideways, her right hand hitting the concrete just before the right side of her head. She did a bounce and rolled into the water.

In scenario two, she was sitting in the chaise longue, which was a foot from the rail. She started to get up, reached to the rail to use it to support her rise, and as she was almost up, her left hand slipped and she fell forward and over.

The third scenario was similar to the first. She intended to sit on the rail, misjudged where it was in the dark and slipped over the edge, hit the cement, rolled to the edge of the breakwall and stopped. Because of the judge's earlier ruling, the animation stopped there.

The jury couldn't see her roll into the water, but McGuire was free to talk about it.

"She could lie there for minutes, or longer? An hour? Two hours?" he asked.

"Yes," said Paul.

"After she's got into the position, if she had a generalized seizure, could it put her in the water?"

"In my opinion, yes. If there's any force that would dislodge her from that position, yes, she would roll into the water."

The fourth scenario was similar to the second and ended with a roll that stopped at the edge of the breakwall.

"And if she had a seizure from that location, could that put her in the water?" asked McGuire.

"Yes."

"Dr. Paul, you're not suggesting to this jury that this is what happened, any one of those scenarios that they saw, is that fair?" asked Pendergast.

"No. I think I'm saying that any one of those scenarios would put her in the same position and would give the same physical evidence."

"Do you understand my question? Once, again, I'm asking you: You're not telling this jury that's what happened, is that right?"

"No."

"Because you don't know what happened, do you?"

"I don't."

"In fact, you originally came up with seven scenarios that possibly could have happened on that deck, is that right?"

"Yes."

"Let me ask you this: Would you agree with me that you can make these animations do anything you want to?"

"Not consistent with physical principles."

"You can make them stop when you want to?"

"Not consistent with physical principles."

"My question is, you could, is that correct?"

"Yes, I could . . ."

"You could make it be murder if you wanted to?" she interrupted.

"I could make the person be Superman, but it wouldn't be consistent with physical principles."

"Would you agree with me there's a number of inaccuracies in these animations?" she asked.

"What does 'a number' mean?" interrupted McGuire.

"Well, let's start with the way the decking goes. Would you agree with me that you have the decking going the wrong way on the deck?" she asked, referring to which way the boards were laid.

"The decking boards are going the wrong way in the animation, which I had never noticed before," said Paul.

"You told the jury that your calculations were based on a one hundred and fifty-pound woman. Where did you get that information?"

"From the coroner. From the autopsy."

"If the testimony in this courtroom was that the body was one hundred and fifty pounds wet, which meant give or take ten to fifteen pounds, your calculation of her weight is about ten to fifteen pounds off, is that correct?"

"I used one hundred and fifty pounds, yes."

"All right. Tell the members of the jury where, in these animations that were prepared under your specific direction and control, the blue comforter is found."

"Nowhere. I did not address the blue comforter."

"And if the testimony in this courtroom was that the blood spot was found under the blue comforter, can you account to this jury how that could have possibly happened if any one of your scenarios was right?"

"Yes. It could have occurred if she had the comforter wrapped around her, and it came off while she was falling, and essentially fell to the concrete after she had rolled past the blood spot."

"Have you ever asked to see the comforter or determine how heavy it is?"

"I did not."

Pendergast asked Paul about a diagram he'd made of Florence's injuries in preparing for the animations. He had sketched in contusions behind her right knee, and Pendergast asked him where that information had come from.

"It would have to be from the autopsy and the photographs."

Pendergast asked him if he had his copy of those things with him.

He did.

She asked him to get out whatever it was that told him about the contusions behind the knee.

"It's primarily based on this photo," he said, handing her a photo.

This was the grand moment they'd been waiting for for six weeks, hoping all along it would play out just the way it had. During preparations, after getting Paul's sketches and animations in March, the prosecution team had wondered about Paul's sketch showing bruises on Florence Unger's leg. There was nothing in the autopsy that mentioned bruising there, and no sign in the photos.

One day in a meeting, it struck both Bilkovic and Skrzynski at the same time. There was a photo showing bruising where her elbow bent. Was it possible Paul had mistaken her arm for her leg? Ohmigod! That must be it!

"This does *not* leave the room. It does *not* leave this room!" Pendergast had said, then.

And they'd been waiting ever since for this moment to see if the vaunted expert had indeed made such a colossal goof.

"Would that be this?" she said, holding up the photo of the arm. Deadpan.

"Yes."

"Doctor, would you be surprised if I told you that this has been identified in this courtroom by Dr. Stephen Cohle as the outside of Mrs. Unger's elbow and arm?"

Chuckles in the courtroom. Paul was calm. There had been a mistake, but surely it wasn't his. Pendergast must have mixed something up.

"Would you agree that this is the photo?" she said, showing him a bent arm and a bruise.

"Yes," said Paul, peering at it, thinking for a minute it was one of a leg, then realizing it wasn't. "I think that photograph is actually the elbow. I'm sorry. Let me look at the photos, again."

Pendergast handed him the pile of photos. He went through them one by one until he was done, the look of confidence slowly morphing into one of mortification. He riffled through the photos a second time. And a third.

There had been two minutes of silence in the courtroom that seemed like ten. Bilkovic hoped it would go on forever, a moment like this being hard to come by.

Paul looked up. "I can't find the other photo," he said.

"Are you suggesting to the jury that there's another photograph that shows a scrape behind the right knee? Or are you conceding that that might have been the photograph that you used to diagram your injury?"

"I need to concede, I guess."

She left that hanging there in the courtroom a beat or two, then moved on to the concrete apron, or, more precisely, the metal edge of it that ran along its length, vertically, sticking up above the concrete from less than an inch to more than an inch.

"In your computer animations, where you have her going over the breakwall, how high is it there?" asked Pendergast.

"Frankly, I don't know," said Paul, his voice quiet, the expert witness now acting anything but cocksure, still not having gotten past the leg for an arm.

"Did you think it might be important?"

"No."

Pendergast asked him if he was familiar with the term "axonal injury"—he was—and told him that testimony earlier had been that an axonal injury has to have existed for an hour and a half, to create the chemistry that causes specific stains used to detect it.

"Doctor, if you accept the axonal injury scenario as true, would you agree that the rolling-immediately-into-the-water scenario is ruled out?"

"I'm sorry. I missed the first part."

"The axonal injury taking an hour and a half minimum to develop, if you accept that premise as true, would you agree with me that that rules out your rolling-immediately-into-the-water scenarios?"

"Apparently, yes."

"I have no further questions, Your Honor."

McGuire had a lot of damage to undo.

"Do you have any reason to believe that the comforter would have played any role in affecting the trajectory of her fall, or affecting the dynamics of her fall, the kinetics of her movement in any way at all?"

"I don't think it would."

"Could the comforter in any way contribute to a trip?"

"Yes, it could."

"Would it cushion her in any way, or prevent any of the injuries that she sustained?"

"It would not."

McGuire asked him whether, if Florence Unger weighed 135 or 140 pounds dry, "Would that have had any appreciable effect on your opinions?"

"It would not. It would obviously change the total amount of energy from one thousand eight hundred to maybe one thousand seven hundred foot pounds, which is still much more energy than [needed] to both cause her injuries and roll her into the water."

Paul was done. Later, over dinner, the prosecution team regaled each other with versions of his testimony, Skrzynski in particular mocking Paul to the enjoyment of the others. Later Pendergast said of that crucial point in Paul's testimony, "After that, he just bailed. He couldn't wait to get off the stand." Up until then, "He sounded like a pompous ass." After? Like a man with a plane to catch.

Harrison played down the damage, saying it caused a laugh but was irrelevant to the points Paul had made, hadn't tarnished his expertise. "I thought Igor Paul was one of the best witnesses I have ever used or seen. I thought he did a great job," said Harrison later. As for the gaffe, "It was nothing. It was so minor."

The judge asked if the defense thought it would need a full day on Thursday to wrap things up. Harrison said they'd probably only need about an hour more, that he had only one more witness. He didn't mention the witness by name. It was Mark Unger.

A PROBLEM JUROR?

Court reconvened Thursday at 9:40 a.m. Seven minutes later, the jury was excused, and the judge and attorneys met in chambers to discuss a problem. One juror, Robert Eggleston, had sent a note to the judge about calculations and notes he'd made during Paul's testimony, based, he said, on his knowledge of high school physics, and wanted to know whether his notes could be passed on to the rest of the jury in the event he was one of the extra jurors dismissed before deliberations began.

That set off alarms with both the judge and defense attorneys.

Eggleston was a retired General Motors engineer. Harrison had reacted to him viscerally at jury selection, but against his better judgment made the tactical decision to keep him on the jury.

"Honest, when I first saw him, my hair stood up. I got a bad feeling," Harrison said later. "We left him on because he was an engineer and we were going to be arguing engineering. So it was good to have an intelligent guy on the jury."

Pendergast argued that the note, itself, shouldn't disqualify Eggleston. Batzer agreed. They then went back into the courtroom to put a follow-up discussion on the record.

Harrison told McGuire and Harrison to come up with

a brief list of questions they'd like him to ask the juror, and they recessed at 10:04. At 11:02 they met again, in chambers.

Lawyers on both sides questioned Eggleston. McGuire and Harrison wanted him removed. Eggleston said he hadn't made up his mind about a verdict. Harrison and McGuire thought he was lying.

The judge kept him on.

"It was so obvious to everyone in the room besides the judge that we had a problem here," said Harrison.

"If I had been a defense attorney, I'd have defecated," said Bilkovic. The prosecution team was elated Batzer hadn't dismissed him. They chalked Eggleston up in their column.

Court reconvened at 11:43. Batzer went over his planned jury instructions with the attorneys, and the jury was brought back in at 11:52.

Harrison had an immediate surprise. He no longer had one more witness to call.

"Your Honor, and ladies and gentlemen of the jury, I have made a decision not to call Mark Unger as a witness, and therefore, on his behalf, the defense rests."

Harrison had mulled it over during the night. He thought reasonable doubt had been clearly established. He was convinced that his client, in his words, "was walking." So why chance things by putting him on the stands?

The jury was excused just before noon, done for the week.

The judge and attorneys discussed possible lesser charges and jury instructions. All agreed they would eliminate manslaughter. State law required the jury have the option of considering second-degree as well as first-degree.

At 2:33, they were done.

GETTING TWEETY BIRD TO DANCE

Court reconvened at 9:50 a.m. on Wednesday, June 14. There was one bit of drama to play out before the jury was summoned. The trap Pendergast had set during Igor Paul's testimony had remained unsprung. She was hoping to keep it set.

"Apparently we're going to have a little scrap," said the judge.

"Minor, Your Honor. Very minor," said Bilkovic. All they wanted to do was show one of Paul's animations during closing arguments, slowed down so it could be seen frame by frame.

The defense objected, again, to no avail.

"To me," began the judge, "it seems like this is similar to those little cartoon booklets that maybe some people remember when we were kids, where you take the little booklet. And you could get, with your thumb or finger or something, run through it very fast and you could get Tweety Bird to dance or something. I just don't see the problem, and so I'm going to allow it in."

If London bookies had taken bets on the least likely phrase to make it into a first-degree murder trial in Michigan in 2006, it probably would have been "You could get Tweety Bird to dance."

The jury was brought in at 10:04.

* * *

Batzer told the jury that they would hear closing arguments and explained that because the prosecution had the burden of proving its case, it would go first, the defense would offer a rebuttal, and then the prosecution would address them a final time.

"Thank you, Your Honor," said Pendergast. Her closing arguments have a reputation for heartfelt passion and a hold on juries that goes well beyond the logic of the words.

"It's horrifying, isn't it?" she began. "A human life reduced to a piece of paper. An autopsy protocol that says that a living, breathing human being was transformed into a corpse on October 24, 2003. A piece of paper that says Florence Unger became a number that day. Number 446 at the Spectrum hospital morgue.

"What this paper doesn't say is equally horrendous. That it happened for no good reason. Really, no reason at all. Other than one. Because the world revolved around Mark Unger. What he wanted, when he wanted it, and how he would react when things didn't go his way.

"On the night of October twenty-fourth of 2003, shortly after Fred Oeflein saw Florence and the defendant on that deck, something didn't go his way. And an ignition point was reached. We don't know if it was [that] he found out about the affair with Glenn Stark. Or if he realized that the reconciliation he hoped to be was not to be. That we don't know.

"I think by now we all know that on that deck that night there was an altercation and there was a struggle, and there were actions on the part of the defendant that would send Florence Unger crashing over that railing to the cement platform below, where she would lay unconscious, immobile and bleeding for at least an hour and a half. While *he* waited for the coast to clear. So *he* could sneak back down, like a rat in the night, to see the end result of his Dr. Jekyll and Mr. Hyde–type behavior, and the end to the life of Florence Unger, when he found her still alive on that platform.

"And he placed her in the water face down, where she would spend the final moments of her life staring blankly at death in the face, while the very life drained from her broken body. And as hard as it is to understand, he made his wife die in the dark of night.

"The final chapter to her life was written in a cold, dark lake. But the final chapter to her story was written in this courtroom. And awaits only an ending which will be written by you, the jury. I beg of you, make sure it's the right one. Because although Florence Unger may be in this courtroom without a choice, she is not in this courtroom without a voice. And she has spoken to you through the evidence.

"There is so much that you don't know about Florence Unger. You don't know her favorite food, her favorite color, her favorite TV show. You don't know what her future dreams were, nor her past regrets. You don't know anything about her, except for a little bit about how she lived. And way too much about how she died. Somewhere in a cold cemetery, she lies in the ground for eternity because of the actions of that man."

Pendergast then summed up the testimony about the Ungers' troubled marriage, his stint in rehab, the various accounts of the day Florence died and its aftermath.

She dwelled, of course, on the linchpin in her case, Florence Unger's fear of the dark. Premise number one of Mark Unger's story, she said, was that he'd left Flo out there in the dark alone. Based on what they'd heard about her fear of the dark, "It just didn't happen. The defendant's story fails from the very first premise . . . and if you understand that, then that makes your job as jurors a whole lot easier. It is very telling that in his brief, roughly five-minute conversation, Florence Unger tells Fred Oeflein that she is afraid of the dark. That's very telling. A very brief conversation with an absolute stranger, and he knows that fact about Florence Unger."

Pendergast reminded the jury that Joan Frank testified that Mark Unger described to her a romantic interlude on the deck, that they were getting along so well that Flo let him put his arm around her.

"Alarm bells, I believe were the words she used, went off instantly when he said that. Because she knew that there was no way that that could be true," she said, asking them why, if it were true, would he then go inside and spend so much time with the kids, reading extra stories, watching DVDs?

"Does that sound like someone who knows that Florence Unger is waiting for him out on that deck? Ask yourself if that makes any sense?"

And did it make any sense that when he woke up in the morning and realized she'd never come in, that he wouldn't go looking for her, that he'd call Linn Duncan and ask him to look, instead?

Or that when he did go outside, he went in the direction *away* from where he'd last seen his wife? Or that when he encountered Linn Duncan, "He beelines directly to the spot where Florence Unger's body is located in the water?"

She told them it was strange that while his wife's body was floating in the lake, he packed the car for the drive home. And that later in the day, in violation of Jewish religious law, he asked Flo's parents if he could cremate the body, when only months earlier he had been adamantly opposed to his father's cremation.

Everything she'd talked about so far, though, wouldn't mean anything if Pendergast couldn't sell the jury on the science. Unless they saw the science the same way she did, she had nothing.

She told the jury that the ninety minutes it had taken for staining to show evidence of axonal injury made sense. That would have been about the time it would take Mark to regroup from whatever happened on the deck. To go back to the cottage, to play with his kids and put them to bed, to make sure the Duncans' light had gone out, to think, What now?

If, after ninety minutes, Mark had gone back out and found, to his surprise, that his wife was still alive despite her injuries, putting her in the water would have been the only way to assure she'd die, that she couldn't point the finger at him.

How did she get in the water? Not by seizure, she said, reminding them of the testimony of Dr. Brian Zink, the emergency room physician.

"You also have bruising on the right wrist, bruising on the right forearm and bruising on the elbow—the leg, according to Dr. Paul," said Pendergast, using the engineering professor's embarrassing misidentification to great advantage. "A high-paid expert that doesn't know an arm from a leg."

Pendergast gave a detailed rebuttal of a litany of statements Harrison had made in his opening remarks, using a PowerPoint presentation to alternately flash on the screen verbatim excerpts of his opening, then verbatim excerpts that contradicted him.

For example: His statement on May 3 that:

Nobody ever walked out to that body to examine Florence Unger to see if she was still alive.

And testimony the next day by EMS technician Mike Trailer:

I reached down in the water to feel a limb, to make sure that we had a situation where we did not have a rescue.

Harrison's statement that:

Dr. Brian Zink, an emergency medical specialist, will testify in this case . . . and he will tell you that if she had a generalized seizure, she would have been able to move up to about two feet.

And Zink's testimony:

Focal seizures tend to be smaller movements, anything from twitching of the face to a movement of the arm. It's a lesser degree of movement, and not involving the whole body.

Harrison's statement that:

Dr. Paul McKeever, this neuropathologist from Ann Arbor, will also tell you . . . that he is nevertheless of the belief that Florence Unger died from her head injuries and not from drowning.

And McKeever's testimony:

I really have little to say about it. Again, I didn't examine the lungs.

Harrison's statement that:

Unfortunately, in this case, the so-called scientists did not search for trace fiber evidence of any kind, which would have told us some things.

And lab technician Frances D'Angela, who said:

I examined very close the break wall to see if there was anything, any fibers or anything that would tell us what happened.

"Now it's time for you, the members of the jury, to write the final chapter, or the end to the final chapter of Florence Unger's life," said Pendergast.

"It's not my words, nor Mr. Harrison's words, nor Mr. Harrison's compelling voice. It's the quiet voice that you weren't able to hear in this courtroom. Because a dead woman has spoken to you in this courtroom, through the evidence. The evidence that points in one direction, and one direction only.

"You, the members of the jury, will never be able to do justice in this matter. The unfortunate truth is that a human life has been ruthlessly and recklessly obliterated. And there will never be enough justice for that. Never."

It was 12:52 p.m. The court recessed for lunch. At 2:33, it reconvened. The jurors had had an hour and a half for Pendergast's passionate last sentences to echo in their minds.

A DRUNKEN FIRST MATE

Harrison's tone contrasted sharply with Pendergast's. He was calm and dispassionate, wise in the ways of the law, which he explained to the jury.

"The only law you are to follow in this case is what Judge Batzer gives you. He is the law in this case. But I would like to tell you what some of these principles mean to me, in the hopes that they will assist you in understanding them," he began.

"The first principle is the presumption of innocence. The presumption of innocence is the most important concept in the criminal law. It is a principle that was born out of hundreds of years of tyranny. Times when dictators and monarchs did what they wanted. They eliminated political rivals with the swing of a sword. They killed people simply because they were political dissenters. They did what they wanted to."

Harrison told them that when the trial began on April 26, and as it wound down on June 14, Mark Unger continued to wear a cloak of innocence "that was wrapped around him, that was made of some material that could not be penetrated by what was referred to as the terrible swift sword of wrongful accusations. Well, those are pretty flowery words, pretty fancy words, but I really can't think of a better way to describe it."

Harrison told them they had to find the defendant guilty beyond a reasonable doubt, which the judge would talk to them about later, but "I want to tell you a little story and hope that the story assists you in understanding it.

"Suppose a little boy complains to his mother about a very, very severe pain in his leg. And the pain persists for a week, and then two weeks, and the mother takes that little boy to the doctor. And the doctor conducts some test, and takes some X-rays and consults something, and then he says, 'Madam, your son has a terrible problem in his leg. We must amputate his leg at mid-thigh. We have to do it, now, today, in order to save his life. I want to call surgery and set it up.'

"Do you think this mother would say, 'Okay, Doctor, go ahead and make the call, and amputate my son's leg'? I think not. I think she would say, 'Hold your horses.' I think she'd get a second opinion. I think she might get a third opinion. I think she would read everything she could find on that subject. I think she would talk to her husband. I think she'd talk to people who were important to her, who she knew she could trust. And I think if anyone spoke against that surgery, with a reason not to do it, she wouldn't do that. She wouldn't allow that to happen."

My God, thought Pendergast. Enough of the whimsy. Get to the point.

"Well, ladies and gentlemen, don't think for even a moment that Mark Unger's life, his family, his liberty, are any less important to him than the leg of the little boy in my example. That's where reasonable doubt comes in," continued Harrison.

And what was the point? That the jury should treat the charges against Unger like a leg injury and get second and third opinions? Trying to make sense of what she'd just heard, Pendergast felt her confidence rising. It had hardly been a stellar start for her esteemed colleague.

Harrison then infuriated Pendergast by saying, "I had to bring out some things that were probably harsh, things that some or all of you may not have liked. For example, even though the prosecutor brought out the affair through Glenn Stark when he was on the stand, I followed it up with other people. And I brought out Florence Unger's shopping and spending, and her resentment about getting a job. And her inability to live on ten thousand dollars a month tax-free.

"And in the process I may have offended or angered you. Please understand this: I knew what I was doing. I wasn't attempting to offend the very people who are going to decide the fate of my client, decide whether his family and him will live in misery forever or not. The purpose of these questions was to simply show you that Florence Unger was a regular human being like everybody else."

Pendergast's blood boiled. Florence Unger's affair or her shopping habits had nothing to do with the issue at hand: Had she fallen accidentally off the boathouse roof, or had she been pushed? Had her husband put her in the water? And Harrison had the gall on top of it to say he wasn't bringing it all up to impugn her, but just to make her seem like a regular gal?

"You know," he continued, "prosecutors have said, 'That man Mark is a cold-blooded killer. A monster.' And he is no monster, and he is no killer, and he is no murderer. Likewise, these prosecutors have portrayed Florence Unger as a perfect angel, a faultless, perfect person. And she was not perfect, just like Mark was not perfect. She had pluses, she had minuses, she had virtues, and she had weaknesses and she had strengths. So does Mark. And that was the only purpose in describing those things to you, not to offend you."

And then he told a story that he said would show them the danger of making false inferences about guilt.

"It's an old story, but I think it illustrates a point. The story is a story about the golden days of the great sailing ships," Harrison began.

This better be good, thought Pendergast.

"A ship was about to leave the harbor in the evening. And the first mate came aboard and he was drunk. And the captain had him searched and he found a bottle of rum in his pocket. And the captain ordered him to quarters and wrote in the ship's log: 'First mate, drunk tonight.'

"On the second day out, the first mate worked like nobody ever worked, to resurrect his position. He volunteered to stand night watch for fifteen straight nights as the ship crossed the ocean. He did everything that anyone could ever hope for. And on the last night, just as the captain was about to go to his own cabin, the first mate approached him and he said, 'Captain, I am so sorry for having been drunk. Please forgive me. And, Captain, please remove that entry from the ship's log that I was drunk. I will lose my license as a first mate.'

"And the captain said, 'No. I am not going to remove that entry. The only thing that matters is what I wrote in that ship's log. And if it's true, that's all that matters.'

"And, so, the captain went to his cabin for the night, the mate stood watch, the ship safely navigated into the harbor, and the voyage was over, and the mate took his quilled pen and wrote in the ship's log, 'Ship safe in harbor. Captain sober tonight.'

"Now, it's true that the captain was sober. So, according to the captain's rule, he could write that. And the inference comes from 'Captain sober tonight.' It conveys exactly the opposite thing from the truth. Because the suggestion is, if he was sober tonight, he must have been drunk other nights. So, true or not, be very, very careful about allowing inferences to carry you off into some fairytale land about what really happened here."

"Huh?" thought Bilkovic. What kind of story was that? He'd been worried about Harrison, respected his courtroom presence, thought him a great lawyer. But this was hardly great lawyering.

It was hard to imagine anyone wavering in his or her opinion because of the repentant mate and his sneaky ways.

"A lot of sound and fury, signifying nothing," thought Skrzynski.

Skrzynski leaned over and whispered something to Bilkovic, who had to bite his lip to keep from laughing out loud.

"We were all lost on that one," Bilkovic said later.

It was time to talk about the evidence, and the morning of October 25, 2003.

Harrison told the jury that what led to his client being charged with murder was not the death of Florence Unger, but the phone call to 911 by Maggie Duncan. That because of the wrong impression she gave the dispatcher, the first policeman on the scene arrived misinformed, and misinformation continued to be passed along from officer to officer as the responders arrived.

"We already know that Maggie Duncan called and said to the dispatcher, 'I believe it is a suicide, or a drowning or something.' And the dispatcher said, 'Do you know if she had been depressed lately?' and Maggie Duncan said, 'Yeah, she has been, I believe.' Now, from that, from that we had the dispatcher contacting Deputy Troy Packard."

Harrison read from a transcript of the dispatcher's call. "'Are you ready for your first one of the day? . . . This lady's husband called her and wanted to know if they had seen his wife, because she had been talking about suicide.'

"Well, we know that's not accurate. It's a mistake," said Harrison. "Mark didn't call Maggie Duncan and say, 'My wife is missing, she's been talking about suicide.' Mark called and said, 'Do you know where Flo is? She didn't come home last night.'"

Word of suicide spread from officer to officer, said Harrison. "And so some things get focused on out there at the scene and others are ignored. For example, anything that might point to accident is ignored. Why look for accident? We have a husband, they mistakenly think, that said his wife died by jumping over a very low railing and killed herself by falling to the pavement twelve feet below."

The investigation's blindness to accident was compounded, he said, by what he called Law Enforcement Class 101, where "cadets are taught where there is a death, to at least look at the surviving spouse, the surviving husband or wife. And that's what they did. They look at the scene and they say, 'Baloney. Baloney. This is no suicide.' I mean, nobody jumps off a twelve-foot-high deck if they're trying to kill themselves, even if it's a death trap out there."

Even if it's a death trap out there.

"So, they believe that Mark, the guy they mistakenly think was promoting the suicide theory, is involved in the lady's death. And the entire investigation goes off in the wrong direction, and it gets compounded to the point where Mark ends up denying something that he never said. 'No. She didn't kill herself.' I can just see these officers, now, out there at Watervale. 'Oh, this is great. Now the jerk is denying what he already said before to the dispatcher. What a liar!'"

From a false starting premise, he said, the police saw all of Unger's actions from a skewed point of view, the way he cried, how he talked to his friends on the phone. When he went down on his hands and knees to retch and moan, it wasn't the way they thought he should retch and moan.

A classic example of conclusions being made from a false premise, said Harrison, was the seeming import of Unger's wet clothing being found in the car.

"Everyone knew he was wet. And so he went back to the Mary Ellen at some point, and he took off his wet clothes and he put them in the car. What was he hiding? He was hiding wet clothing that everyone knew was wet?" asked Harrison.

Harrison told them that the investigation was botched in numerous key areas. They never, for example, took Florence Unger's core body temperature.

It was 3:28. Harrison asked if they could take a short recess. The jury left the room, and the judge asked the attorneys to come forward for an off-the-record bench conference.

At 4, the jury was excused.

The case was going to the jury the next day. Until now, the trial had been held Wednesday through Friday so other business could be attended to on Monday and Tuesday. The judge told the lawyers that, anticipating lengthy deliberations, the trial would now be held on Monday and Tuesday, if needed.

SAVAGING DRAGOVIC

Harrison's closing arguments continued at 10:03 on Thursday morning.

"My point to you is, anybody can go in the wrong direction if they are given wrong information, and it leads them somewhere where they wouldn't be going but for that wrong information. And it snowballed in this case. And that's what I want you to know," he began.

He recounted the list of Florence's friends who testified they didn't know she was afraid of the dark, and that Lyle Wolberg had testified that Florence had walked several blocks to his house in the dark the week before she died.

He said if it was true, as Kathy Stark had said, that Florence had called her and her husband frequently at night, there was another perfectly good reason: She was hoping to see, or at least talk to, her lover.

Harrison reminded the jury that they would need their common sense during deliberations, and there was no better place common sense would come in handy than when thinking about Fred Oeflein, the Duncans' caretaker, and what he'd had to say.

"Thank God," he said, "for Fred Oeflein." He reminded them that as Oeflein was about to take his boat across the dark lake, "Florence said to him, 'Oh, I could never do that. I'm afraid of the dark.' "

Harrison said the timing, if you believed the prosecution's theory of murder, made no sense. Having introduced himself to Oeflein by name, having heard your wife tell him she was afraid of the dark, would it then make sense at that point in time to hatch your plot?

"You'd have to be stupid or nuts to decide to kill your wife at that moment. You'd have to be a fool to tell the police that Florence told him to go and check on the kids while she stayed out on the deck, if that wasn't actually what happened, because Florence had just gotten through telling a perfect stranger that she was afraid of the dark," said Harrison.

"Mark has to say, if he's thinking and deliberating, 'Whoa, man, if there's any bad time to do anything bad, it's when I introduce myself by name in front of a stranger who's going to be around here.' It just doesn't make sense. We talked about using common sense. It's that kind of analysis that defies common sense."

Pendergast thought if there was one thing that didn't make sense, it was the argument she'd just heard. Harrison had just made her argument for her. Harrison had said, basically, it's stupid to say your wife told you to leave her alone in the dark just after she told a stranger she was afraid of the dark.

Harrison debunked the notion that Mark's behavior was indicative of anything, even if he had been alternately crying and not.

"Nobody should be judged and called a criminal because of how he acts on the day when his wife has died, his children are now motherless, and the police officers are pointing the finger of guilt at him," he said. "I can't imagine, other than war time, what would be more likely to cause a person to be in some form or some state of shock. And when you are in a state of shock, all bets are off in terms of what you're going to do."

He ridiculed the prosecution theory that a motivation

for Mark to kill his wife might have been that she'd dis-abused him of any hope things could work out by telling him on the deck about her affair with Glenn Stark.

"The truth is, Mark didn't know anything about the af-fair until long, long after Florence's death. Not one girl-friend of hers knew anything about it. It was apparently the best-kept secret in Huntington Woods, where apparently nothing else is a secret about anybody.

"And there's no way Florence Unger would have told Mark on that night, on that deck, about that affair. Fred Oeflein said that Flo was very happy on that deck. She was bubbly. It would be idiotic, in that very short frame of time, when Oeflein got in his boat, for Flo to say to Mark, 'By the way, Mark, I'm having sex with your best friend, Glenn.'"

Harrison ridiculed Dragovic.

"You've heard us argue about his publicity-seeking in-jection of himself into notorious cases. You know about his civil practice. You know about his personality and his delight in criticizing other pathologists, and his belief that he and only he knows the answer to pathology questions.

"This is the kind of witness the prosecution has asked you to find a man guilty of first-degree murder, based on this man's testimony," said Harrison, as a printed tran-script scrolled across the video screen of back-and-forth between Dragovic and McGuire as Harrison read:

"'Question: I'm asking about how long she would have survived after impact. Interpreting the staining evidence, you did testify that you thought it would take at least an hour for her to die.

"'Answer: Right. Based on the staining evidence, an hour, hour and a half. Maybe even longer. Maybe even two hours.

"'Question: You testified in this case in January of this year?

"'Answer: Yes, sir.'

"And what he testified to in January was: 'Question: Do you have an opinion as to the length of time that she may have lain on the cement concrete surface before she went into the water?

" 'Answer: That would be measured by minutes. How many minutes, I cannot tell.

" 'Question: Well, one hundred and twenty minutes?

" 'Answer: Well, we are talking minutes. Minutes may mean five minutes, ten minutes, fifteen minutes. I don't believe that she was in there for an hour . . . I indicated, sir, that I believe that her body was placed in the water within minutes after sustaining the head injury.'

"And so then McGuire said, 'Now, that's what you said when you testified under oath before. Now, which is true, Doctor? The evidence that you gave in January or the evidence that you gave from the witness stand?

" 'Answer: Both of them.'

"McGuire's next question was: 'Doctor, are you making this up as you go along?'

"What I'd like for you to do for me, if you would, is try to visualize this case without Dragovic's testimony. Just try to put it out of your mind. What creates images in your mind about guilt beyond a reasonable doubt without the testimony of Ljubisa Dragovic? What is there? Of course, it falls down. There is nothing. Nothing here."

ELATION FOR THE DEFENSE

Finally, Harrison had hit his stride. He might have been well served to ask for a recess, let his words linger in the jurors' minds awhile. Or to have finished his close with his attack on Dragovic.

But without pause, he was on to Dr. Cohle, and then the rest of the medical witnesses for the prosecution.

He reminded them of how reluctant Cohle had been in determining the manner of death as homicide, that he finally used a standard of preponderance of evidence, that is, that there was at least a 51 percent probability, not the criminal standard of beyond a reasonable doubt.

"So what does that mean?" asked Harrison. "It means that if Dr. Cohle was on this jury, he'd vote not guilty. He doesn't even believe the manner of death was beyond reasonable doubt. The official pathologist in this case."

As for Dr. Brian Zink, the emergency room physician the prosecution brought in to head the defense off at the pass on its suggestions that a seizure could have propelled Florence Unger into the lake, Harrison said, "I found him to be—trying to be careful on the word I use, I want to be polite—I found him to be a bit *surprising* in some of the things he said.

"He is an assistant dean and spends seventy-five percent

of his time, and has done so for a long time, in administration, what school administrators do, and twenty-five percent in the emergency room. And he is a very fancy, highfalutin' guy, and I thought to myself, 'Gee, I wonder how much time he actually spends in the emergency room getting his hands dirty, or getting his hands bloody?' "

Harrison asked why Zink, if he was such an expert on brain trauma, said twenty-five percent of those with Florence Unger's injuries could be expected to make a full recovery and fifty a partial recovery, in contradiction to the testimony of Dragovic, Cohle and Dr. McKeever that her injuries in all likelihood were fatal?

"The other thing that bothered me about Dr. Zink was that for some reason, he was like a man with a mission. He didn't seem to come in here and just be trying to provide information to you to help you. He seemed to be a guy who came in ready to fight. And I don't know why. He sure seemed that way to me, the way he answered questions . . . Why would a guy do that? If he was a disinterested expert?"

And then he, in Pendergast's mind, crossed the line.

"I also don't remember him telling us that he had written anything, any research papers or textbooks or anything like that. And I kind of wondered whether his presence here as an expert witness had anything to do with the requirements in major universities that persons in those kinds of positions have to do research and have to do writing or have to do something outside their academic sphere in order to continue to maintain their position. And that he hadn't done anything like that," said Harrison.

"And I wondered to myself, 'I wonder if this guy *has* to be here, and *has* to testify, in order to satisfy the requirements necessary to hang on to his tenure job. It's kind of a sad thought, maybe even a harsh one, and I hope it isn't like that.'"

Yeah, I bet you do, thought Pendergast. *This* was something shredable on its face. If he was tenured, he'd have a job for life, and if he didn't and was in trouble for a lack of published papers, testifying in a trial wasn't going to help him out. The saying was *Publish or perish*, not *Publish or perish or testify*.

That led Harrison to Dr. McKeever. He was Pendergast's key witness, who could tip the scale of doubt about contradictions between Cohle's testimony and Dragovic's.

Harrison said that McKeever's prime task for the prosecution was to take some slides of Florence Unger's brain tissue and test them with some stains, though it was clear from McKeever's own testimony that this was hardly his area of expertise.

Harrison put up on the projector and read portions of the cross-examination of McKeever by McGuire.

"Question: 'Now, do you know how sensitive NSE is as a stain? Can you tell us with any assurance that it will or won't work at a particular point in time after a traumatic event has occurred?'

"His answer was: 'I think that I can refer to some of the citations that you mentioned before in regard to that, because the answer is, I don't know personally, which is why I go to these studies.'

" 'Is it beyond your expertise?'

" 'Not after I see what the studies have to say.'

"Question: 'You folks in hospital pathology don't have a need to know, I would assume, whether an injury produced axonal damage within minutes or seconds of trauma. That's not something that you'd be concerned with in a hospital setting, is it?'

" 'Right. That's why I go to the literature to find out.'

"So, the bottom line is that Dr. McKeever is probably a terrific hospital pathologist. But his contribution to this case was pretty minimal, if nonexistent. Although he's obviously a very learned man, he knows very little about staining techniques."

Harrison put up on the screen excerpts from McGuire's cross-examination of State Police Lieutenant Rains, who had written that one possible scenario was that Florence Unger had sat down on the top rail, lost her balance and fallen over backwards.

"We have the accident reconstruction expert giving you a scenario that certainly looks like an accidental fall to me," said Harrison. "That's the quality of the case that they're asking you to convict this man of first-degree murder based on. And it makes no sense."

Harrison reminded them that John Zarzecki had testified that once the police and the Exponent crew were done dismantling the railing, he and Dave Ruby were able to go up on the deck and break off pieces of the badly rotted wood that was left with their bare hands. And Zarzecki had discovered there was another roof below the current one, which explained why the railing was so low, too low to prevent someone from falling over in the event of an accident.

After a break for lunch, Harrison picked up with Igor Paul. He recounted at length Paul's extensive credentials and his contention that there were several scenarios, at least, that could explain Florence Unger's fall and death by accidental means.

He finished recapping his witnesses' testimony with Dr. Schmidt, the Wayne County Medical Examiner.

"He told you about studies that had been done that show that during wartime, when persons were killed almost immediately by missiles and shells, that even though there was instantaneous death, there was also virtual instantaneous pulmonary edema, the fluid in the lungs, that it can happen exceedingly quickly, almost upon receipt of a serious head injury."

He told them Schmidt said the manner of death should be indeterminate, that there wasn't enough evidence to make a definitive call.

"Witnesses like Igor Paul, like Carl Schmidt, like John Zarzecki, like David Ruby are powerful witnesses. And I believe we were fortunate to have people like them here to assist you in interpreting the facts," he said.

Harrison derided the prosecution's theory of events.

"These prosecutors would ask you to believe that Mark

went out to that deck and caused a horrible, horrible, psychopathic thing to happen. That he took his wife, who he adored, and somehow kicked or threw or pounded her over that deck railing down to the pavement below.

"A monster, is what they want you to believe. And then he calmly went back to the Mary Ellen, and he had the boys brush their teeth, and he got them ready for bed, stories, Red Wings games on the radio, whatever. That he kissed them, and that he left and went back out to the scene of his horrible crime, and that he then, without any evidence to back it up, kicked or pushed or placed her body in the water.

"And then what? He came back in and he kissed his sons, again, after just destroying their mother. Hannibal Lecter, in *Silence of the Lambs*, couldn't even do that. It is outrageous to suggest that anybody could destroy the life of the mother of these children and act like that. It's outrageous and absurd, and it's a lie.

"You haven't seen any kind of evidence worthy of a criminal charge in this case. There has been nothing in this case that even approaches things like fingerprints, or eyewitnesses, or confessions. No real evidence in this case. You have the worst kind of circumstantial evidence, and I hate even dignifying the nature of the testimony that you have by calling it any kind of evidence, let alone real or solid evidence.

"This case was in the trash can of this courthouse out in the back before it started, and where it belongs. And it's already started to rot like these sixty-plus-year-old posts. You may only convict on proven evidence beyond a reasonable doubt. And you could not possibly convict Mark Unger without making an awful lot of wild guesses, for which you don't know for sure, beyond a reasonable doubt, are true."

At 3 p.m., the court recessed. The jury was brought back in at 3:32 to hear Bilkovic wrap things up.

BILKOVIC SHINES

It struck some courtroom observers as a surprise choice to have Bilkovic do the rebuttal. Pendergast was the star, the one with the nearly perfect record in homicide cases. Then there was Skrzynski, eloquent, dramatic, a strutter who took command of a courtroom.

Bilkovic had a commanding presence. "He's an alpha dog," says Pendergast. He is tall, 6 foot 4, and broad-shouldered at 260 pounds. Despite his size, he moves with grace and fluidity, a former college baseball player who played in the Little League World Series for his Grosse Pointe team in 1979, getting eliminated by the Taiwan team that went on to win the title.

(Like Unger, Bilkovic coached his boy's baseball team, a travel league team made up of the best players in the northern suburbs of Farmington and West Bloomfield. The summer of 2004, just before the preliminary exam, Bilkovic's team played Unger's. Before the game, Unger strode up to Bilkovic, as Bilkovic's wife, who knew Mark, watched wide-eyed, afraid there might be trouble. Instead, Unger said, "Mark, Max isn't on the team, anymore. It's okay if I'm here," referring to the Family Court decision that he give up custody pending the outcome of the trial.)

But despite his presence, and his smarts, Pendergast had her doubts.

"Are you sure you don't want John to do it?" she asked a day or two earlier, second-guessing herself.

"I can do this, Donna," he'd told her. An athlete, he could tell the difference between knowing you had it, and hoping. Today, he had it.

"Unfortunately, in our society, bad things happen. Terrible things happen. Husbands kill their wives. Husbands with children kill their wives. Husbands who have been rejected by their spouse, and who do not want the relationship to end, kill their wives," he began.

"Mr. Harrison talked to you about the presumption of innocence. And this protective cloak. Well, just like that blanket was separated from Florence Unger on October twenty-fourth, 2003, that cloak has been ripped away from Mark Unger by the evidence in this case."

Bilkovic scornfully dismissed the testimony by Ruby and Zarzecki that the deck was slippery, or that the railing in question could be rocked back and forth by five or six inches, in contradiction to what police on the scene concluded in their tests.

Zarzecki had a video camera with him that day in February of 2004 when he visited the scene. If a loose railing was so important to his testimony, why hadn't he captured it on tape for everyone to see?

He said Lyle Wolberg had lied about Florence not being afraid of the dark. "Ms. Pendergast referred to him as the helper. I refer to him as the shopper. He's got a grocery list, and he's picking up items one by one. Let's go to the first item. Got to get rid of her fear of the dark. He tells you that just hours after Florence Unger sees Ron Loeb and is crying and is telling him, 'I don't want to go to Watervale, I'm scared, I'm afraid,' that she shows up at Lyle's house, and she's happy as a lark. And she walks there. And she walks home.

"Contrary to the testimony of Harold Stern, Peter Stern,

Ronald Loeb, Laurie Glass, Kathy Stark, Glenn Stark. Contrary to Fred Oeflein. They know this fear of the dark is a huge thing. Because if you believe the evidence that has supported the fact that there is no way, in pitch dark, on a cold, rainy night, over three hundred feet away from the Mary Ellen, that Florence Unger would have stayed out on that deck by herself, their case is done. It's that simple."

Bilkovic criticized Schmidt. "Dr. Schmidt told you that in his opinion, she hit, died instantly and rolled into the water. For that to have happened, every single injury she had had to have bloomed instantly," he said. "Upon impact, immediately she inhales one last breath and fills her one lung up to ten percent of volume that was blood."

Or, he said, you could look for a more reasonable excuse for how a woman's lungs got filled with fluid who was found floating face down in a lake.

As for Paul, "For $25,000, you get Igor Paul and his cartoons," he said. "Reasonable doubt at reasonable prices? Look at what he testified to. You would think that if you were going to pay an expert that much money, an expert in biomechanical engineering, somebody that's supposed to be an expert in anatomy—*if you're going to pay an arm and a leg for him, you'd better get one that knows the difference between an arm and a leg!*"

Courtroom observers stifled their chuckles.

It was a line he had run past Pendergast earlier.

Pendergast was worried it might seem like piling on, in case there were members of the jury sympathetic to Paul. Bilkovic wanted to do one better than that—in addition to the line, he actually wanted to have a lifesize manikin in the courtroom, one with removable parts arranged so that one arm and one leg were switched.

"Absolutely not," said Pendergast. She let him keep his line.

Bilkovic said that McGuire had worked with Paul before and, needing help on this case, called Paul and said, " 'Hey, we got a problem, we need you to come up with a scenario that shows that this could have been an accident.' Well, you know what? You can do whatever you want with animation. You can make people fly. It's not real evidence.

"Igor did what he was paid to do."

Paul's animations might look at first viewing like a clear explanation for how Florence's body got into the lake without Mark's intervention, he said, but they weren't believable.

And then he sprung the trap they'd set earlier. With Batzer's permission, he slowed one of Paul's animations, frame by frame.

When the prosecution had gotten the animations in March, near panic briefly set in. Paul had serious credentials, and the animations looked good. From an armed robbery case they'd once worked together, Bilkovic knew a techie at the state police, Sergeant Bill Torkey, who handled all sorts of computer-related evidence and testimony. Bilkovic took the animations to him and asked him if there was any way to slow them down.

Torkey got them a slowed-down version. "I ran it by a bunch of people to see what they thought," Bilkovic said after the trial. "You see it at normal speed, you think, 'Wow, that looks good.' But you see it slowed down, it looks like a cartoon."

Slowed then, what you saw, instead of a landing by Florence and a smooth roll into the water, was the body landing, sliding several feet to the front and side, at about a 45-degree angle, then changing course by another 45 degrees and proceeding straight into the water.

Paul needed to account for where the rails bowed out, the blood on the apron and where the body was in the water. If the body got into the water on its own, it needed to connect three dots that didn't line up, hence the glide to the side.

The prosecution's theory, though, accounted for the zig-zag—the body landed and stopped, where it bled awhile before Unger dragged it into the water.

The prosecution team thought the animation looked absurd in slow motion. They hoped the jury agreed.

Bilkovic told the jury the prosecution wasn't alleging that Unger had gone up north with the premeditated intention of killing his wife. The prosecution wasn't alleging he went out on the deck intending to kill her. But that doesn't mean there wasn't premeditation.

"Premeditation means, did the person have enough time to weigh the pros and cons of their decision and then commit the act? It can be hours, it can be minutes, it can be seconds," said Bilkovic. "But after he caused her to go over that railing and she was lying down below, unconscious, gurgling in her own blood, he then made the decision to end her life by putting her in the water. That is premeditation. That is first-degree murder."

Bilkovic put a picture showing Florence at her radiant best.

"This is Florence Unger prior to October twenty-fourth, 2003," he said.

He put up a picture of her dead body, shot at her autopsy.

"This is Florence Unger when the defendant got done with her. A lifeless body, assigned a number on a cold metal slab. The evidence in this case has proven beyond a reasonable doubt that the defendant is guilty of murder. He knows it. Show him with your verdict that that you know it, too."

If it had struck some as a surprising tactic to have Bilkovic finish up, it didn't, now. The second he stopped, Skrzynski said to himself, "That's it. We just won."

It was 4:35 p.m. The judge told the jury it was too late to give them instructions today. He told them to report back at 9:15.

IN THEIR HANDS

Court reconvened at 9:48 on Friday, June 16. The judge and attorneys spent the first few minutes agreeing on specific language for Batzer's instructions. At 9:57, the jury was brought in.

Much of what the judge told them regarding the law and what was required for one verdict or another was boilerplate, word for word from state statutes downloaded from the Internet.

Unger was presumed innocent unless the prosecution had proven each element required beyond a reasonable doubt. As for reasonable doubt, the law was intentionally vague and circular, allowing each juror to decide what it really meant.

They were free to choose which witnesses to believe, and free to believe or disbelieve portions of a witness' testimony. They could decide for themselves if a witness had lied, and to what extent. They heard, he said, testimony from many police witnesses. Their testimony should not be held in higher regard than that of other witnesses.

The defendant had been charged with first-degree murder. The elements were that the death of Florence Unger was caused by the actions of the defendant, that the defendant intended to kill her, that the act was thought out in advance, and that the killing was deliberate.

The premeditation needed only be long enough to give a reasonable person a chance to think twice about whether to proceed. "The killing cannot be the result of a sudden impulse, without thought or reflection," said the judge.

Under Michigan law, the jury was also free to consider the charge of second-degree murder, which required that he'd intended to do great harm or created a very high chance that death or great harm would likely result from his actions.

Batzer told them to consider the charge of first-degree murder, first. If they agreed that Mark Unger was guilty of the charge, there was no need to discuss the lesser charge. But if there was some disagreement, they were free to discuss the lesser charge before returning back to the charge of first-degree.

One would-be juror was dismissed because lengthy deliberations might conflict with a long-planned trip to Alaska, two more were dismissed after their names were drawn by the clerk.

The judge told the remaining jurors to go into the jury room and wait until all the exhibits were brought in before they began their deliberations. He said to deliberate until noon, then send a note out saying whether they preferred to have lunch brought in or whether they wanted to go out for lunch.

The jury left at 10:38.

Normally, when the jury went out, Bilkovic was nervous. This time? He'd never been more relaxed. "They don't have a snowball's chance," he said to himself, of the defense.

For weeks, Bilkovic's confidence had been growing. At the beginning of the trial, he couldn't eat his dinner. He'd pick at it and let it get cold. "By the end, I was having some of the best meals of my life," he said.

McGuire and Harrison thought they knew, too. "There was so much reasonable doubt you could build a bridge and walk on it," Harrison said later.

"At this point, we'll recess to await further word from

the jury," said the judge. "Counsel, I've said it's certainly no consolation to the side which doesn't prevail, but we've had just excellent quality of advocacy and lawyering from all the lawyers, both sides, throughout this trial. Court is in recess."

The jury went to the Brookside Inn for lunch.

At 4:50, the judge sent them home for the weekend.

WEEK EIGHT
VERDICT

Monday was a long, tedious, nerve-wracking day for Mark Unger, his attorneys and the prosecution.

No one expected a quick verdict, and no one was disappointed. Beulah is a beautiful small town, gorgeously situated at the east end of Crystal Lake. The beach is just a block from Main Street. The lake lives up to its name, a surreal shade of blue when the sun is out. It was a perfect place for killing time, unless you were in your suit, awaiting a verdict in one of the biggest cases of your career.

Other than the beach, or wandering into Crystal Lake Adventure Sports to window-shop for kayaks or to look at its racks of Patagonia outdoor gear or strolling into a couple of antique stores or the upscale market whose pizzas and submarine sandwiches are considered by many the best in northern Michigan, there wasn't much to do. Three blocks in any direction and you were out of town.

At 5:56 p.m., the judge reconvened the court and told the lawyers there had been no verdict and they were done for the day.

Tuesday was another tick-tock day in paradise.

There was a bit of excitement when the lawyers were

summoned just after 11, too early for lunch. But it wasn't a verdict.

The jury wanted some testimony read back to them. They had their own notes of the trial, and the exhibits, but didn't have written transcripts. They had been told earlier that if their discussions bogged down over specific testimony, parts of the transcript would be read to them.

The foreman had knocked on the door for the bailiff and said they needed to hear Dr. Cohle's testimony about lividity, the pooling of blood that occurs after death.

Court reporter Kathy McBride found the portion they needed. In addition to defining lividity, and how it differed from bruising—bruising was considered a "vital" process, meaning it happened during life or in the first few minutes after it ended—Cohle explained rigor mortis.

About 3, the lawyers were summoned, again, for more testimony, this time what Sergeant Beth Baesch of the Benzie County Sheriff's Department had to say about her interview with Max Tyler and the contents of the Mary Ellen and Unger's SUV.

She had recounted how Max's mom was supposed to have slept in the downstairs bedroom and his dad upstairs; that his mom had taken a blue blanket out to the deck; his dad had come back without their mom in the middle of the second movie he and Tyler were watching and told them it was time for bed and tucked them in; Max listened to the Red Wing game on the radio awhile after going to bed and the last he remembered it was 3–0 for the Wings; he awoke in the dark to feel himself being kissed by his father—he could feel his whiskers—and when he woke up, again, it was light out and his dad and brother were already up.

McBride continued to read, Max telling Baesch that their dad had then taken them over to the Inn and broken the news about their mother, and that his mom and dad had been "sort of not getting along."

The jury went back to its room at 3:36.

At 5:02, the judge asked the jurors if they wanted to stop for the day. They did.

Early Wednesday afternoon, McGuire and Harrison were in Frankfort catching a rare lunch outside the courthouse. Most days, they had eaten lunch with Unger in a conference room, with Roger Wotila often going for takeout from L'Chayim.

Today, they'd decided to break with routine, expecting another full day of deliberations. But during lunch, they got the call: There's a verdict.

No matter how long you'd practiced law, nothing would stop that jolt of adrenaline when you heard those words.

At 3:08, the jury entered the room and took its seats.

"Mr. Eggleston, are you the foreperson of this jury?" asked Judge Batzer, referring to Robert Eggleston, the juror who had been questioned during the trial by the judge and defense attorneys because of the note he'd written about his knowledge of physics.

Bad news, thought Harrison.

"Yes, that is correct."

"Mr. Eggleston, the court is informed that the jury has reached a verdict. Is that correct?"

"That is correct."

"If you would hand the form of the verdict to the bailiff, the bailiff will hand it to me," said Batzer. Eggleston passed it on the bailiff, who passed it to the judge, who passed it to the clerk.

"The clerk will publish the verdict," said the judge.

The moment before the verdict was read seemed frozen. Lives were about to change, but in which diametrically opposed way? Every second since Mark Unger had called the Duncans had been aiming toward *this* moment, and there was no chance of its being anticlimactic.

Harrison stared at Pendergast as everyone waited in stop time. His client was in all likelihood walking out a free man. He wanted to see, and remember, the look on her face when she got hit with the third loss of her long career.

Some of his buddies in the print and broadcast media at the trial had told him when deliberations began that it was a sure thing.

"I didn't have that level of confidence, because I've seen too many of these things," he said later. "I've tried a lot of cases in my life and I think I'm pretty rational, but I had a hard time keeping my feet on the ground, our defense was so strong."

He, unlike McGuire, liked Pendergast. Nonetheless, he'd enjoy seeing her face.

(Once, at a deposition before trial, McGuire had told her: "You make me sick." She, in turn, dismissed his background of medical malpractice and his base of scientific expertise: "He did all *foot cases*," she sneered. *"Foot cases!"*) Harrison respected her. He thought of her as a friend and prided himself on being an elder statesman of the law he fancied she looked up to. He wanted to enjoy that moment when it hit her what had happened.

He stared at her, and the verdict was read, and the look on her face *was* one of shock. Her lower jaw dropped. If one of the photographers in the room had Harrison's angle and captured that moment on film, or more likely, captured it digitally, the image would have revealed one of two things: a prosecutor surprised that she *hadn't* lost her third murder case, or one surprised that she did.

"*People of the State of Michigan* versus *Mark Steven Unger*," intoned the clerk. "We, the jury, find the defendant guilty of murder in the first degree."

Gasps in the courtroom.

"Members of the jury, was that and is that your verdict, so say each and every one of you?" asked the judge after a moment or two to let the room quiet down.

The jury said as one: "Yes."

The clerk then polled each of them in turn, Sondra

Anderson, David Anthony, Katherine Couturier, James Zoulek, Kristina Robideau, James Priest, Curt Cooper, Jane Weisbrodt, Fred Walton, Robert Eggleston, Lucinda Mc-Gregor and Rebecca Tarker.

Each said "Yes" when asked, "Was that and is that your verdict?"

"All right," said Batzer. "Anything further from counsel?"

"Nothing on behalf of the People," said Pendergast.

"No, Your Honor," said Harrison.

"All right," said Batzer. "Members of the jury, I want to thank you for the time and attention you've brought to this lengthy and difficult matter."

The jury left the room at 3:11.

Batzer announced that a probation officer would conduct a pre-sentencing investigation and write a report, and that the defendant and defense attorneys would have the right to read it before sentencing.

It was all moot, the sentencing report and the chance for the defense to read it and, at sentencing, rebut it.

Under Michigan law, there is only one sentence for first-degree murder: life without parole. Unless Unger could get the verdict overturned on what would be, by law, a mandatory appeal, Batzer would have no choice but to sentence him to die in prison.

"This case was, I mean, it's a heartbreaking thing," said Harrison, after he'd had time to ruminate on the trial, the verdict and what might have gone wrong. "There's nothing I've worked on that's more disappointing than this case. When you take on everything they can throw at you and you not only knock it down, but you present your own evidence about what really happened, it's heartbreaking. I thought we put on an absolutely fabulous defense."

He said the look of shock on Pendergast's face was proof, to him, that she'd expected to lose the third case of her life. "Her jaw dropped," he said. "She'll deny it till the day she dies, but that verdict was a shock to her."

"Till the day I die," said Pendergast, when told of Harrison's comments. "Till the day I die. We knew we had him."

After a pause, she added: "I will concede I was surprised it was murder one. Murder one surprised me. But I thought murder two. We were cautiously optimistic, but we thought we had him. At least murder two."

Which was an odd admission to make. The case was argued as a first-degree case. The crux of it was McKeever's testimony that Florence Unger had to have been on the concrete apron for a substantial period of time, about ninety minutes. And that after that amount of time, with the injuries she had, she could not have gotten into the water by herself.

That time element made it premeditation, or so Pendergast's case went. Short of her dying day, she was admitting doubts she'd made her case.

THE FOREMAN'S LETTER

On September 8, Eggleston, the juror whose note to the judge at the end of the trial had caused such turmoil, wrote a ten-page letter to Pendergast. Like the Duncans, he, too lived on a lake, Crystal Lake, which, as his letter showed, informed some of his thought processes during the trial.

The letter read, in part:

> I'm going to recount to you my experiences and observations during the Unger trial with the thought that you might find them helpful in understanding what the jury thought and how they reacted.

Pendergast, who prided herself as a square shooter, provided a copy to Harrison, who in turn provided copies to the the attorneys who would handle Unger's appeal.

"Let me begin at the end," Eggleston began, an end he claimed he'd fashioned.

> On Wednesday, mid-morning, the jury was ready for a verdict. Tina, Lucy, Cathy and Becky came out for second degree. I could sense the jury was going to move quickly to a second-degree verdict when I said: "Let me tell you what I think happened."

Five minutes later, when I was finished, it was first degree, and there was no doubt in anyone's mind. It took several hours of crying and all the emotions associated with the tension of the trial, but everyone was resolute.

Eggleston broke his report into sections, including "least deliberated areas," "best witnesses," "some miscellaneous kudos/observations," and, by far the lengthiest section, "the deliberations."

Surprisingly, Eggleston said that, despite the weight defense attorneys put on the testimony, the jurors barely discussed anything said by Schmidt and Paul—"or should I say Abbott and Costello?" he wrote.

No juror during deliberations mentioned either, except for Schmidt's testimony and slides regarding [Florence Unger's] lungs.

Eggleston also treated another crucial part of the defense case dismissively—the railing around the boathouse, its low height and state of disrepair.

Many decks have seats instead of railings. I replaced mine that was pre-1985 code two years ago and it was 20 inches high.

Perhaps most surprising of all was his claim that Florence's fear of the dark was irrelevant to the jurors, given the importance put on it by the prosecution.

Everyone in Northern Michigan knows that you would never stay out in the rain on a windy late October night.

Eggleston's roster of best witnesses included patrolman Troy Packard, Dr. Paul McKeever, Dr. Brian Zink, Linn Duncan and Dragovic.

Of Duncan, he wrote:

An honest man. His description of lowering the porch furniture the same day as Flo's murder added credibility to the strength of the railing and nonslippery condition of the deck.

Of Dragovic, Eggleston wrote:

Very entertaining . . . his testimony made us believe beyond a reasonable doubt drowning was the cause of death.

But then he added, bewilderingly:

The jury was resistant to his showmanship and discounted his testimony.

Under a section labeled "miscellaneous kudos/observations," he wrote:

Mark Bilkovic: Best salesman, a true closer if I ever saw one.

John Skrzynski: He was more effective in impeaching witnesses than Mr. McGuire with all his yelling and theatrics . . . A welcome oasis of calm and reason in a desert of yelling.

Sgt. Wally Armstrong: Detective I would least want investigating me if I were Mark. A seasoned no-nonsense professional that I sensed the defense was a little afraid to pick on. Like the Mounties, he got his man.

Judge Batzer: He was fair and wanted the jury to deliver justice. He did everything possible to ensure a fair trial that would be difficult to overturn on appeal.

He was hardly so kind to McGuire:

We were afraid he would have a heart attack during one of his cross examinations. We found the yelling unsettling and distracting.

In a section he labeled 'jury trivia,' Eggleston wrote that two of the jurors had graduated from high schools in the Grosse Pointes, a collection of five small, very affluent communities just outside Detroit; that two of them were graduates of the University of Michigan; that one of them had a daughter attending U-M; that two of them had lived in affluent Oakland County as adults; and that "half of us were not local." It somehow seemed important to him that Pendergast not see him as a yokel.

Eggleston also reminded her in the "jury trivia" section that a "fudgie is a Mackinac terminology, not Benzie County."

The last struck Harrison when he read it as proof that the juror had been prejudiced against him from the start of the trial. At the least, he hadn't gotten over being perturbed at the "fudgie" reference in Harrison's opening argument, "fudgie" being a perjorative synonym for "outsider" or "tourist" that is used by locals on Mackinac Island, a tourist island in northern Lake Huron, who are perpetually ticked off at the flood of day-trippers clogging Main Street and buying fudge at all the fudge shops the island is known for.

Igor Paul got two pages to himself. Eggleston said he was

a pompous ass [who] upset me when he looked at the jury in that East Coast condescending look and said, "I won't bore you with the details of the mathematics because I'm sure you're not interested," or words to that effect. He looked like he was talking to people too stupid to understand or care. By this time in the trial, the jury was a unit. "All for one and one for all" was our creed, and we had just been insulted. Just writing about it now is upsetting.

Eggleston wrote that the slow-motion animation during close was "aptly described as a cartoon" and that when he started to rebut Paul's arguments during jury deliberations, "none of the jurors wanted to listen to my explanations because they had toally discounted his testimony."

Eggleston wrote that he felt honored to be voted foreperson and tried to keep his own opinions in check so other members would feel free to express theirs. But after the first poll only had eight votes for guilty, Eggleston said it was time to speak up.

What he told them was his theory of the chain of events leading up to Florence Unger's death, a theory that would send chills up Harrison's spine, and anger into his heart when he read the letter:

I said that I thought from Tuesday until Thursday night or sometime Friday the week of Flo's death, Mark tried to exercise his control over Flo and get her to drop the divorce. He intimidated [sic] and was perhaps physical, but it didn't work. Time for Plan B. Plan B was to remove the problem. If Flo wouldn't rescind the divorce, then he had no choice but to kill Flo . . . He would have to make it look like an accident. How and where could he do it?

Couldn't push her off his deck in Huntington Woods. He was very familiar with the boat house deck at Watervale. So he told Flo that he finally had seen the wisdom of a divorce, which caused an unsuspecting Flo to be relieved and hopeful for the first time in a long time. That would account for her cheerfulness on the cell phone to her friend on Friday.

Mark got her to the boat house deck under a pretense of his ideas to make settlement of the divorce easier. Not wanting to talk in front of the kids, of course she would go with him to the boat house deck. There they met Fred Oeflein. Flo was bubbly. She was happy that Mark was ready to end the mar-

riage. A short time later . . . Mark surprised Flo and
forced her over the railing. Then he kicked it to make
it look like she had stumbled over the railing and ran
down to the apron to check on Flo.

Nuts! She was still alive

Eggleston wrote, melodramatically.

Back to the cabin, where he waited, reading an extra
story to the boys. Once the boys were in bed, he went
back down to the apron and saw Flo was still alive.
Either at this time—or he came back one more time
later in the night—he rolled Flo into the water and
blood.

Eggleston's take on things involved events never discussed in court, for which no evidence existed nor was any
presented. Mark told her he was ready to agree to a divorce? He asked her out to the deck to discuss divorce
terms? He took Flo north with the plan to push her off the
deck and kill her? Even in private conversation, no one,
not Pendergast, not Skrzynski, not Bilkovic, had said that
Unger planned the murder in advance. The prosecutors
thought that it likely was an argument gotten out of hand,
with premeditation entering the chain of events only after
she had landed on the concrete apron and Unger decided to
put her into the water.

My feeling was that this version of events explained
the evidence. When I completed my version, everyone
was silent. Dave said, "He staged it." That was it. All
the jurors now believed he logically had motivation to
know Flo was alive when he put her in the water.

Later, Harrison, and the Wolbergs, would claim there
was a culture divide that played a crucial role in the trial's
outcome, a divide Eggleston agreed with. Harrison, he
wrote:

didn't understand the real cultural difference between Benzie County and Oakland County (Detroit, etc.) lies in accepting responsibility for one's actions and not blaming someone else.

He didn't comprehend that because of the lower population density, we are more interdependent on each other and work with the establishment to support the community.

Eggleston concluded his letter by telling Pendergast,

You are a hero and my hero.

Of her opposite lead counsel, he said:

Mr. Harrison has a meter running and can take satisfaction every minute of every day that his wallet is getting fatter. The longer the trial, the better it is. He even gets rewarded by losing because now he can prepare an appeal and bill more money.

In fact, Harrison had nothing to do with the appeal other than passing Eggleston's letter on to the attorneys who handled it as possible evidence of jury malfeasance.

AFTERWORD

On Good Friday, March 21, 2008, a three-member panel of the Michigan Court of Appeals upheld Mark Unger's conviction of first-degree murder.

The state Supreme Court announced on October 24, 2008, that it declined to review the case. The family didn't expect relief, there, but appealing to the Supreme Court was a requirement before they could file an appeal in federal court.

The family was buoyed, though, that two of the seven justices wanted to conduct a review about possibly ordering a new trial based on prosecutorial misconduct by Pendergast. The judges said she'd crossed the line on numerous occasions with her characterization of the defense using "smoke and mirrors" and comments such as "a deliberate attempt to mislead," "red herrings," and the like.

The two also said the prosecution had committed misconduct in its comments about Igor Paul.

Connie and Jerry Wolberg had a falling-out with Harrison, and they no longer talk. Connie felt he'd botched the trial, that he'd spent too much time impugning local police, and that not making better use of Roger Wotila, the highly regarded attorney from nearby Cadillac, was a mistake.

"He's an Atticus Finch, and they didn't use him," she says.

Like others, she is under the impression that Mark declined an offer of a manslaughter plea, a plea the prosecution said was never offered. "Mark was so passionate about never, ever, ever letting the boys think he'd done anything to hurt their mother," she said.

In part, her anger at Harrison may be disappointment over what to her was a shocking verdict that flew in the face of Harrison's reassurances during the trial that things were going well.

"Harrison kept telling Mark, 'This is a no-brainer,'" she said.

Jerry and Connie visit Mark regularly and cheerfully bear the financial brunt of his frequent and expensive collect calls from prison.

"Roger was really a valuable resource to us, a fabulous guy and a great lawyer," said Harrison. "Having said that, he just wanted to be in the background and not greatly involved. He didn't say that so much in words, but that was the sense we got."

Harrison and McGuire both say there was a bias against them by the locals who made up the jury, that they resented the lawyers' expensive cars and, moreover, resented a defense that had of necessity to try to attack the skills of the police and sheriff's deputies who showed up at Watervale that morning.

"We were facing a culture clash between those who live up north and the downstaters," said McGuire. "We've got a Jewish urban defendant with urban lawyers and they're driving expensive cars. And to an extent we were taking on the local police force. So it became us versus them. We were attacking their institutions."

And, said Harrison, jury members must have known there would be a civil suit against the Duncans "who were pillars of the community, if they acquitted Mark. If he wasn't to blame for his wife's fall, the poor condition of the boat-house deck and railing would have been."

What could or would he have done differently? "I don't know what we could have done. I wish I could say we learned from it," said Harrison. "Our guy should have walked. He probably would have if he'd been tried in Oakland County. Tom and I both say we'll take this case to the grave with us."

Harrison thought Batzer was very tough on them in his rulings, and would have normally been angry about it, "but he was the most accommodating judge you can imagine. He was so good to us personally that it took away the zeal to bitch."

After the trial, Schmidt reviewed McKeever's testimony and remains unimpressed. "There was nothing really conclusive about his testimony," said Schmidt. "Had he tried to present his findings in the context of a scientific meeting, he would have received a lot more criticism."

As for Igor Paul's testimony, he thought "the physics was quite extraordinary, but it didn't help the defense that he came up with so many alternative scenarios. Had he been able to narrow it down to one or two . . .

"One of the things that remained with me from the Unger trial is that the way people perceive things versus the facts are two different things. Ever since that trial I've thought about how to present complicated information in a way people can understand better.

"I saw one of the TV shows on the case and a juror said that Florence Unger would have had to roll three or four times to get into the water, and she couldn't have done that with her injuries. He just didn't understand the evidence. It was only forty inches from where she landed to the water. She had a waist of twenty-eight inches. So she only had to roll one and a half times. That inability to understand the evidence bothers me immensely."

Another thing that continues to bother him is what he perceives as the politics behind Unger's prosecution.

"One of the things that most struck me about the Unger case was the politics. I called Steve Cohle when I decided to help on the case, and he told me about Dragovic and the other Oakland County people driving to see him. He told me it was one of the most uncomfortable moments of his life.

"What could you think of the justice system in Oakland County? We in Wayne County are blessed by a county government that leaves us alone. We're independent of the prosecutor's office. I've never had a prosecutor come in and tell me to change my findings, much less a prosecutor from Lansing and a prosecutor from a different county."

Does he think Unger murdered his wife? He doesn't know. If he pushed her from the roof, it was murder. If she fell on her own, it was an accident. But he thinks the evidence was ambiguous, and reasonable doubt the only logical conclusion.

What he is sure of is that Unger didn't drag her into the water. "If you look at the autopsy report, there wasn't a single drag mark on Florence Unger's body. Not a single bit of physical evidence that she was dragged. It's mind-boggling to me they were able to support that. I think she rolled into the water and didn't die right away. The water was only four inches deep there. She could have laid there awhile without drowning."

Was he surprised by the verdict? "No. I think he was an unsympathetic defendant. He was a hard guy to feel sorry for. His life circumstances up in Benzie County were hard for people there, who work hard to make ends meet, to sympathize with. What was he making? Ten thousand dollars a month tax-free? For not working?"

Mort Meisner still coaches a travel team made up of Huntington Woods' finest young baseball players. He is on the list of people Unger is allowed to make collect calls to, and Unger calls him weekly.

"We talk about the Tigers and the Pistons and the Red Wings," said Meisner. "You forget he's in prison."

Seymour Schwartz, the defense attorney who is also active with the Alley Cats baseball team, said he is still angry at the Sterns for keeping Max from the team and for the divisions that have lasted in the community.

Max and Tyler live with the Sterns, who formally adopted them after their dad's conviction.

Bilkovic is still in private practice. He said he understands when people tell him that they think Unger is innocent, that the contradictory science at least made for reasonable doubt.

"But this is one time the jury got it right," he said.

For Skrzynski, the medical expert, the scientific evidence was not ambiguous. The stain McKeever used to show Florence's axonal injuries left no doubt she'd been alive on the concrete apron for ninety minutes and someone then put her in the water.

Pendergast's theory of the crime is: "He was having a warm and fuzzy moment. She said, 'No, it's over.' And he lost it. He pushed her. She fell. It was an accident, basically. I think he looked around. 'Did anyone see me or hear me?' And went back to the cottage to regroup.

"He comes back. She's still alive. If she recovers, it's over for him. She'll tell people he pushed her. Her injuries are all on him. He'll lose his kids. I think he came back, and he goes down to the apron and sees she's breathing and says, 'Oh, shit.' And puts her in the water. 'It's okay, no one saw me. It's gonna be okay.'"

In November 2006, the estate of Max and Tyler Unger got a default judgment of $10 million against their dad. The estate's lawyer, Alan May, who used to be Harold Stern's boss, said assets included $250,000 in life insurance on Florence, which had been held in escrow; Unger's highly mortgaged and vacant home in Huntington Woods, which had a listed value of $600,000; and about $80,000 in other properties Mark and Flo had owned jointly.

Even in the event of a possible reversal of Unger's life sentence on appeal, the default judgment will stand.

"If he ever tries to do anything like O. J. Simpson did, we'll go after that, too," said May, referring to the book *If I Did It*.

Unger told reporters after the trial that he was reluctant to cooperate in any would-be book projects because he wanted to write his own book. He reluctantly and after much delay agreed to be interviewed during a series of phone calls for this book, with the caveat that he would not be directly quoted. He doesn't think he had a trial of his peers. He thinks it was, for him, a case of guilty until proven innocent.

Unger made headlines again, briefly, in November 2007 when he was assaulted by a fellow inmate at the St. Louis Correctional Facility in northern Michigan. His neck was cut and required only minor medical attention.

Soon after, he was transferred to a prison in Muskegon, and in the spring of 2008 he got the good news that his status was being changed from level four to level two, meaning he was no longer considered dangerous.

The change meant he would be allowed out of his cell for many more hours each week, and allowed to make more frequent calls to friends and family.

"He says he's just happy to be able to see the sky. To look at the flowers and the grass," said Connie Wolberg.

Unger tells friends he has hopes of getting out of jail on appeal. He tells them he knows that's what Flo would want, so he can get back together with his kids.

He has a wide range of family and friends he calls and who visit him. He likes talking about his kids, about what he misses, welcoming the frequent tears he says keep him human in a place packed with those who fill their days in an emotionless stupor. He tells his friends he thinks about Flo all the time so he won't forget how much he loved her.

A convicted defendant is entitled under American law to appeal his conviction, in an effort to overturn the jury's finding of guilt. As of going to press, an appeal of Mark Unger's conviction in federal court is planned.